PRAISE FOR
INVESTING FOR BETTER

Daniel skillfully blends academic theory with practical asset management, crafting a pivotal book for grasping market dynamics and the essence of the field. It delves deeply into the industry with an engaging and accessible narrative, making complex concepts both understandable and enjoyable. It is a great read if you want to stay ahead of the curve in the evolving asset management industry.

> **—Marina Balboa**, Professor of Finance, Universidad de Alicante

Investing for Better provides a comprehensive guide to the asset management industry, mapping its evolution and the forces that drive the industry, including the important role that asset managers play in implementing Environmental, Social, and Governance (ESG) risks and opportunities into the investment process. ESG issues are no longer niche or nice-to-have add-ons for investors; they have moved into the mainstream. Anyone working or wishing to work in the asset management industry today needs to understand this fast-evolving space and will need to be able to demonstrate that understanding beyond just paying lip service to them. Gone are the days of "Greed Is Good" Gordon Gekko style of investment, where making money at any costs—to people, the planet, and society more broadly—is acceptable. While many people see it as the role of governments to address the issues of climate change and human rights, the reality is that the private sector has a large role to play; without investment at scale and the ability to deploy capital, keeping the world to the aims of the Paris agreement will not be possible. To all young people wanting to make a difference in the world, my advice is always to follow the money; the finance sector, including asset management, can be an area of influence and importance to addressing some of the world's biggest issues and to providing investable solutions.

Whether you are an industry practitioner, student, policymaker, or simply interested in the role of the assessment industry, this book provides valued insights and a road map for navigating its evolving landscape.

> **—Fiona Reynolds**, former CEO of PRI and Chair of the
> UN Global Compact Network Australia

We are living in times of immense change, and it is up to us to ensure the winds of change blow in the right direction. And nowhere is this transformation more important than in the asset management industry. In a short space of time, driven by Europe, sustainability has started to be adopted around the world. There has also been positive change around gender inclusivity and at directing the forces of capital markets toward improving future businesses and societies.

To address the leadership challenges on the horizon, it is vital that the changing complexities of asset management, with its complex inter-workings and embedded systems, are well understood. We have seen sustainability take a more prominent role as well as the democratization of investing. The emergence of younger generations of investors bringing more diversity and gender balance is one of the fastest growing segments today.

Dr. Daniel Seiler has written an essential guide to help those who want to delve deeply into this exciting industry. This compelling text is a valuable tool for those hoping to shape its future progress. As new technology driven by the AI revolution brings even greater disruption and transformation, this book will provide a valuable guide for those wishing to influence the asset management industry over the coming decade.

—Deborah Yang, CEO and cofounder of Daizy

Daniel is one of those rare breeds of people who can successfully bridge the gap between academic theory and practical applications. This book is, therefore, a must-read for all those who wish to understand the conceptual underpinning of financial markets and the real-life functioning of asset management. I particularly like Parts III and IV of the book, where Daniel rises above the fray in the ever-growing (and often pointless) debate between active and passive. Instead, he cogently presents a new framework of asset management industry that also addresses societal preferences like ESG. Please read and spread the good word!

—Amit Goyal, Swiss Finance Institute at HEC at the University of Lausanne

INVESTING
FOR BETTER

INVESTING
FOR BETTER

HARNESSING THE FOUR DRIVING FORCES
OF ASSET MANAGEMENT TO BUILD
A WEALTHIER AND MORE EQUITABLE WORLD

DANIEL SEILER

New York   Chicago   San Francisco   Athens   London   Madrid
Mexico City   Milan   New Delhi   Singapore   Sydney   Toronto

1 2 3 4 5 6 7 8 9   LCR   29 28 27 26 25 24

ISBN   978-1-265-06691-8
MHID   1-265-06691-4

e-ISBN   978-1-265-06717-5
e-MHID   1-265-06717-1

This publication is designed to provide accurate and authoritative information in regard to the subject matter covered. It is sold with the understanding that neither the author nor the publisher is engaged in rendering legal, accounting, securities trading, or other professional services. If legal advice or other expert assistance is required, the services of a competent professional person should be sought.
> —*From a Declaration of Principles Jointly Adopted by a Committee of the American Bar Association and a Committee of Publishers and Associations*

McGraw Hill books are available at special quantity discounts to use as premiums and sales promotions or for use in corporate training programs. To contact a representative, please visit the Contact Us pages at www.mhprofessional.com.

McGraw Hill is committed to making our products accessible to all learners. To learn more about the available support and accommodations we offer, please contact us at accessibility@mheducation.com. We also participate in the Access Text Network (www.accesstext.org), and ATN members may submit requests through ATN.

For Anna, Annick, Elijah, Sophie,
and all other upcoming asset managers.

CONTENTS

PREFACE

Asset management is in need of a higher purpose.

My colleagues and I have been passionately managing capital using quantitative methods for the last 20 years. As a group, we have top-notch mathematical, computer programming, and data management skills. Because these skills are sought out by virtually every other industry today, the question arises of why a new grad—or even a more experienced worker—with these skills would choose asset management as a career.

I found that as the battle for highly skilled employees picked up over the years, more and more of my colleagues were getting poached by competitors. By competitors, I do not refer only (or mostly) to other asset managers—my direct commercial competitors—but to companies that were mining for talent in the same skills strata I was, often high-tech firms.

The attractions offered by high-tech firms often turned out to be soft benefits rather than strictly economic ones (though hefty high-tech company option packages do admittedly make a formidable argument for some workers). Some of these soft benefits are trivial and easily replicable, such as loosening up dress codes (replicable so long as you are not a Swiss private bank, of course). However, I believe many of the other soft benefits are more profound.

High-tech companies sell candidates on the idea that they will be able to make a positive impact on their society and the world. For example, tech firms are the ones leading the push to become net-zero emitters of greenhouse gases and pointedly offer benefits to employees suggesting an openness to confronting all types of social discrimination. The enormous profitability of some of these firms let them offer employees paid time off to participate in community-based charitable activities or to work on nonprofit projects using company time and resources. In short, these firms are putting their money where their corporate mouths are by supporting social and environmental causes and incentivizing their employees to do so too.

You may believe this social and ecological activism is a bunch of woke mumbo jumbo, but there is good evidence that young employees value these sorts of initiatives even more than they do base salaries. In February 2023, former Unilever CEO Paul Polman published the results of a survey of more than 4,000 workers across the United States and the United Kingdom (Polman, 2023). Polman finds that the twenty-first century workforce is "entering an era of conscious quitting," where employees forgo paychecks and walk away from businesses that fail to demonstrate commitment to supporting social and environment values.

One of my reasons for writing this book is I have realized that to attract and retain the people with the kinds of skills asset managers need to *invest better* during the twenty-first century, the industry must dedicate itself to the pursuit of a higher purpose. Gone are the days where the model for a skilled financier is a morally ambiguous Gordon Gekko character, bent on the unapologetic pursuit of profit above all else. I believe that if asset management is to attract the best minds and create the most value for its clients, it is time to step up to the plate and set our sights on changing the world for the better.

I argue in this book—and believe I have ample historical justification—that asset managers are the ones who shape the face of the world for decades in the future. This proposition might seem far-fetched to you, but keep in mind that without smart capital allocators competing to find the best, most useful ideas, there would be no innovation.

The world has changed a lot in the last 30 years. I graduated from one of the finest schools for environmental sciences in the world, ETH Zurich, in the mid-1990s, trained as an environmental chemist and ecologist. At that time, I couldn't find a job in my field, but was lucky to get hired as what was then the obscure position of "sustainable investing analyst." The fact that I stumbled into this position at the time led me to get both a master's and a doctoral degree in finance, and then to pursue a career as an asset manager for almost three decades.

At the time I entered the asset management business, the world was agog over the possibilities of a crazy idea, born in part in a Swiss laboratory at CERN, called the internet. Everyone was going nuts for anything.com, and no one cared about environmental degradation and climate change.

Nowadays, the situation is different: there is high demand for talent in ESG (environmental, social, and governance) issues—a trend I'll have plenty to say about in Chapters 13 and 14. While my views on ESG are nuanced, I believe the emphasis on sustainability is entirely justified and proper, considering where we find ourselves vis-à-vis the dual crises of climate and biodiversity loss. It is my opinion that as an industry we must do more to identify the best and brightest candidates and to take great pains to nurture them as the colleagues who will be instrumental in shaping the world of the twenty-first century. Considering the serious issues we face, the success of this cohort of asset managers may even play an instrumental role in determining the fate of human civilization.

This book aims to equip novice and experienced asset managers, as well as interested stakeholders, with a conceptual framework—one based on the core principles of financial intermediation—that goes beyond the current (and stale) dichotomy between active and passive investing. I have organized the book into four parts:

Part I (Chapters 1–4) provides a thorough explanation of the larger ecosystem in which asset managers operate. Namely, in Chapter 1, I offer a high-level map of the ecosystem and follow up by discussing buy side, sell side, and other players in Chapters 2 through 4. This part of the book is likely to be most helpful to students, asset managers early in their career, and politicians and journalists, but my guess is that more seasoned asset management professionals will also probably pick up a few tidbits reading through it. You will be able to follow the reasoning and enjoy the topics in subsequent sections of the book without reading Part I, but you will have a better grasp of the nuances behind the arguments if you understand my map of the industry and how each of the players fit (and sometimes meld) together.

Part II (Chapters 5–8) describes the conceptual framework that now governs the industry, especially the drivers that have channeled everyone's attention into a debate between "active versus passive." Chapter 5 offers an overview of fees, size, and competition for investing talent, and the rest of the chapters in this part take a closer look at the interplay between these drivers. The last chapter in this part discusses the active-passive dichotomy and why I think it is at best meaningless and at worst value destructive to the asset owners who have hired us to manage their financial futures.

Part III (Chapters 9–14) introduces my preferred framework for conceiving of the asset management industry, based on the principles of financial intermediation. In this part, I make the point that there is a good reason for people to have spent so much intellectual time and horsepower rehashing various points related to active and passive investing approaches. Both active and passive investing styles exist in a world of intense competition, so they must have some characteristics that confer "evolutionary" advantages. Therefore, I look at the characteristics that make each approach attractive from a financial intermediation point of view. These characteristics are investing cost, investment risks, information asymmetries, and societal preferences. Further, I explain how the intermediary model based on four driving forces allows the asset management industry to build attractive, robust businesses that help society.

Part IV (Chapter 15) is a manifesto for the asset management industry based on the arguments I make in Part III. Short and sweet.

To maintain the standard of living in developed countries and improve those of what we know now as the developing world, all while protecting the irreplaceably valuable biosphere that supports our complex civilization, the asset management industry needs to provide its best and brightest with more than just a paycheck. The asset management industry needs to provide a vision of the future and a higher purpose for young people entering it. My hope is that this book will provide the spark that ignites that fire.

ACKNOWLEDGMENTS

My major *thank-you* goes to Erik Kobayashi-Solomon, an extraordinary positive force in the finance industry. His sharp feedback allowed me to develop a vague idea into the tangible model described in this book.

A big *thank-you* goes to four different groups that I call professors, role models, roadrunners, and companions.

The professors group includes the academic guidance from Amit Goyal, Pedro Santa Clara, Markus Schmid, Rossen Valkanov, and Heinz Zimmermann who admirably continue to contribute to an ever-growing understanding of the forces shaping the asset management industry.

The next group includes not only role models but also great mentors of mine who taught me the business mechanics of asset management from various perspectives: Elisabeth Stern (ESG investing), Martin Brenner (ESG investing), David Owen (ESG investing), Olivier Cronenbergh (alternative investing), Hans-Jörg Baumann (alternative investing), Stefan Wittmann (quant investing), Peter Oertmann (quant investing), Axel Schwarzer (asset management).

But no asset management business is successful without its irresistible distribution champions. Therefore, a special *thank-you* to the tireless roadrunners in various regions and across different distribution channels, who gave me the opportunity to explore the nuances of different local and global client segments: Jared Buell (United

States), Brian Engle (United States), Sheridan Bowers (United Kingdom), Andreas Faeste (Australia), Helen Lo (Korea, Japan, Taiwan, Hong Kong), Anja Nieberding (Germany), Florian Schepp (Germany), Lorenzo Corrias (Italy), Daniel Keller (Nordics), Patrick Sege (Switzerland), and Othmar Gubelman (Switzerland).

Last but not least, my companions and friends who were part of an incredible exciting journey building up an asset management franchise over the last decade from a single-digit asset base to almost US $50bn at its peak—day by day: Yun Bai, Markus Becker, Nicolas Burkhardt, Bratislava Brown, Manuel Egger, Michael Ehrig, Kerstin Hottner, Franziska Kirner, Daniel Schild, Yves Schläpfer, Alexander Schmidt, Stephan Schneider, Olga Voldiner, Franziska von Haase, and Natascha Waldschmidt.

PART I

The Asset Management Ecosystem

A Map of the Asset
Management Industry

For an adventurer in any field, a good map is an essential piece of equipment. The first four chapters of this book offer a well-calibrated description of the various players within the industry, how their managers are incentivized, and what their objectives are—in a phrase, a crisp overview of the asset management industry and the environment in which the industry operates.

Before I proceed, I will say that creating a comprehensive map of the global asset management industry is almost impossible, and creating one that is simultaneously interesting and engaging for a reader is an unqualified impossibility. First, there are differences from one jurisdiction to another; even countries as geographically and historically tied as the United Kingdom and France show significant differences due to diverging legal traditions, for example. Second, there are differences in perspective depending on what part of the industry to which one is exposed; the industry appears very different to those who are operating in different spheres and attempting to accomplish different tasks. Finally, the tendency is for actors operating in one part of the capital markets ecosystem to expand into other parts of the ecosystem, blurring boundaries and definitions as they go.

The start of this chapter presents a simplified version of the ecosystem that depicts each part as entirely separate, but as each division is explained, you will soon see how much overlap and blurring of lines exists.

Although creating a high-resolution map of the capital markets ecosystem that includes every situation, country, and nuance is impossible, my goal is to focus on the key functions and entities. My hope is that creating this broad-brush picture will allow readers to understand the arguments I make in later chapters of the book. Although you will be able to understand the later chapters without reading this chapter, keeping a general picture of the asset management ecosystem in your mind while you read the rest of the book will allow you a much better understanding of the importance of the industry for our society.

By the end of the chapter, you will have a good understanding of the differences between principals and agents, how the industry is split between the buy side and the sell side, and how the various buy-side and sell-side agents interact within the asset management ecosystem.

PRINCIPALS AND AGENTS

Let's start out by defining the most basic separating line in the business of investing—principals and agents.

For all the complexities that have developed for various reasons, capital markets are essentially very simple. There are two sets of actors that have either too much or too little cash. These two groups we will call *principals* because it is principally their needs that drive the development of capital markets.

The first group of principals we will discuss are those that have too much cash. We will call this group of principals *asset owners*; some asset owners are people, others are organizations.

The second group of principals are those that need cash. We will call this group of principals *issuers*; most issuers are organizations, but some of the organizations aggregate the issuances of individual people as well (e.g., mortgage-backed securities are pools of loans made to individual homeowners).

Issuers seek asset owners' excess cash in return for either future payments (bonds) or an ownership stake in the business (stocks). We will call the bonds and stocks paid for by the asset owners' cash *investment opportunities.*

Investment opportunities always exist due to a contractual relationship. A bond issuance contractually requires a business to make repayments according to a certain schedule and at a certain rate. If the business does not fulfill its contractual obligations, holders of that instrument—owners of the bonds, in other words—have legal rights specified in the contract. Similarly, stockholders have certain rights enumerated in corporate documents and can sue the company in cases where they believe the company's managers did not uphold the terms of the agreement. Because investing deals with contractual ownership agreements, a lot of the language used here refers to "contracts," meaning either bonds or stocks.

In the bad old days, asset owners had very limited access to issuers outside of their local area. A wealthy farmer might invest in the construction of a mill situated on a local river, but would not know about, let alone be able to invest in, an inventor's steam engine company in another part of the country, for instance. Investments were constrained to networks of personal relationships, and before advances in transportation and communications, networks of personal relationships were local.

Another issue in the bad old days was that raising large amounts of money was difficult without coordination of many asset owners.[1] As the number of asset owners increased, it became more and more necessary to develop clear rules relating to the contractual relationships between parties—both between the issuers and the asset owners and among different asset owners as well. Efforts to coordinate groups of principals favored the development of a class of specialists who could coordinate communications, bookkeeping, legal challenges, and the like between a network of asset owners to meet the needs of a certain issuer.

These specialists are what we call *agents*. Agents are not issuers or asset owners but are employed to highlight the investment opportunities presented by issuers to asset owners.

In the first example of blurring of lines between divisions, I'll say that even in the old days, the distinction between principals and agents was not clean. Agents tended to be entities that had excess cash, so they would pool their cash with other entities holding excess cash to fund an investment opportunity presented by an asset owner. As such, these early agents also became principals.

Eventually, the investment opportunities and situations became so complex that further specialization was required. This leads us to the topic of buy-side and sell-side agents.

BUY AND SELL SIDES

Some agents specialize in helping issuers raise money. Agents whose duty is to issuers are said to be part of the sell side. Conversely, agents specialized in helping asset owners find and allocate capital to investment opportunities are said to be part of the buy side.

Both buy-side and sell-side agents function as intermediaries to enable the principals they respectively represent to find and create investment opportunities. Financial intermediaries help society through four main functions:

1. **Transforming the notional size of investments.** This function is usually related to "packaging" or "structuring" assets in a way that asset owners will perceive them as investment opportunities.
2. **Transforming the liquidity of investments.** This function relates to the establishment of a market on which financial instruments can be transacted.

3. **Reducing the cost of investments.** This function typically refers to a reduction in transaction costs for a given investment; however, it also includes other costs—the cost to find an attractive investment, for instance.

4. **Transforming the risk of investments.** Asset owners must deal with a variety of risks: idiosyncratic risks related to the actions of the issuers, market risk, interest rate risk, and credit risk, to name the main ones. Buy-side agents mainly use the miracle of diversification to reduce asset owners' risk of losing money in investment opportunities.

One might not think about financial intermediaries as being helpful to society—certainly not as helpful to society as pharmaceutical companies—but consider what our economy would look like if buy- and sell-side intermediaries did not carry out the functions previously mentioned. Essentially, the world would be trapped in a medieval system with no access to financial markets, diversification strategies, and investment opportunities open to anyone other than the mega-rich. Regarding value-adding industries like pharmaceuticals, if there were no buy- and sell-side intermediaries, pharmaceutical companies would certainly not have the capital to make the world a better place.

Now that we have the important distinction of principals and agents, and buy side and sell side sorted out, as well as having an idea about the roles of financial intermediaries, we can turn to our initial 30,000-foot overview of the asset management ecosystem and understand the role of the players within that ecosystem.

ASSET MANAGEMENT ECOSYSTEM

Our map of the ecosystem, depicted in Figure 1.1, is bookended by our principals—asset owners on the far left and issuers on the far right. Notice that actors in these two groups overlap. Issuers simultaneously raise money for their own projects while investing in opportunities offered by other issuers. For example, I have a mortgage (which makes me an issuer), but I also own shares in my retirement portfolio, purchased with excess cash (which makes me an asset owner). As such, you can imagine cutting the diagram out of the book and taping the two ends together so they overlap; issuers are issuing securities to entities very much like themselves while also owning stakes in entities very much like themselves.

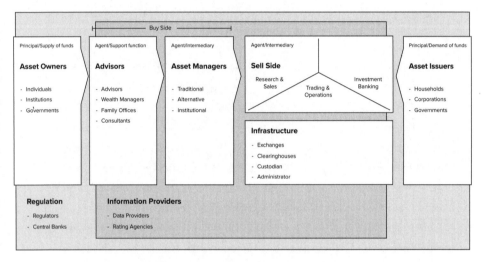

FIGURE 1.1 Asset management ecosystem

You might look at this diagram and say, "If the issuers are issuing to entities like themselves, why not cut out all the middlemen and just issue to themselves?" In fact, this observation leads to what some believe is the great advantage of blockchain-based investment vehicles: the process of "disintermediation."[2] A structure that disintermediated the buy and sell sides and saw issuers issuing securities directly to asset owners might be "efficient" from a process perspective, but the functions carried out by financial intermediaries listed in the previous section would be necessary to make the market "efficient" from a financial economics perspective.[3] I will have much more to say about the role of blockchain and blockchain-based technologies later in the book, but let me say that I do think that the process of disintermediation often increases cost, risk, and the potential for financial fraud.

Moving in from the left side of the diagram, we see that the asset owners deal directly with buy-side agents by interfacing with a group of buy-siders we call *advisors*. Advisors help asset owners find asset managers that meet the owners' risk/reward criteria. As we will see, there are a great many asset managers—running more funds than there are financial instruments to purchase—so advisors help owners sort through the jungle of asset manager offerings. In general, the type of advisor asset owners deal with depends on the amount of capital they have to invest, with investment advisors serving the lowest net worth owners, private wealth managers serving well-off owners, family offices servicing the needs of the very wealthy, and investment consultants advising very large, institutional owners.

This book is primarily about the next block in on our diagram— asset managers. By that term I mean the organizations and people that form the tip of the buy-side spear—those who are responsible for expressing asset owners' opinions about the relative value of different investments. The function of asset managers within the capital markets is simply to allocate asset owners' capital to the ever-changing set of investment opportunities.

Any process related to the allocation of capital and the distribution of capital gains or losses is part of the asset management process. We broadly split the asset management group into three different types—traditional, alternative, and institutional—and will explain what we mean by those divisions as follows.

Once money finds its way to asset managers, those asset managers must pool the funds and find a way to allocate them to investment opportunities. They do so by contacting the level of sell-side agents that are closest to the market, the broker-dealers and market makers responsible for filling client orders, either out of their own inventory or through transactions on the "secondary" market.[4] Markets are established with another class of intermediaries about which I will write in a moment. But now that we have followed asset owner capital through the buy-side process and placed our order with the sell-side agents, let's look at the process issuers go through to place securities on the market—in other words, we will work through our ecosystem map starting now from the right side.

The block at the far-right side of the diagram represents the issuer principals that we have already discussed. When issuers wish to raise money, they speak with sell-side agents: investment bankers. Investment bankers function as advisors to issuers in much the same way that the advisors and asset managers do for the asset owners on the other end of the diagram.

Investment bankers are sell-side agents that deal with primary markets. The work they do is legally separated from the work the sell-side agents working in the secondary markets are doing through what is known as a "Chinese wall." Investment bankers are working on behalf of issuers, whereas broker-dealers are working ultimately on behalf of asset owners; to avoid conflicts of interest, these two groups are separated within the firm. Usually broker-dealers sit lower in the headquarters building (so they don't waste as much time going up and down elevators), while investment bankers' offices are higher up in the building near the executive suites.

Both divisions of the sell side serve as conduits to investments through its connection to another class of intermediaries—listed in the map under the label "Infrastructure" and consisting of exchanges, clearinghouses, custodians, and administrators.

The buy side and the sell side communicate with one another and have a common "language" for discussing investments, thanks to another class of intermediaries called "Information Providers" in the map—these are companies like Bloomberg, MSCI, and Moody's Investor Service. Information suppliers also provide data to principal investors (e.g., any retail investor can look up the Moody's bond rating for a certain corporate bond), but the primary purpose of information suppliers is to facilitate transactions, and that means they mainly focus on serving the needs of buy- and sell-side agents.

All the players in our ecosystem swim in a sea of laws, rules, and oversight frameworks made possible by regulators—for instance, the US Securities and Exchange Commission (SEC).

With this 30,000-foot overview in our minds, let's look at each player in turn, all from the perspective of what an asset manager needs to know.

Asset Owners'
Buy-Side Agents

Different types of asset owners have different needs and different criteria on which they make decisions. An asset manager must understand the needs and criteria of each type of owner—individuals, institutions, and governments—and because the role of go-betweens that I have called "advisors" is so important to asset owners, the perspectives of the advisors is important as well.

Asset owners and advisors are usually divided up by the level of assets under management (AUM) an entity controls. Tables 2.1 and 2.2 provide an overview of how I think about the different groups.

TABLE 2.1 Characteristics of Individual Asset Owners and Their Advisors

INDIVIDUAL OWNERS			ADVISORS	
Type	Objective	Characteristics	Type	Incentives
Retail Individual (Low financial literacy. Tens to hundreds of thousands USD.)	The goal of a retail investor is capital growth. Their main objective is to preserve quality of life after retirement.	Retired individuals are counting on their savings of their working lives to supplement any income they receive from insurance programs. Graduates joining the workforce can figure on about 50 years' worth of savings before harvesting investment profits, but most do not start until they are well older. A reasonable time horizon is in the 10–20-year range. The typical allocation of this group is a traditional equity and fixed-income blend.	**Stockbroker** **Online broker** **Robo advisor**	Gather assets at high fees. Potentially churn.
Wealthy Individual (Low financial literacy. Hundreds of thousands to millions USD.)	Wealthy individuals aim for capital preservation, which enables them to provide a comfortable life, good medical care in old age, and passing on property to descendants.	Many individuals in this group are professionals or small business owners who are looking to manage excess savings or proceeds from the sale of their business when they retire. The time horizon for this group is in the 20–30-year range. As a retail individual they invest along a traditional equity and fixed-income blend. Potentially this group could also add more exotic products or themes to their portfolios.	**Private Banker** **Wealth Manager**	Gather assets. Cross-sell financial products.

INDIVIDUAL OWNERS		
Type	Objective	Characteristics
High Net-Worth Individual (Medium to high financial literacy. Tens of millions to billions USD.)	HNWI aim for growing their asset base. The main objective is to typically pass on property to descendants or philanthropic projects. As such, minimizing tax withholding is important.	HNWI are not worried about near-term cash flow needs and have enough excess savings to feel secure in providing for themselves throughout their lives. Their focus is to establish a foothold in the upper class for the next generations and hence have a time horizon in the range of 50-year plus. Consequently, this group tends to move away from the traditional equity and fixed-income blend to the endowment model investment approach.

ADVISORS	
Type	Incentives
Single-Family Office **Multi-Family Office**	Maximize profit. Maintain relationship with family.

15

TABLE 2.2 Characteristics of Institutional Asset Owners and Their Advisors

INSTITUTIONAL OWNERS			ADVISORS	
Type	Objective	Characteristics	Type	Incentives
Foundations and Endowments (High financial literacy. Hundreds of millions to hundreds of billions USD.)	Capital growth to finance a specific cause or a specific area of research.	The objective of an endowment or a foundation is specific and long-term in nature. Hence, this group invests according to the model named after them: the endowment model. Their investment horizon is 50-year plus.	**Asset Managers**	Continue to manage funds and maintain good relationship with owner.
Corporate Pension (Medium to high financial literacy. Hundreds of millions to hundreds of billions USD.)	Fulfilling obligations to provide contractually defined benefits.	Pension funds rely upon demographic trends and on economic growth to fulfill their obligations—taking payments from many younger workers and routing some proportion of those to pay the claims of a smaller number of retired workers. The investment approach and horizon—typically in the range of 20–30 years—is determined by their liabilities.	**Pension Consultants**	Maximize profit of business relationship.
Mutual Insurer (High financial literacy. Hundreds of millions to hundreds of billions USD.)	Fulfilling obligations to provide contractually defined benefits.	Insurers need to match the liabilities of their insurance contracts. Insurers are highly regulated and monitored. In line with their liabilities, insurers do have a lower risk appetite and an investment horizon that is in the range of 50 years.	**Asset Managers**	Maximize profit of business relationship.

INSTITUTIONAL OWNERS		
Type	**Objective**	**Characteristics**
Forex Reserve Fund (High financial literacy. Up to trillions USD.)	Balancing payments and manage the exchange rate of the currency of a country.	Forex Reserve Funds implement an investment policy, typically given by the central bank, and, as such, do have a nonprofit motive. The investment horizon is short, i.e., 1 year, since portfolio reflects what is going on in the world.
Sovereign Wealth Fund (High financial literacy. Up to trillions USD.)	Capital growth to provide funds to its citizens to further political and social goals.	The investment approach of SWF can vary substantially. Some follow the endowment model; some simply want to mimic a global market portfolio following an almost traditional equity and fixed-income blend.
Public Pensions (High financial literacy. Up to trillions USD.)	Fulfilling obligations to provide contractually defined benefits.	See "Corporate Pensions."

ADVISORS	
Type	**Incentives**
Central Bank	Fulfill political mandate.
Asset Managers	Maximize profit of business relationship.
Pension Consultants	Maximize profit of business relationship.

The buy side is composed of asset managers who have a fiduciary responsibility to asset owners and who help society by acting as an intermediary performing the four basic functions described in Chapter 1. Each of these functions is made easier through the pooling of investor assets.

Consider an asset owner trying to buy 2,000 separate shares on different global markets to create a personalized global broad market index. First, buying all these shares would be cost prohibitive due to transaction fees; when a large fund buys the same 2,000 shares, however, it can split the transaction costs across all the fund's investors, greatly lowering the fees each investor pays. Second, some of the notional values might be too large to appropriately weight against other shares; however, with a large pool of assets, granular control of percentage exposure is much easier. Also, the ability to buy and sell on certain markets (e.g., India or China) might be limited to investors with certain approvals, which only large asset managers would be able to apply for and gain. Third, by buying so many stocks, idiosyncratic (i.e., company-specific) risk is significantly attenuated.

While there are many ways to group asset managers depending on focus and specialization of the fund, I like to think of dividing them in terms of why, what, and how the asset manager invests client money. Considering these criteria, there are three main divisions of managers I discuss:

- Traditional managers
- Alternative managers
- Institutional investors

Traditional and alternative asset managers are alike in that they are responsible for the day-to-day management of investments they select on behalf of clients, and they seldom invest in products of other asset managers.

Traditional asset managers typically invest in standard, "plain vanilla" asset classes—stocks and bonds—and are often restricted in the ability to invest in instruments considered more speculative, such as derivatives. While traditional managers are usually split by the asset class in which they invest (i.e., an equity fund/manager or a bond fund/manager), there has been a trend to create holistic funds that allocate client assets to equities, bonds, and sometimes other asset classes such as commodities.

Alternative asset managers serve specialized clients and usually very wealthy ones. They may invest in plain vanilla products but can also invest in more exotic asset classes such as credit derivatives, asset-backed securities, syndicated loans, options, futures, and the like. In addition to investing in asset classes in which traditional managers do not typically invest, alternative asset managers often use strategies not used by traditional managers, especially leverage (borrowing money to invest) and short-selling (selling borrowed securities and hoping to buy them back later at a lower price).

All the products and strategies I've mentioned here are those that can be used on financial exchanges, but there is another type of alternative asset manager that invests in companies not listed on an exchange—private companies, in other words. Some of these private companies are going concerns (in which the asset managers are engaged in *private equity* investing) or in companies that are starting up and attempting to bring a new product or concept to market (in which case, the asset managers are said to be engaged in *venture capital* investing).

The third group of asset managers is that of institutional investors. These managers typically manage assets for a specific purpose such as a university endowment. This group also has an enormous overlap with institutional and governmental asset owners, so many of the entities already discussed—pension funds (both public and private), insurance companies, sovereign wealth funds—also fall under the category of institutional investors within the asset manager category.

The amount that each group of asset managers manages is presented in Figure 2.1.

Traditional Asset Managers	Estimated Size [T USD] 160.7[1]
Asset Managers	131.7[2]
Wealth Managers	29.0[3]
- Broker/Dealers	
- Banks	
- Advisors	
Examples of Investment Products	
- Mutual Funds	
- Exchange-Traded Funds	

Alternative Asset Managers	Estimated Size [T USD] 13.9[1]
Hedge Fund Managers	4.1[4]
- L/S Equity Managers	1.4[4]
- Event-Driven Managers	0.1[4]
- Global Macro Managers	0.7[4]
Private Equity Managers	9.8[5]
- Venture Capital Managers	1.8[5]
- Buyout Funds, etc.	8.0[5]
Examples of Investment Products	
- Hedge Funds	
- Private Equity Funds	

Institutional Investors	Estimated Size [T USD] 97.2[1]
Private Institutions	58.3[1]
- Pension Funds	38.5[6]
- Insurance Companies	19.8[7]
Public Institutions	38.9[1]
- Foreign Exchange Reserves	6.5[8]
- Sovereign Wealth Funds	11.4[9]
- Public Pension Funds	21.0[9]
Examples of Investment Products	
- Unit-Linked Insurance Plans	
- Pension Schemes	

FIGURE 2.1 AUM by type

[1] Own estimation based on AUM of subcategories.
[2] Thinking Ahead Institute 2022. Data as of end 2021.
[3] Mukerjee, 2021. Data as of end 2020.
[4] IOSCO 2022. Data as of end 2020.
[5] McKinsey, 2022. Buyout funds and so on include private debt and real asset funds. Data as of H1 2021.
[6] OECD, 2023. Data as of end 2021.
[7] OECD, 2022. Data as of end 2020.
[8] Own estimation based on the five largest foreign exchange reserves of funds: People's Republic of China ($3.2 trillion as of end 2022), Japan ($1.2 trillion as of end 2022), Switzerland ($0.9 trillion as of end 2022), Russia ($0.6 trillion as of end 2022), India ($0.6 trillion as of end 2022).
[9] Global SWF, n.d. Data as of end 2022.

Note that Figure 2.1 is slightly misleading. Recall that institutional investors allocate some portion of their capital pools to traditional and alternative asset managers. As such, the $97.2 trillion of assets under institutional investor management are at least partly reflected in the $160.7 trillion managed by traditional managers and the $13.9 trillion managed by alternative ones.

The careful reader might look at the map in Figure 1.1 and become a bit indignant. After all, I've spent many words making distinctions between principals and agents and discussing how advisors and other intermediaries work on behalf of asset owners to direct investments to asset managers. However, in Figure 2.1, we see advisors, banks, and broker-dealers listed among the asset manager group.

In fact, trying to draw bright lines between advisors, banks, asset owners, and asset managers is about as easy as removing saltiness from seawater. Any institution with some relationship to asset owners will attempt to leverage that relationship to generate economic benefits for itself. An advisor that works for a bank, for instance, might direct some of their clients' money to mutual fund companies, place some of their capital in annuity products, some into a fund of hedge funds (FoHF), and perhaps have discretionary control over some subset of the asset owners' securities accounts (a *separately managed account*, or SMA). If an owner is the beneficiary of a pension fund, the owner's proportion of pension's assets might be directed into hedge funds or private equity investments as well. Industry observers try to estimate the AUM controlled by different management groups, but these observers often have no way to prevent the double counting that arises naturally from these overlapping relationships.

TRADITIONAL ASSET MANAGERS

Among traditional asset managers, there are mutual funds and exchange-traded funds (ETFs). Both types of traditional managers carry out the same essential functions of financial intermediaries, but their legal structure differs some.

Mutual Funds

Most people invested in a mutual fund probably do not have a sense of this, but when they buy shares in the fund, they in fact become owners of a special type of company whose purpose is to invest in a diversified basket of assets. This type of firm is generally called an *investment company* and has different legal forms in different jurisdictions (e.g., SICAV in Europe). In the United States, a mutual fund is structured as an open-end investment company, which can be conceived of as a separate, special-purpose company with its own management and governance, whose purpose is to invest in the securities of other companies.

The asset management companies you have heard about (e.g., Fidelity, Vanguard) are the "sponsors" of many of these special-purpose companies. Sponsors incorporate and file paperwork for a new fund/special-purpose company when they perceive customer demand for investments meeting certain criteria. Sponsors will set the fund's mandate, which specifies the risk and return goals of the fund, describes any position size limits, establishes a benchmark if applicable, and in general, paints the lines of the field where the fund will play its game. In short, the asset management company functions as a sort of parent or umbrella entity for a diversified group of special purpose investment companies that is often called a *family of funds*.

A mutual fund is capitalized with investors' funds, and the company's directors are responsible for finding and hiring an investment advisor to carry out the day-to-day activities of purchasing and selling investment assets as well as other third-party providers that take care of bookkeeping, custodial, and other operational and legal duties.

The sponsor of a family of funds maintains a business unit that employs fund managers. For instance, Fidelity—a prominent sponsor—runs a business unit called Fidelity Management and Research. Funds sponsored by Fidelity usually contract out investment advisor duties to employees of Fidelity Management and Research, but fund directors can also select "subadvisors" from other companies to manage the fund's assets.

Funds' boards have both related and independent directors, with the former being employees of the sponsoring company. Once funded, a fund's board is required to maintain a majority of independent directors—people who are not employees of the sponsor nor members of employees' immediate families. These independent directors must be nominated to the board by other independent directors.

Funds' directors are responsible for five main duties: fund performance evaluation, contract approval, fee approval, pricing of funds' shares, and oversight of the third-party functions (e.g., portfolio management and compliance issues).

A mutual fund—as an open-end fund—does not trade on an exchange; instead, an investor wishing to sell some or all his shares will sell them back to the special-purpose company. This is possible because the mutual fund has the power to create new shares if demand for the fund is high, so its capitalization can theoretically increase indefinitely.

Another type of fund, called a closed-end fund, raises capital through an initial public offering (IPO) and the number of shares created in this process are all the shares that will ever trade. After the IPO, the price of a closed-end fund is determined on the exchange as the fund is traded like any other stock.

The price at which shares in the open-end fund are transacted are set each day at the close of trading. In other words, if an investor enters an order to buy a stake in a fund at midday, she will not know the price at which she bought the fund until the settlement prices for all the stocks held by the funds are finalized at the market close. Any orders that are placed after the market close are considered as those to be filled on the next trading day at the next day's closing price.

Exchange-Traded Funds

ETFs have become a very popular investment product, likely because they combine the main advantage of closed-end funds with the main advantage of open-end funds mentioned previously.

The most common legal structure of an ETF is the same as mutual funds (open-end investment company), and both are governed by the same regulations. As such, the words used to describe the participants are also almost the same.

An ETF sponsor is a company that manages the portfolios containing assets underlying the ETF. The sponsor files paperwork with the regulatory body describing the ETF, and once that plan is approved, the sponsor finds an "authorized participant," usually a large broker-dealer.

The authorized participant buys shares in the market according to the ETF sponsor's plan and places those shares in a fund. The fund bundles those shares as "creation units" and swaps these creation units for the value of shares that the authorized participant had placed into the fund in the first place. After that, the authorized participant slices up the creation units into the correct denomination for the ETF and puts those newly created ETF shares up for sale on the secondary market.

Because shares of the ETF are listed on the market, they can be traded intraday—mirroring the main advantage of closed-end funds. Because the ability to generate new creation units is unlimited, the number of ETFs available is not restricted—mirroring the main advantage of open-end funds.

Any assets can be placed in the fund and used as creation units, and whereas the earliest ETFs were structured as index trackers (e.g. tracking the S&P 500 index), over the years, ETFs have been structured to replicate the inverse returns of an index (i.e., if the index price rises by 1 percent in one day, the inverse ETF's price will fall by 1 percent on that day), levered returns of an index, levered inverse returns of an index, and recently, the price of cryptocurrencies.

One important thing to note is that multiple ETFs can (and do) track the same underlying basket—two ETF sponsors can define their ETF in the same way and set up trusts and creation units independently. Usually, one of these will be much more liquid and heavily traded than the other, so is more investable.

ALTERNATIVE ASSET MANAGERS

Alternative managers use instruments and strategies not used by traditional managers, and/or invest in private securities (i.e., those not listed on an exchange). This section will look at three of the most prominent strategies for hedge funds and discuss the main divisions between managers that invest in private securities.

Alternative asset managers all typically use a partnership structure to manage their investment activities. The managers themselves form an entity that has decision-making authority for the partnership, so they are identified as *general partners* (GP). Clients enter the partnership without the right to decide how the partnership will operate, a status that is legally termed a *limited partnership* (LP). We will discuss the origins of this structure and explain it in detail in Chapter 5, but for now, just be aware that in the alternative asset management world, a GP means a fund manager and an LP means a client—one often hears these terms used in this world.

The other similarity between alternative asset managers is the fee structure. "2-and-20"—a 2 percent management fee and 20 percent of profits in excess of some benchmark—are typical, though this simple formula is made more complex in certain private equity investments.

Hedge Fund Managers

Hedge fund managers sell themselves as—and are often considered to be—investors possessing a high level of investment skill. In the hierarchy of the industry, they are at the pinnacle of the profession. Many are known, not only for their investing skill, but for their skill in public speaking, since much of their work deals with attracting assets to manage. These superstars appear at investment conferences, on cable TV channels, and at international gatherings like the World Economic Forum in Davos, and often portray larger-than-life personalities and lifestyles.

Despite several enormous (to the point of threatening global financial stability) blowups and cases of egregious law-bending and breaking, the hedge fund industry has shown stellar growth over the past three decades.

In 1990, hedge funds managed AUM of less than $50 billion (Getmansky et al., 2015). At the end of 2020, the total assets under hedge fund management summed up to at least $4.1 trillion—representing a compound annual growth of over 15 percent per year.[1]

Hedge funds are overwhelmingly a feature of the US capital markets, with 75 percent of hedge fund assets managed by US managers (but of course with both US and international clients). Roughly a fifth of hedge funds are managed in Europe (mainly the United Kingdom, suggesting an Anglo-American cultural explanation) and about 5 percent in Asia (mainly in Hong Kong, to continue with the "Anglosphere" theme).[2]

Private Market Managers

Traditional investment managers and hedge fund managers transact in more or less liquid securities listed on public markets. Liquidity is, in fact, a big deal to a public investment manager.

In contrast to those buy-siders, asset managers who specialize in investing in nonpublic securities (i.e., securities that are not traded on an exchange) are accustomed to having absolutely no ability to liquidate their position for years at a time. The two main groups of these kinds of investors are venture capitalists (VC) and private equity (PE) bankers, with which I am including private real estate investors as well due to the similarities in the characteristics and leverage of the investments.

Not only does the process of withdrawing money differ, the process of placing money is also different from simply buying mutual fund shares. VC and PE firms both require clients (the partnership's LPs) to sign subscription agreements. These subscription agreements sometimes require LPs to partially fund their investment up front, but often simply stipulate that the limited partner will pay up to a certain amount within a certain number of days of the funds being requested. The process of an investment manager requesting investment funds from a pledged partner is termed a *capital call*. Until the client receives a capital call, the client's assets can remain invested in some liquid instrument under the client's control.

VENTURE CAPITAL

A venture capital fund invests in startup companies that run along a continuum of commercial capabilities. Many VC funds prefer to invest in companies in a similar stage of commercial development, and the venture world discusses startup investing in terms of these stages.

There are roughly five separate VC stages that are separated by the startups' business activities and the asset owners that typically fund startups at each stage. Different people and organizations have different definitions of the stages, but in general, you can think of them as:

- **Pre-seed:** Developing a business concept
- **Seed:** Developing a prototype
- **Series A:** Conducting initial commercial tests and engaging with clients
- **Series B:** Developing a repeatable formula for commercial success
- **Series C and beyond:** Scaling up the operations of the business and preparing for listing on a public exchange

At one end of the spectrum are pre-seed stage companies—those that may not have more than an initial idea about a product or service, that may not have any assets or have even done the paperwork to form a legal entity. On the other end of the spectrum are well-known private "unicorns"—companies that are well-known and whose level of commercial maturity is high (e.g., Stripe, SpaceX, Klarna) with valuations above $1 billion.

The geographic split for VC funds is similar to that of hedge funds, with roughly 75 percent of AUM managed by US fund managers and something like 25 percent managed in Europe, with relatively small amounts managed in Asia. Within the United States, California is the most active state for VC, followed by Massachusetts, New York, and Texas. California is especially important for software ventures—centered around Stanford and Palo Alto (Sand Hill Road in Palo Alto is to the VC world what *al-Ka'bah* is to Muslims). Massachusetts gives rise to more biotechnology startups, centered on Boston's Harvard and MIT ecosystems (Massachusetts's Route 128 is Sand Hill Road's little brother on the East Coast).

A VC fund is typically structured as a 10-year limited partnership, and the partner of a VC fund thinks of the partnership in three different chunks of time. The first year or two of a fund's existence is focused on "sourcing" deals—speaking with entrepreneurs, assessing business plans, and making decisions about which startups the fund will invest in. The next three to five years are focused on pouring energy into the companies in the portfolio that are still up and running to "scale" quickly—in other words, to increase the number of customers they serve so that revenue growth rates are very high. The last few years are focused on "harvesting" the investments in their portfolio—trying to either arrange a sale to a "strategic investor" (i.e., a listed company or a large private company that is buying startups to increase their own products' feature sets and/or to stifle competition) or to plan for an IPO.

In addition to private VC firms, corporate venture capital (CVC) firms also exist. Many large companies from widely different industries (e.g., Google, Occidental Petroleum) establish VC arms to supplement traditional research and development (R&D) efforts within their firms.

VC funds tend to be successful in proportion to the quality of their networks. Especially at early stages, using a discounted cash flow model to try to value a startup is folly.[3] As such, VCs tend to pay the most attention to startups that come to them through introductions via other VCs that they've worked with (and succeeded) in the past, trusted entrepreneurs that have founded or worked for the VC's portfolio companies in the past, or mentors/colleagues in academia who are often the first ones to see new scientific ideas in labs or research papers.

PRIVATE EQUITY

Whereas VC firms invest in startup companies—some of which do not yet have any customers, let alone a well-developed business model—PE funds look to invest in businesses operating in well-understood industries and/or with mature, proven business models.

Typically, a PE firm wants to find an existing company with a history of operations that extend through at least one business cycle and that is poorly managed or not otherwise generating a good return on its assets in place.

The PE firm's strategy typically uses leverage—in other words, the fund will invest $10 of their client's money, then borrow $90 from banks to buy an asset selling for $100—and after purchasing the firm, uses the firm's own cash flow to service the debt from the investment. For this reason, PE funds are often known as *LBO*, or leveraged buyout funds.

PE funds tend to prefer underperforming assets on the theory that they can replace the management team, make other business model changes (e.g., selling off noncore units), and improve profitability. The theory is that if they are unsuccessful at improving the firm's operations, at least the debt payments are covered by cash from operations. If they are successful, the increased profitability pays them and their LPs a good rate of return, and they can turn around and sell the (now improved) company to a strategic investor (i.e., a larger company) or take it public via IPO.

PE funds are successful in proportion to the quality of the network contacts of its managing directors. Typically, sell-side bankers will approach PE firms with prospective transactions, so the quality of PE bankers' connections to the sell-side are important. Then a PE firm will typically retain former leading executives in the industries in which it typically invests and relies on these executives to lead the turnarounds of the struggling acquisitions. After a few years of cleanup work, the PE banker's connections to the sell-side pay off again as they look to exit the investment through sale to a strategic investor or through a stock exchange listing.

PE transactions obviously tend to focus on companies that have been shown to generate dependable, steady cash flows, or that have the prospect to do so if the firms were run more competently. This situation—a cash-flow producing asset that is bought using a healthy amount of leverage—looks very similar to the situation of commercial real estate investors, so I tend to think of private real estate investments as just a subcategory of PE.

AUM AND RETURNS FOR PRIVATE MARKET MANAGERS

The entire private investments market—including VC, PE, private loans, and real estate—represents roughly $10 trillion of AUM, of which one-fifth of this amount is managed by VC funds and about 45 percent by PE funds. Because these funds have minimum investment requirements and require individuals to be "accredited" (i.e., meet a regulatory mandate for income and net worth), the majority of AUM in private market funds are institutional—corporations, pension funds, endowments, and the like.

Trying to assess the performance of private market managers is very difficult, since the assets do not trade on secondary markets.

The common wisdom about VC and PE funds is that they are attractive investments that tend to outperform the broader market (and whose returns are not necessarily correlated with the market—making them doubly attractive). However, looking as objectively as possible at LP returns in private market funds gives a decidedly more nuanced picture.

A performance survey by Steven Kaplan and Berk Sensoy found that PE funds (which they call "buyout funds") had outperformed the S&P 500 by an average of 20 percent over the life of the funds, but there is evidence that PE outperformance net of fees is deteriorating as more and more money flows into this asset class (Kaplan and Sensoy, 2015).

The relationship of asset class inflows to fund performance is such an important one that we discuss it in detail later in this book as one of the driving forces of the asset management business. Suffice it to say that the performance of PE groups raising funds over the past two decades—a period during which the number of funds and the associated capital commitments were historically high—has been slipping. There are good reasons to expect this slippage to occur, as laid out by the academics Berk and Green in a 2004 paper we discuss in more detail in Chapter 6.

The picture of VC returns is even sadder. The Kaplan and Sensoy survey found that venture funds raised in the 1990s (i.e., the ones that would have harvested going into the dot.com boom and crash) outperformed the S&P 500, whereas those raised in the 2000s underperformed. A 2018 paper entitled "Risk Adjustment in Private Equity Returns" by Arthur Korteweg (Korteweg, 2019) found much the same result: "the average venture capital (VC) fund earned positive risk-adjusted returns before the turn of the millennium, but net-of-fee returns have been zero or even negative since."

What's the moral of the story? If you have the chance to invest in a VC fund in 1994, you'd better take it!

INSTITUTIONAL INVESTORS

Any entity that is already pooling resources from asset owners can be considered an intermediary of sorts. That said, if the pooling entity was founded and constituted by the asset owners and is acting as a single representative of them, it should also be considered an asset owner. The most significant institutional investors are just this sort of asset owner—an entity like the ones listed in Table 2.2—a corporate or government pension, a sovereign wealth fund, or a mutual insurance company that acts on behalf of all the members of a particular group.

The characteristic that sets this class of owners apart from others is that it splits the duties of investment management between itself and external managers. Because some of the assets are allocated to external managers, this group of institutional investors is often termed *allocators*.

I have already offered an overview of each of these classes of allocators, so there is not much left to say here except to discuss the economics of why a large asset owner might want to also function as an asset manager in its own right, which follows in the next section.

Also, there is one other institutional investor that is not an "asset owner cum asset manager" but rather a pure-play allocator—funds of hedge funds (FoHF). FoHFs are agents in every sense of the word, so they are different from other institutional investors that also act as principals. Because FoHFs share so many similarities with other allocators, I describe them here.

Asset Owners cum Asset Managers

Why a large pension fund, SWF, or insurance company would choose to "in-source" its investment decision-making is simple mathematics. If I oversee a pension with a $10 billion AUM and I outsource the management of those funds at a cost of 50 basis points, I will end up paying $50 million a year to outside parties. $50 million will buy a lot of investment talent, and a portfolio of $10 billion will attract salespeople and research analysts from the sell-side firms like flies.

As mentioned, owner/managers are usually investing for a specific purpose tied to some future liability. For instance, a pension fund has the liability to its members to provide certain benefits to them after retirement; an insurance company has the liability to meet the lawful claims of its customers when they suffer a covered loss. As such, the timing and nature of the institution's future liabilities defines its investment policy—risk tolerance, investment time horizon, and liquidity constraints must all be sensibly aligned.

Pure-Play Allocator

FoHFs are structured like hedge funds, pooling capital from HNW owners and institutional or government allocators. While the benefits of pooling capital are as previously described, the fact that FoHFs charge management and performance fees in addition to fees charged by the hedge funds where the FoHFs are placing owners' capital has caused many investors to question whether allocating to these institutional investors is value-creative or value-destructive to owners.[4]

Large funds of funds do pool significant amounts of capital (e.g., UBS Hedge Fund Solutions, the largest FoHF, oversees an AUM of more than $40 billion), have the negotiating power to force smaller hedge funds to accept lower fees, and are notorious among hedge fund managers for negotiating the cancellation of lock-up periods, which allows them to make redemptions on a quarterly basis. An FoHF might withdraw their clients' money if a hedge fund under-performs its benchmark even over a single quarter.

Part of the reason that FoHFs throw their negotiating weight around when placing capital with hedge funds to remove lock-up provisions is because they typically allow for their own clients to request a capital redemption more or much more frequently than hedge funds allow—monthly in most cases.

Issuers' Sell-Side Agents

The sell side has three different sides. One side faces the buy side, another faces the issuers, and the third faces the market.

In Figure 1.1, note that the sell-side box is split into three sections, with each facing a different constituency. The buy side interfaces directly with sell-side research analysts and salespeople.[1] Securities issuers interface directly with investment bankers.[2] A sell-side institution's traders and operations employees interface directly with the exchange or with other market participants on the secondary market.

Before we go much further, I should say something about nomenclature. In the business, people simply refer to "the sell side," but in media, these institutions are talked about as "banks," "investment banks," "brokers," and "broker-dealers." These names court confusion, because while there is overlap between a sell-side institution and a bank, investment bank, broker, and broker-dealer, they are not exactly the same. A bank is an institution that receives deposits and lends them out again; an investment bank is one function within a sell-side shop; a broker sounds uncomfortably like "stockbroker," and someone on the sell side would rather wear white shoes after Labor Day than speak to a retail investor; a broker-dealer is yet another function within a sell-side shop.

By far, the most important thing to understand about the sell side is that it is a flow business—transaction volumes count, and a good part of sell-side salaries are tied to the transaction volumes flowing through their purview.

With this general rule in mind, let's look at each part of a sell-side shop.

SALES AND RESEARCH

Salespeople sell stocks, bonds, or derivatives. Most people assume that most investment volume is in stocks, but bond volumes are much, much larger, thanks to the heavy borrowing needs of "sovereign borrowers" (i.e., countries).

In 2012 the global fixed-income market and the global equity market had capitalizations of $87 trillion and $57 trillion, respectively. In 2021, both markets had capitalizations of $127 trillion and $124 trillion, respectively (SIFMA, 2022).

However, in terms of issuance volume the fixed-income market is still much larger. For example, in 2021, $13,437 billion in fixed-income securities were issued in the United States compared to only $436 billion in equity issuance (SIFMA, 2022). The two drivers of fixed-income issuance are government bonds and mortgage debt.

Mortgage-backed securities also represent a large percentage of the bond or fixed-income markets; these securities are created by aggregating (i.e., pooling) the mortgages of many homeowner borrowers. What this means is that in fixed-income markets, we have many more potential issuers—governments and individual homeowners—than in equity markets, where only companies are issuing securities.

Because the market sizes between fixed-income and equity markets are so large, the value of bonds traded is much larger than the value of stocks traded; per-day dollar volumes in the US bond market total around $955 billion versus "only" $565 billion in stock markets (SIFMA, 2022).

Product sales and trading are split up by geography and type (e.g., US equity, European sovereign debt), and employees dedicated to managing trade flow of that type of product are said to "sit on a desk." For example, if I am a salesperson who specializes in European equity, I will tell people that I sit on the European equity desk.

Salespeople (sometimes known as "sales-traders" on the equity side of the business) live and die by transaction volume. A good salesperson knows his buy-side counterparty[3] well and tries to the extent possible to encourage the buy-sider to trade with him or her as often as possible.

The best way to encourage the buy side to trade is to offer some "important" bit of information. To offer important information, the salesperson's best weapon is the research analyst. Research analysts have the responsibility to "cover" (i.e., research, analyze, and write reports about) about a dozen stocks and have familiarity with a few dozen more associated stocks. Research analysts are divided up by industry or by geography and industry, depending on the competitive dynamics of the sector. Research analysts speak with executives at their coverage companies, create financial models for the companies while considering industry conditions, and use the results of those models to make recommendations to buy, sell, or hold the securities the company is issuing.

Sell-side analysts may be drawn from the executive ranks of companies in a certain industry, so have a good understanding of the competitive dynamics of the firm and may also meet more or less frequently with upper management (especially the CFO) at the companies they cover.

However, while analysts do meet with executives of the companies under coverage, they do so strictly as third-party analysts, as if they were representing investor interests rather than the sell-side institutions they work for.

The sell-side research analyst does not directly sell the product of his or her work. The reports produced by the research analyst are used as an inducement for asset managers to interact with the sell-side institution for which the analyst works. The result sought by the sell-side institution is for the buy-side institution to transact through the sell-sider's sales and trading arm.

Remember that the key to understanding the sell side is the number of transactions they complete. Leading research analysts get up in front of large audiences of clients, appear on cable TV shows, and are quoted in the *Financial Times* and the *Wall Street Journal*. They look like superstars, but really they are slaves working on behalf of the sell-side institution's sales desk, specifically, the managing director who acts as the "desk head." As such, sell-side reports must offer some reason to transact, because the sales desk only gets paid commissions and fees when a client transacts with them.[4]

It is likely for this reason that quarterly earnings announcements have become such an important part of the sell-side calendar. Before corporate earnings statements are released, sell-side research analysts make predictions about what the company will say and opine on the possible implication of certain statements.

After the earnings calls, the analytical team will produce an earnings report and perhaps even change the rating they have assigned the company (from "buy" to "hold" is a bearish signal, obviously; from "sell" to "buy" is the most bullish signal possible). The sales desk loves it when a research analyst publishes a change of opinion note! When this happens, the salespeople on the desk start calling each of their buy-side contacts prompting them to transact based on the change in researcher opinion.

TRADING AND OPERATIONS

As much as it feels natural to talk about investment banking now, let's follow the transaction to its logical conclusion and finish up with the part of an investment bank that touches the buy side before moving on to the part of the bank that deals with issuers.

After a client places an order with a salesperson, that order must get routed to a market to be transacted. Anyone with experience in trading for their own accounts will have the impression that the routing and transacting parts are done pretty much instantaneously and automatically. However, for a large-asset manager, this is most decidedly not the case. We will discuss the limitations put on asset managers by the amount of a security's liquidity in a later chapter, but for now suffice it to say that often a good bit of work needs to be done to execute a trade on behalf of a client.

The most important thing when filling an order is that the execution of that transaction should not be allowed to affect the price of the stock. In the pursuit of this, there are four very important letters: V, W, A, and P. *VWAP* means volume-weighted average price, and its calculation should be obvious from the very name.

A sell-side trader wants to fill a client order at VWAP or (hopefully) better. Doing so makes the client happy, and when the client is happy, the salesperson is happy. One sell-side trader friend of mine calls himself a "VWAP monkey" because the execution of these trades does not usually take enormous (or any) skill or insight. You just need to know to dribble out the order a little bit at a time, buy more during dips accompanied by higher trading levels, and you should be OK.

If it's easy enough for a monkey to do it, you'd better believe that it's easy enough to be programmed into a computer to do it. Starting back in the mid-aughts, this is exactly what large investment banks started doing—figuring out how to automate the execution of trades so the company could fire a bunch of those highly compensated traders and replace them with Sun Microsystem servers (at the time, Sun Micro offered the biggest bang for the computing buck).

Operations is the last step of the line for a buy-sider's transaction. Even though from your perspective as an investor it looks like you possess the stock as soon as you click the "Buy" button, in truth, all securities transactions "settle" at a different time. Settlement is the process of exchanging securities on the one hand for money on the other, and this process takes place several days after the trading day, depending on the jurisdiction and security traded.

In addition to settlements, a bank's operations department has a risk control function, in that it makes sure that trades are being made on behalf of actual clients and that the clients' account details are correct. An unethical trader without operational oversight could theoretically specify that moneys from the transaction could be sent to his private account in the Cayman Islands, for instance. This would mean that the buyer would pay the trader rather than the counterparty for the stocks in question and that the seller would receive nothing in return.

INVESTMENT BANKING

Investment banking is a business tailored to help securities issuers sell equities and debt on public markets, to plan and advise on mergers with or acquisitions of other companies, and to take part in other capital activities necessary for a large company like spinning off or selling businesses.

Investment bankers, being part of the sell side, are rated by the number of transactions they finish. One often hears about "M&A league tables," for instance, showing which sell-siders effected the most transactions during the period in question.

In the old days, investment bankers represented the greatest source of income for a sell-side institution and the employees working in investment banking were the most highly compensated. Bankers tended to be drawn from the best families from the best schools because those families had the best connections to the industrialists who were running the companies with which the investment bank wanted to do business.

But starting in the 1980s, the traders—those guys (and at that time they were all guys) from the business that deals with the secondary market—started generating more money and gaining more political power within banks. At that time, the people with a sales and trading background were aggressive, smart, and commercially oriented, but they did not have to have graduated from the top schools nor were they expected to attend garden parties with the Guggenheims, for instance. As time has passed and the business has matured, I am not sure that there is a huge difference now in background between the two sides of sell-side institutions, but somehow the investment bankers still have the reputation of running in more rarified circles.

Other Industry Players

The dance between the buy side and the sell side does not take place in a vacuum. The dance floor designed by regulators, infrastructure providers, and information providers plays an important role too.

For asset managers, having an efficient and stable market is crucial. Although it's possible to make money in less favorable market conditions, achieving consistent profits and long-term success becomes challenging without these essential market characteristics.

REGULATORS

Humans can get pretty smug. The massive postwar rebuilding effort in Europe and Japan, powered by US multinational companies, gave rise to a period of unparalleled economic growth. The collapse of the Soviet Union and the rusting through of the Iron Curtain in the early 1990s underscored the advantages of capitalism, free markets, and representative democracies. By the time the chairman of the US Federal Reserve (the Fed), Alan Greenspan, was welcoming the new millennium on his way to receiving an unprecedented fifth nomination as the head of the most powerful and influential bank regulator in the world, he and a lot of other economists believed they had figured it all out. Tweaking interest rates when necessary but basically giving markets free rein had created the Great Moderation—robust economic growth, low inflation, and healthy employment statistics.

Just three months after taking the chairmanship in 1987, Greenspan testified to the US Congress, advocating for the repeal of the Glass-Steagall Act. This landmark legislation, established after the 1929 stock market crash, had enforced a separation between commercial banks, investment banks, and insurance companies.[1] Greenspan's stance foreshadowed the forthcoming era of relaxed regulation. During the buildup to the Global Financial Crisis (GFC), asset managers reveled in the indulgent atmosphere of loose regulation, akin to a bacchanalian party. However, when the music eventually stopped, the absence of responsible oversight proved to be highly unpleasant.

The 2008–2009 GFC effectively disproved the lenient approach to regulation and sparked widespread regulatory reforms worldwide. As a result, regulation has increasingly become a vital factor for asset managers.

Who Regulates?

The most important regulators are those whose purview is a nation-state (e.g., the Fed and the US SEC) or in the case of the European Union, a collection of nation-states (which established the European Securities and Markets Authority [ESMA] in 2011). Every top-level regulator, however, approaches the task of financial supervision in a slightly different way, and the models used vary on a spectrum between "functional" (where supervisors for each type of financial business—banking, insurance, and securities—are established) and "objective" (where a supervisory agency regulates multiple types of institutions to insure, for instance, prudential management or proper business conduct).

The ESMA is a bit of an oddball because it is super-national rather than international. There are also international regulators that exist to coordinate the activities of nation-state and super-national regulators and set standards to which these bodies may refer.

It's easy to get lost in the alphabet soup of regulatory body names, but Figure 4.1 will at least give you a head start on understanding who the participants are.

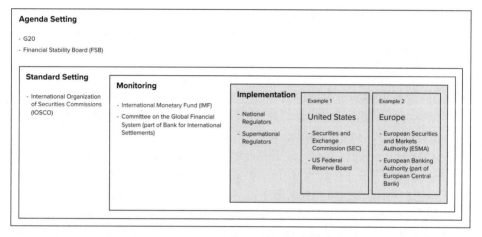

FIGURE 4.1 Asset managers' regulatory landscape

Looking at Figure 4.1, you might be forgiven for thinking that these organizations fit together in a neat hierarchy. In a perfect world, dispassionate regulators might sit at the highest level and develop standards that august international bodies would communicate to local regulators and monitor implementation of those regulations in each nation-state.

The reality is, however, that just as the lines between buy-side institutions are blurry, the relationships between regulators and standard setting organizations are also quite fuzzy. The International Monetary Fund (IMF) is, in a real sense, the grandfather of all international financial organizations and set forth a framework for international financial cooperation as the World War II was starting to grind to its bloody conclusion. It might be placed into a "meta-agenda setting" level higher than the highest level displayed in the figure, because it provides the framework within which the other organizations are built and operate. Right now, it sits at the third highest level, below the standards bodies, because part of its function in the modern day is to monitor crises and to "war game" potential responses to theoretical scenarios. As a final illustration, the Group of 20 (G20) is shown at the highest level—an agenda setter—but its appearance on the global stage is relatively recent, so it is clear that the global regulatory system was not constructed from a top-down process.

In the end, an asset manager who has clients in a given jurisdiction must ultimately answer to the (sometimes overlapped) regulatory bodies in that jurisdiction. The rules are similar from one jurisdiction to another but not the same, because international standards bodies have no authority to force regulations on member states. The rules for a certain jurisdiction are heavily influenced by the financial tragedies that have taken place in that jurisdiction and, to a lesser extent, from notable tragedies that have occurred in foreign jurisdictions. Rules are also an outgrowth of the culture of the home country, the development of its judicial and legislative systems, its political processes, and on the influence of industry players on the rule-making process. Twisting the kaleidoscope containing these elements gives similar but different pictures for the regulatory framework within nation-states.

What Is Regulated?

The old saying on Wall Street is that there are only two emotions: greed and fear. It would be nice if regulators could control those emotions, since the combination of greed and fear lies at the heart of every tragedy since the beginning of organized markets.

Since regulating human emotions is beyond the scope of any government agency, the goal of a regulator is to create the conditions that attenuate the greed and fear of market participants to create a stable, efficient market. A stable and efficient market is one that is characterized by rational analysis of economic conditions and trading that reacts appropriately to new material information becoming public.

As anyone who was alive and active in the markets in 2008–2009 can attest, an unstable, inefficient market caused by failures somewhere in the financial system can cause an enormous amount of damage to companies, investors, and society at large.

Regulating a system to prevent or attenuate systemic risk is not easy though. One of the main lessons learned from the GFC of 2008–2009 was that financial innovation moves much too quickly for static regulation to be up to the task of preserving stability. I believe that rather than creating a rulebook to cover all possible cases, the goal of financial regulation should be to continuously improve the strength and resiliency of the financial system. Viewed from this perspective, it's clear that regulation is very relevant to asset managers, since perceptions regarding what steps will strengthen the financial system are always shifting.

Traditionally, the focus of regulation has been more on entities like banks, investment banks, and exchanges—actors that take large positions on their own behalf or are responsible for the maintenance of an orderly, efficient market. However, another thing the GFC taught us was that asset manager behavior could, in times of extreme stress, synchronize investment activity in a way that exacerbated systemic stress. The sell-everything mentality showed that there are effectively no safe-haven assets when enough stress is applied to a financial system.

Rules that address asset manager reactions in times of extreme financial stress are an area regulators have thought a lot about since circa 2010.

Another area of interest to regulators related to asset managers has been that of protections that should be afforded to the consumers of asset managers' services—asset owners. As the markets started to fall apart in the GFC, a prominent hedge fund manager who had posted continuously impressive, continuously consistent returns—one Bernard Madoff—was shown to have generated such impressive returns by simply paying one set of investors' money from another set of investors, what's known in the business as a Ponzi scheme. Clearly, the asset owner consumers of asset manager services will be reluctant to invest money in funds if they are worried that they have no legal protection from such nefarious schemes.

As such, there are really three regulatory areas that directly affect the day-to-day operations of an asset manager: investor protection, market efficiency, and financial system stability.

INFRASTRUCTURE PROVIDERS

If regulators provide the rules to the financial game, infrastructure providers provide the actual field on which the game is played. This section will mainly focus on the exchanges but also cover other infrastructure providers such as custodians and administrators.

Exchanges

With the largest, most famous stock exchanges all themselves listed entities and owned by huge, international conglomerates, it is worth reminding oneself that exchanges all started out and in fact are still starting out as kinds of private clubs for sell-side companies.

The sell-side brokers of old paid capital into the club (known as "buying a seat on the exchange") and gained certain advantages for their membership. Like any club, exchanges wanted to police their members, making sure to invite only people who would not upset the apple cart by defrauding clients or otherwise negatively influencing trading activity on the market. Recall that sell-side entities are simple toll takers—their compensation is based on transaction volume—so any actions that might impede the growth of trading volume was frowned upon.

The main benefit of having a seat on the exchange was the ability to become a "market maker" in certain stocks, and being a market maker guarantees making a profit in most situations, because only a market maker is allowed to buy at the bid and sell at the ask.

The bid price is always lower than the ask price, so as long as the market maker manages his or her inventory sensibly, the market maker is always buying low and selling high—the age-old recipe for success in the markets. By "managing inventory sensibly," I mean not building inventory that is too much greater than the demand for the security.

A market maker can expect to live a good life, making a nice salary and bonus working sensible hours that leave most of the afternoon free. However, the right given to a market maker to mint money is offset by the exchange requirement that the market maker preserve an orderly market and provide necessary liquidity for the name on which they make their market.

What this means is that, in times of stress, when markets are falling rapidly, and everyone is (rationally or irrationally) afraid, the market maker must continue to post bid and ask prices and must trade a certain minimum number of stocks or contracts (in the case of options) with whoever is willing to pay the bid price or sell at the ask.

This responsibility—to maintain a market even under conditions of great uncertainty—is great for investors. It ensures the benefit of "price discovery," which simply means that a market participant has some sense of what the price will be for a certain quantity. If this advantage doesn't seem profound to you, think about how you might price assets that do not trade on an exchange, like fancy wristwatches. The only way you as a potential buyer or seller of a wristwatch might know what a watch is worth is to ask what a watch like that last traded for. A rare watch might have last traded 13 months ago, so there is no way to know what the supply-demand picture for that watch is today based on a price that is more than a year stale.

The requirement for a market maker to post prices at which he or she will trade a given number of shares of a particular stock at that moment is very valuable—even essential—to the smooth functioning of our financial markets in other words.

Central Clearinghouses

Back in the old days, if Investor A wanted to trade with Investor B, each counterparty was dependent on the solvency of the other. Let's say I'm Investor A and I own 50,000 shares of ABC stock that I'd like to sell to Investor B for $2 a share. I am dependent on Investor B having $100,000 and being able to deliver it to my bank; Investor B is dependent on my having and being able to deliver 50,000 shares of ABC at the appropriate time.

This dependency makes it hard for markets to function efficiently, because everyone needs to know everyone else and make sure they are only dealing with solvent and honest counterparties.

This problem was solved hundreds of years ago in Osaka, Japan, with the establishment of what we would now call a "central counterparty" (Moss and Kintgen, 2010). The central counterparty was originally a part of the exchange, and each of the members of the exchange capitalized the central counterparty. The central counterparty sits between all buyers and sellers for every transaction on the exchange. In other words, Investor A is not selling to Investor B, but rather to the central counterparty, which then sells the security to Investor B. Investor A need not worry about the solvency of Investor B or vice versa; both just need to have confidence that the central counterparty is solvent and will act in good faith.

In the modern day, central clearinghouses are no longer owned by the exchanges, but exist as nonprofit corporations funded by fees on each transaction. Like an underground water main, the work the central clearinghouse does is unglamorous, unseen by most market participants, and completely irreplaceable. If central clearinghouses did not exist, the market would simply not be as liquid and efficient as it is.

Custodial Banks

Custodial banks (aka *custodians* or *administrators*) are also essential to the smooth functioning of modern markets, but I won't spend much time on them simply because their impact on asset managers is small.

Custodial banks do not accept cash deposits, so they are nothing like the retail banks described earlier; they also are not involved with issuing or trading securities, so they are nothing like the investment banks discussed either.

Custodial banks are simply charged with making sure that they have the definitive record of names and contact details of all beneficial owners of all stocks, bonds, and commodities—any security that is now or was formerly transacted in physical form. This task is phenomenally important to anyone who receives dividends, interest, or principal payments, because without the custodian, those payments might go to someone else. They also make sure that other corporate actions, such as acquisitions, stock splits, reverse splits, delistings, spin-offs, and the like, are processed accurately.

INFORMATION PROVIDERS

Market efficiency deals with the wide availability of information to investors. Information is a synthesis or interpretation of raw data, so the provision of data and its management have become increasingly vital to market participants in general and asset managers in particular. This section will discuss both raw data providers—called *information systems*—and those that turn the raw data into information—called *rating agencies*.

Information Systems

Information systems include companies like Bloomberg, Reuters, Compustat, and FactSet. A few companies belonging in the rating agencies group, such as Morningstar, also have products that offer pure data.

Data are becoming increasingly central to the practice of finance, and it is obvious to me that the volume and importance of data will do nothing but increase into the future. Government agencies provide data from filings in a special format that allows every numerical element of an annual or quarterly report to be easily pulled into a database and analyzed. Asset price data is widely available as well, and lagged data is very nearly free.

More and more, there is too much data for a single human to process, but too much data is never a hindrance to machines and machine-learning algorithms.

It is not hard to believe that soon investors will have all possible information necessary to understand a company and to see how this company information is reflected in securities prices. The crucial question now for investors is to what extent access to these vast quantities of data help them make better investment decisions.

Rating Agencies

This section, specifically refers to credit rating agencies like Moody's Investor Service, fund rating agencies like Morningstar, and index creators like MSCI.

The business of rating agencies is a delicate one. Kenneth Arrow (Arrow, 1962) summarizes the theoretical challenge to the business in his comment: "There is a fundamental paradox in the determination of demand for information; its value for the purchaser is not known until he has the information, but then he has in effect acquired it without cost."

Arrow's paradox affects the relationship of asset managers and rating agencies. As we know an asset manager can gain an edge through data processing, and so do rating agencies. As such, there is a fine line between the two, and this ambiguity leads to issues at times.

For example, after the GFC, credit rating agencies were widely accused of contributing to the breadth and severity of the subprime mortgage crisis by having been too lax, credulous, and haphazard in assigning rating to complex mortgage-backed structured instruments. The credit agencies analyzed very complex structures with different payment tranches and assigned ratings to each tranche. The credit rating agencies did not engage in these complex analyses out of the goodness of their hearts and the desire to see fixed-income products appropriately priced by the marketplace—they were paid fees by the issuers of the securities themselves. This obviously brings into question the reliability of the opinions expressed by the agencies, since presumably, a securities issuer would try to exert a positive influence on the outcome of the analysis.

In addition to what appears to be a clear conflict of interest, ratings for the highest credit quality tranches inappropriately assumed two things as axiomatic: the data provided by the mortgage issuers were correct and the ability of the highest-quality tranches to pay would remain high even under extreme economic stress.

Unfortunately, both assumptions were wrong. Mortgage issuers were incentivized to issue mortgages to risky clients, so sometimes they bent the truth regarding the ability to repay the loan and the credit quality of the top tranches were not stress-tested for a historically large financial shock.

In a double misfortune, many asset managers simply outsourced security analysis to credit rating companies and said, in effect, "Show me some Triple-A rated paper with a decent yield and I'll buy it."

When thinking about fund ratings and model portfolios/index construction, we can also see some deleterious effects stemming from rating agencies' influence. For example, in the case of Morningstar's fund ratings, one study found that changes in the star-rating of covered mutual funds had more effect on flows in and out of funds than did changes in the actual underlying performance of the funds (Del Guercio and Tkac, 2008). This effect was especially notable after 2002, when Morningstar adjusted its rating methodology.

Now that we have a nice overview of the players on the field, who the referees are, and how the field is set up, let's turn to the three forces that drive the asset management business.

PART II

The Forces Shaping the Active-Passive Dichotomy

The Driving Forces of the Asset Management Industry

Reading a typical book about asset management, you would be forgiven for forgetting that it is a business. While all the equations and clever math are fun for philomaths, it's easy to lose sight of the fact that, at the end of the day, people running an asset management business need to design a differentiated product offering that attracts a certain demand volume at a certain price to generate revenues and ultimately profits.

The purpose of this chapter is to lay out the three driving forces of the asset management industry and to show you how those forces relate to the concepts of price, quantity, and differentiation found in all businesses.

The asset management industry's three driving forces are:

1. Fees
2. Size
3. Investment talent

Revenues are generated by selling a quantity of something at a certain price. We can think of the driving force of fees as equivalent to "price" and the driving force of (investment pool) size as equivalent to "quantity." Investing talent is the driving force that allows asset managers to differentiate their product offering in a way that allows them to generate profits by raising prices, increasing quantity sold, or both.

Just as in a manufacturing business, asset managers use two main approaches to generating revenues. Some manufacturers—Rolls-Royce, for instance—produce very few units but sell each one at a high price. Rolls-Royces are massive, solidly built automobiles that come replete with custom-crafted, high-end interiors that are designed to provide its riders with every comfort while reminding them that they are traveling in the motorcar of choice for the global elite. Other manufacturers—Kia, for example—mass-produce vehicles, each one of which is sold at a fraction of the price of a Rolls-Royce. Kia bodies are small and light, and the interiors are spartan and undifferentiated. The car is designed to allow the owner to get from point A to point B just as any other person might, with a minimum of fuss and expense.

In the case of automobile manufacturers, Rolls-Royce competes based on the uniquely differentiated characteristics of its product. Kia, on the other hand, largely competes on price. Similarly, there are asset managers that take a Rolls-Royce approach and those that follow Kia's lead.

One of the big, obvious differences between selling automobiles and selling asset management services is that in the case of automobiles, you can see exactly what you are getting when you sign the contract and take delivery. In contrast, asset management companies sell their clients a certain vision of the future. Asset managers charging a high fee are essentially signaling that their clients they will receive a Rolls-Royce future rather than a Kia one.

Let's take an initial look at the driving forces of this differentiation. We'll dig more into the nuances of these forces in the following chapters.

DRIVING FORCE: FEES

Asset management fees come in several different forms. A *management fee* is calculated as a percentage of assets under management and is used to pay for operating and administrative duties related to holding securities. The management fee does not include trading costs—the fees that the asset manager must pay the sell-side broker to transact securities. Another form of fee is the *load*, which represents a commission charged to an investor when the investor buys or sells an interest in a fund (a *front-end load* is charged upon the investor purchase, and a *back-end load* is charged upon the investor sale). Sometimes, loads are split between the front end and the back end, and additional fees, called redemption fees, are charged if an investor pulls money out of the fund within a specified short time after investing. The ratio of the total fees paid by an investor to own a share of a fund is called the *expense ratio.*

Like all businesses, the asset management business follows the fundamental laws of economics. One of these fundamental laws is that of supply and demand: scarcity drives price up and ubiquity drives it down.

What are scarcity and ubiquity in the context of investments? Remember what asset management companies are selling—a promise of the future.

A future that everyone agrees will occur is ubiquitous, so financial products promising that future should be cheap. A great example of a financial product based on an easily foreseen future is one that tracks a broad-based market index. While no one can claim to know what the index will trade for in five years, there is no doubt that the value of the investment account of a client who invested in the index-tracking product will be closely and directly related to the value of the index.

The manager in charge of investing money in a fund tracking an index like the Russell 1000 does not have any discretion over the stocks she buys or the proportion of the total portfolio that the asset represents. When companies enter or leave the index, she must buy or sell those companies as soon as possible to create as small a discrepancy between the index value and her portfolio value as possible.

Since the future of an index-tracking fund is 100 percent defined by the index, and since the manager of the fund has no discretion over which stocks to buy and in what proportion, it follows naturally that the fee for managing this type of investment portfolio should be very low. Indeed, these types of fund products trade for just a few basis points.[1]

Let's say that another investment manager can convince clients that she can reliably select stocks for an investment portfolio whose performance will consistently exceed that of the index by one percentage point in her version of the future. In such a case, trust is essential, since clients are willing to pay much more than they would have paid for an investment fund that exactly followed the index.

She decides to charge a management fee of 50 basis points (0.50 percent) to compensate her for her rare investment skill. Clients would expect that once management fees were deducted, they would be better off compared to the index-tracking portfolio by 0.50 percent (1.00 percent outperformance minus 0.50 percent fee).

Clearly, the key ingredient in the setting of fees is a perception that the manager can select a basket of investment securities that consistently generates returns superior to some baseline. This is where another driving force of asset management—competition for investment talent—comes in. More talented investors should be able to reliably paint a more precise version of the future, meaning select baskets of stocks that generate higher returns than a baseline, and they should be compensated for their skill by being able to charge higher fees.

The problem is that while money management fees might be set high by a particular manager, the high price does not necessarily signal that the client will receive superior returns. I will discuss the research behind this counterintuitive dynamic later in this book.

But before we do that, let's have a look at how the concept of investing fees developed over the years and get an intuition of why investors believe higher fees will lead to better results.

Years ago, when the asset management business experienced its first tidal wave of demand, several studies were undertaken to understand the environment for fees in publicly traded instruments like mutual funds. The first study, commissioned in the early 1960s by the US House of Representatives and written by the Wharton school, was responding to the enormous growth in AUM by mutual funds starting in 1958. That year, the mutual fund sector grew from around $8.7 billion at the beginning of the year to $13.2 billion at the end—an increase of over 50 percent in 12 months. Consumers began to complain that fees being charged were too high, so Congress responded with a study that was subsequently followed up by another in 1966.

These studies revealed that the base management fee had remained fairly constant throughout the 1950s and early 1960s at 50 basis points per year. However, the reports also mentioned that other fees, covering the cost of processing dividends, custodying assets, and the like, could be tacked on as well. In total, the end cost to investors for mutual funds was found to be hovering in the 1 percent per year range, in addition to fees paid through to brokers selling the mutual fund shares to end clients—what we call the "load" today.

Around the time the Congress commissioned these studies, the first hedge fund was born. The April 1966 edition of *Fortune* magazine ran a story (Loomis, 2015) entitled "The Jones Nobody Keeps Up With" about a onetime financial journalist, Alfred Winslow Jones, who had formed a novel investment vehicle in the form of a general partnership. Under this structure, all three partners invested capital and all three made investment decisions.

After several years of outstanding investment returns, some of the original partners' friends and family members begged to be allowed to invest with Jones and friends. In 1952, according to *Fortune*, Jones changed the form of the partnership from a general one to a limited one to allow for "passive" partners.

In the limited partnership structure, only the general partners (Jones and his original partners) could make investment decisions.

Limited partners (friends, family, and hangers on) would invest money and pay the general partners a portion of their investment gains.

Jones set the fee at 20 percent of the realized annual profits, net of any realized losses.

Jones was using what we would now call a *long/short equity* strategy to invest in the postwar boom market. He and his general partners would look for companies that they thought would perform well and bought—or "went long"—those shares. The fund would often buy shares "on margin." Buying on margin means borrowing money from a broker to enable the purchase of more shares than one has capital. "Borrowing money" means using financial leverage, so Jones's partnership was a levered vehicle.

Jones and his general partners would also look for companies they thought would perform poorly. When they found one, they would borrow the company's shares from a broker (in exchange for a *stock borrow fee*) and sell those shares in the open market. If the shares went down, Jones would be able to buy them back at a lower price, return the borrowed shares to a broker, and pocket the difference between the buy and the sell price. This is known as "shorting" or "selling short."

Note that Jones was borrowing shares, and since borrowing means using financial leverage, he was levered on the short side of his trades as well.

However, the point of the short trades was that if the entire market fell, the profit from the shorts would ameliorate losses from the long positions, so that the portfolio would be partially "hedged."

Jones called his strategy a "hedged fund" because of the financial protection presumably provided by the short positions. Whether Jones would have admitted this or not, he probably used the term *hedged fund* as a marketing device as well as to portray the fund as "hedged" and safe despite the fact that the fund was actually levered (which is risky).

While the description in the *Fortune* article and my summary make Jones's strategy seem quite staid and theoretical, reading between the lines of the *Fortune* article, it is clear that Jones was making a lot of bets on market timing in addition to picking stocks that he thought would go up or down. According to the article, Jones's fund was aggressive—sometimes taking a position that was net 120 percent long (i.e., even deducting the short positions, he had bought $120 of stocks with every $100 of his investors' capital). Being aggressively long in the US market of the 1950s and 1960s, when the United States was the global hegemon, was a good strategy. The *Fortune* article describes Jones's fund's enormous outperformance compared to the highest returning mutual fund at the time. Over a five-year period, Jones's fund increased 325 percent after fees, 100 percentage points higher than the Fidelity Trend Fund (managed by Gerald Tsai, a man whose name you should remember as you read on in this chapter). In other words, a $100 investment in Jones's portfolio at the beginning of that five-year period would have been worth $425 at the end of the period and after Jones and his partners took a 20 percent cut.

After the *Fortune* article was published, folks whose names you may have heard—George Soros, for instance—took a page out of Jones's playbook and set up *hedge funds*, dropping not only the letter *d* but also, in many cases, Jones's focus on structuring the portfolio in a way to protect from downside market risk.

Essentially Soros and Jones's other "children" inherited many features of Jones's fund, including the limited partnership structure, the use of leverage and short selling, aggressive market positioning and a sensitivity on market timing, and—last but certainly not least, especially with respect to our discussion of fees—the practice of taking one-fifth of limited partners' profits for themselves.

According to a *Wall Street Journal* article (Mallaby, 2010), Jones originally picked the 20 percent fee structure based on his understanding that in ancient times, the captains of Phoenician merchant ships kept a fifth of successful voyages' profits. Whether this is true historically or not matters much less than the impact that Jones's fee had on the asset management industry.

The performance fee of 20 percent that Jones cribbed from ancient Phoenician mariners became standard.

Note that Jones did not take any other fee from limited partners. If his clients were successful in the markets, he would enjoy part of that success. If his clients were not successful, Jones and his general partners had to pay the price of the office rent, subscriptions, whatever salaries they paid employees, and all the rest out of their own pockets.

Jones was trained as a sociologist, held deeply egalitarian views, and was concerned with matters of social progress. Suffice it to say that his particular brand of beneficence did not catch on in the industry in the way his taking of one-fifth of realized profits did.

DRIVING FORCE: SIZE

The amount of client money an investment manager has to invest—size—is the second driving force of the asset management industry and equates to "quantity" in the formula for revenue generation. The most common way to speak about fund size is *assets under management*, or AUM.

In the asset management business, even very high fees—like the 2 percent of AUM that hedge funds typically ask for—look pretty low.

A 2 percent fee will allow a manager to live quite comfortably with an AUM of $1 billion ($20 million in revenues) but will qualify him to receive government welfare payments with an AUM of $1 million ($20,000 in revenues). Given the difference in revenues generated from a large fund versus a small one, it is natural that investment managers prefer to manage large funds.

However, a large fund size also brings with it its own problems, which we will discuss in the following chapters.

Just as we did with fees, let's now make a brief review of how size has come to dominate conversations in the money management industry over the last 50 years.

In the 1960s, new theoretical work in financial economics set a foundation for an enormous change in the asset management world. In 1964, William Sharpe published a paper entitled "Capital Asset Prices: A Theory of Market Equilibrium Under Conditions of Risk" (Sharpe, 1964). This paper showed that the key systematic driver of equity returns was that of all other equity returns in aggregate. While it might seem obvious that most stocks make money in a bull market and lose in a bear market, Sharpe's capital asset pricing model (CAPM) related the likely future returns of an individual stock to its historical covariance with the market at large. A few years later in 1968, Michael Jensen published a 20-year history of review of mutual fund prices in a paper entitled "The Performance of Mutual Funds in the Period 1945–1964" (Jensen, 1968), which drew upon the work of William Sharpe and other theorists like Jack Treynor and showed that it was quite challenging for an asset manager to consistently outperform the market as a whole. These insights grew into the asset management methodology we now call passive investing.

In 1975, John Bogle—formerly the head of the Wellington Fund but pushed out of that position due to an unwise merger—started a new fund named after the flagship of Admiral Nelson's fleet during the Battle of the Nile, the HMS *Vanguard*. In 1951, Bogle's 130-page senior thesis at Princeton had been a study of mutual fund returns, many of which he found did not surpass those of the overall market. Nearly a quarter of a century later, Bogle IPO'd the first S&P 500 index fund, selling only $11 million worth of shares versus expectations for $150 million worth. Despite the slow start, Bogle's Vanguard Fund ended up changing the face of asset management forever by focusing on size and cutting management fees to the bone. From that $11 million start in 1975, index tracking funds now manage almost $11 trillion capital in the United States alone, an annualized growth rate north of 20 percent over the last 10 years. During the same period active equity strategies witnessed an annual growth rate less than half of that (see Figure 5.1).

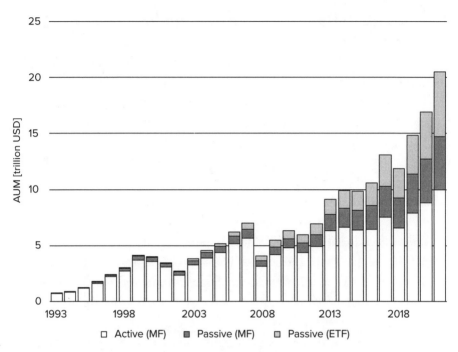

FIGURE 5.1 AUM of US funds by investment approach (mutual funds and ETFs)

Source: Data from Investment Company Institute.

Advances in computer technology and the enormous fall in price of both computing power and financial data have enabled the growth of indexing technology and continue to allow asset managers to offer plain vanilla index-tracking products to clients for nothing but the agreement that clients will allow their shares to be lent out.

Another trend, which you can see clearly from Figure 5.1 is the birth—at around the turn of the twenty-first century—and the subsequent rapid growth of exchange-traded funds (ETFs) as a tool to receive passive investment exposure. As we know from Chapter 2, ETFs do essentially the same thing as index funds—acquire broad market exposure—while also allowing investors additional operational flexibility.

DRIVING FORCE: INVESTMENT TALENT

In any competitive market, selling goods or services at a profit is made more difficult because one must compete with other players that are trying to do the same thing. Competitors may be offering their goods or services at a price that is lower than the one at which you are offering your own. The only way to survive such competition is by offering a differentiated product that is perceived as more valuable than the low-priced alternative.

As we have seen, in the asset management world, the way to make a fund more attractive is to convince investors that it has access to investing talent unavailable at other funds. One would be forgiven for thinking that investors would be convinced about a manager's access to investing talent through the analysis of quantitative data. That is the way the world *should* work but does not, as we shall soon see.

Thinking back to our automobile example, if we are shopping for a new car and somehow develop brand amnesia, we would be able to look at the price of a Rolls-Royce and instantly know that it was a more highly differentiated, high-quality automobile than a Kia simply by the price. In the stilted language of financial economics, the price of a good or service serves a signaling function to prospective buyers—a higher price implies greater differentiation and higher quality.

The confounding thing about the asset management world is that, far from signaling high returns, high fees often signal lower returns—fee levels seem, in other words, *inversely* proportional to the returns generated by the funds.

Yes, there are the high-fee managers that generate very high returns, but there are plenty that charge high fees, invest in risky assets, and barely return the risk-free rate. An unlucky subset of investors has personal experience placing capital in high-fee funds that invest in risky assets and return a partial or total loss of their money!

Keep this confounding fact about performance in the back of your mind, and we will return to discuss it in greater detail in the next chapter. Before we do that, let us look at the talent pool from a wide perspective and understand what drives dynamics related to the pool of talented investors in general.

Finance education has improved enormously over the last 50 years, especially with certifications such as the Chartered Financial Analyst program. In addition to knowledge, the proliferation of cheap and readily available market prices and corporate data has opened investment analysis to a wide pool of investing aspirants, allowing for many more people to try their hand at investing.

Data and training are two logistical hurdles that have allowed for greater representation in the industry, but I also think that there has been a cultural transformation as well, the importance of which should not be overlooked. Namely, for hundreds of years, finance was essentially boring and staid—structuring and transacting in fixed-income instruments, bonds, real estate, and the like.

In the 1980s and 1990s, several overlapping factors—deregulation, increased pay for financial services employees, and the granting of options and other share-based compensation—led to an influx of highly skilled employees looking for a big payoff.

One of my favorite studies looking at this dynamic was published in 2012 by Thomas Philippon and Ariell Reshef (Philippon and Reshef, 2012). They studied the allocation of human resources and the level of compensation to financial service workers in the United States during a nearly 100-year period, from 1909 and 2006.

Philippon and Reshef found that financial deregulation was the key driver of financial services job complexity, skill intensity (i.e., how much specialized knowledge one needed to compete effectively), and consequently, of salaries within the industry. When regulation is relatively low, finance sector salaries tend to be high and vice versa.

If we converted the findings of their study into a graphical format, it would clearly show a smiley face graph that mirrors the graph of income inequality in the United States over the same period. Namely, their graph shows that from 1909 to 1933, financial industry salaries grew and were paid to employees with increasingly high skills—the finance sector was soaking up the best candidates and starving other industries of talent, in other words. The Black

Monday crash started off a process of regulatory oversight into financial markets resulting in the erection of the legal frameworks that are so well-known today: reporting requirements, SEC oversight, banking regulations, and the like.

The regulatory boom prompted by the pain of the Great Depression ended up dampening financial services salaries, such that salaries and skill levels in the sector were similar to those in other corners of the economy; this trend continued for nearly 50 years, until the election of President Reagan, who campaigned, in part, on the promise that he would release American industry from burdensome regulation.

Like clockwork, from 1980 through to the mid-1990s, the US finance industry started to hire highly skilled workers, paying an attractive wage. As more skilled people began to see financial services as a potentially lucrative career, competition became fiercer, and salaries rose. By the mid-1990s, salaries tipped over from *generous* to *excessive* compared to other industries' workers' compensation.

The academics found that by the turn of the twenty-first century, financial service salaries, relative to those of other industries' workers, had returned to the pre-Depression peak; in 2006— unfortunately, the last year covered by their study—Philippon and Reshef calculated that the average US-based financial services worker earned 70 percent more than the average worker in the rest of the private sector.

The study is so sweeping in its historical scope and so convincing in its conclusions that I wish they or another group would do a follow-up. The dot.com crash brought about the Sarbanes-Oxley legislation, which was passed in 2002—just a few years before the Philippon-Reshef study concluded. But the GFC of 2008–2009 brought a wave of worldwide regulation: Dodd-Frank Act in 2010, Basel 3 in 2013, MiFID II in 2018. According to the hypothesis that regulatory intensity drives financial services salaries, this increasing regulation should have brought down salaries.

There is one study, published in 2018 that does look at financial service salary levels after 2006 (Boustanifar et al. 2018); this study—in line with the regulation hypothesis—suggests that compensation levels peaked in the industry shortly after 2005 (just when the scramble to comply with Sarbanes-Oxley regulations was at a peak) and decreased continuously in the years afterward.

Another factor that made more people want to enter financial services was a shift in pension culture that moved investing responsibilities to workers in general.

In the 1980s, US pensions generally transformed from defined benefit to defined contribution plans, and thus shifted the onus of responsibility of investing to the workers themselves (Ippolito, 1995). These cultural shifts started, I believe, to provide impetus to a more entrepreneurial attitude toward investment and saving. From this entrepreneurial attitude, more creative financing structures arose and a greater infrastructure (lawyers, accountants, bankers, and the like) sprung up to support the new style of investing. Add to this also the amazing ability to buy cheap computing power, which made what ultimately turned out to be very dangerous financial structures (credit default swaps and collateralized mortgage obligations) possible, but now allow for innovations such as blockchain and nonfungible tokens (NFTs) to be created.

The point behind all this is that now, as we are already on the verge of being a quarter of the way through the twenty-first century, we have a large pool of investors that have the training, data, and spirit to invest in the market.

With this background, it is without a doubt that product differentiation will become more challenging.

WHAT DOES HISTORY TELL US ABOUT THE DRIVING FORCES?

Hedge fund managers added a management fee roughly double what public mutual funds were charging—around 2 percent—in addition to a 20 percent performance fee, à la Jones's Phoenician model.

If you ask the man on the street (or on the Street) which part of the typical hedge fund 2-and-20 fee structure they want, most say "20." Twenty is larger than two; larger is better. It follows that having a piece of the 20 percent performance fee would be better.

Let's see what the smart money says.

Recall Fidelity fund manager Gerald Tsai, who had the best five-year performance after Jones in the period covered by the *Fortune* article.

Mr. Tsai passed away in 2008 as a billionaire. Mr. Jones, 29 years Mr. Tsai's senior, passed away in 1998 with a comfortable amount of wealth, but not on a track that would have put him onto the billionaire path, even if he lived for another 20 years.

The difference between these two asset management pioneers is, I believe, that Tsai focused on gathering AUM and collecting management fees, whereas Jones focused on beating the market and maximizing performance fees.

After investing successfully for Fidelity, where Tsai worked from 1952 to 1965, he struck out on his own and started the Manhattan Fund, which held concentrated positions in a few high-profile companies (the Facebooks and Googles of his time) in what we would now call a momentum-based strategy.

He sold the Manhattan Fund in 1968 as his performance started to flag. Upon selling the fund, its hot stock portfolio was caught in the 1969 crash. Over the next few years, the fund lost 90 percent of its value.

While Tsai's performance was not nearly as good as Jones (whose fund only had 3 years of net losses during its 34-year history), Tsai parlayed the payment he received from selling the Manhattan Fund eventually in an asset gathering insurer and financial services company, Transamerica, and hired a young Sandy Weil, founder of Citigroup, to manage it—allowing someone else to worry about financial performance, while he could enjoy the benefits of collecting the management fees on a large pool of assets.

Any insurance company is essentially a management fee-based business, that allows for relatively small premia to be collected regularly, year after year, invested in the markets, with any customer claims paid out from the investment proceeds. No one buying an insurance contract thinks they are writing a check to an investment vehicle, and they certainly do not raise a bunch of troublesome questions about how the insurance company's investment performance has been over time. Insurance company managers, on the other hand, are happy to pocket the spread between the amounts they are obliged to pay out to policy holders and the premia they reel in each month.

It is interesting to note that Warren Buffett also ended up owning an insurance company. In a paper entitled "Buffett's Alpha" published in 2013 and updated in 2018 (Frazzini et al., 2018), a team of researchers found that Buffett's investing success boiled down to his ability to buy well-run companies with low operating risk coupled with his insight that the returns of such firms could be enhanced by financial leverage.

The researchers found that Buffett's average leverage was 160 percent and that a large portion of this leverage came from the "float" from his privately held insurance and reinsurance business.[2] The researchers also found that the effective cost for the insurance float was below that of the average Treasury Bill rate—in other words, Buffett was borrowing money to invest for the long term at a rate lower than the US government borrows short-term funds!

Both Tsai and Buffett created a structure that allowed them to maximize their AUM—their size—and derive consistent payments from those assets, investing them in the public markets, and taking part of the upside of the returns, while promising a fixed return to their insurance clients.

The conclusion is simple, taking a piece of the management fee is like owning the bank. Getting a piece of the performance fee is like working at the bank.

What history tells us is that focusing on size is the natural incentive for all asset managers. Focusing on performance and justifying high fees alone does not do the trick.

Collecting a large amount of client assets is, as should be clear, a double-edged sword for asset managers. On the one hand, expanding

AUM means more management fees. The first law of common sense tells the manager of a business that more fees are better than less fees. On the other hand, at some point—and this point differs for different strategies—additional client assets present organizational and logistical problems that we will discuss more in Chapter 6.

THE INTERPLAY OF THE DRIVING FORCES

We have seen that asset management is no different from any other business in that it must respond to customer demands to generate revenues. The formula for generating revenues (price times quantity) and the point of differentiation for an asset manager (investment talent) make up what I am calling the three driving forces of asset management.

The only way asset managers can position themselves in a very crowded competitive field is by either reducing fees below those of competitors or by convincing clients that the clients' future economic situation will be much better if their capital is invested by the manager.

For a manager to choose the first business strategy—the Kia approach—essentially, she must decide not to decide. In other words, she must become an index tracker and provide a perfectly certain future to the client. The reason for this is that making decisions requires time and effort, and time and effort are expensive on Wall Street.

This train of thought means that a manager focused on creating a successful business competing on cost must focus solely on rapid execution of transactions. The manager must mechanically and instantaneously express the clients' desire to receive the index's return.

If cash sits in the portfolio for very long before being invested, it will provide a drag on the portfolio—or more accurately, it will provide a difference in asset allocation to the index it is supposed to be tracking (since indices do not hold cash). If the organization publishing a certain index changes the index's components and the fund does not respond to the change close to instantaneously, again the fund is out of sync with the index, creating a difference between the fund returns and those of the index.

If the process of running a passive fund sounds robotic, it is. Building and maintaining robots costs money, and the only way to make sure that the manager will be able to pay for these robots is by building scale. Every dollar flowing into the fund ends up sharing the cost of creating the robotic infrastructure necessary to carry out each transaction, so it makes sense that collecting more dollars means sharing the costs over a broader client base.

Because this robotic, execution-focused investment strategy removes the necessity of the manager to choose what assets go into the portfolio, it is known as *passive* investing.

An asset manager wanting to use an idiosyncratic strategy— selling a vision of a future that is materially better than the certain one offered by an index tracker—must take the opposite track. This Rolls-Royce manager must offer a unique insight into the markets and developing this unique insight requires time and money.

This manager must hire consultants to analyze aerial photographs of shopping center parking lots to see how the holiday shopping season is really going. He must hire analysts to count the number of oil tankers moving from Saudi Arabia to European refineries to make a more accurate assessment about how "tight" the market for refined products is likely to be in a few weeks' time. One manager told me once he had hired a plane and some infrared cameras to detect the activity in power plants—don't ask me how that works. Alternatively, managers must pay exorbitant fees to "expert networks" comprised of moonlighting executives and engineers at firms in a certain industry to understand pricing dynamics, recent technological advances, and the like.[3]

The manager of a Rolls-Royce fund charges a lot. Whereas a Kia fund may charge a management fee of only 4 bps, a Rolls-Royce fund will try to charge 2 percent—fully 50 times higher—and more, if possible, as well as charging an extra fee for extraordinary performance.

A manager of a Rolls-Royce fund that oversees $1 billion in client capital will be charging a management fee of around $20 million—plenty enough to hire a team of smart, hungry analysts; pay consultants, lawyers, and administrators the eye-watering fees they charge to the fund; and maybe even have enough left over to enjoy traveling to Davos in a private jet.

Because this idiosyncratic, research-centric investment strategy requires a manager to actively choose which assets to buy and sell, it is known as *active* investment management.

Still, for an active Rolls-Royce manager with a $1 billion fund, the temptation exists to try to leverage some of the expensive research about shopping malls or oil tankers to find a reason to buy or sell another few stocks.

Indeed, this temptation to buy or sell more stocks might not only be a whim but may be required as part of the manager's mandate. Mandates typically limit the amount of capital that can be invested in an individual investment or might limit the proportion of ownership of a company that the manager can take. In these cases, the manager has made a legally binding promise to find something more to do with the money after position size reaches some threshold.

The fact is that managing $1.5 billion does not require 50 percent more time or resources than managing $1 billion. So all things equal, a manager will want to maximize the "quantity" term to generate more revenues while being stubborn about not lowering the "price" term (i.e., dropping fees).

Eventually, the strategy of collecting more investor capital to maximize revenue generation starts to cause performance problems for reasons we discuss in the next chapter. This is the dirty secret of asset management: namely that the longer an active manager operates and the more successful she is, the closer the fund becomes to looking like a passive investment vehicle, albeit a passive vehicle that is charging clients 50 times the going rate.

Now that we understand the industry landscape, the driving forces, and the basics of how those driving forces shape the market, let's take a closer look at the interplay of the driving forces.

A Closer Look at the Interplay Between Size and Fees

This chapter describes the mechanics of fees and size in detail, drawing especially from academic literature concerning these driving forces.

Flows and size have an obvious relationship: the higher the net inflows (i.e., inflows less outflows), the larger the size of the fund. However, the relationship of size to returns is not as obvious, and most people don't realize that it is of central importance until they get into the industry. Capacity, we will see, is a key element driving diseconomies of size.

SIZE AND FEE DYNAMICS

The most effective marketing strategy for a fund is to produce attractive returns. Doing so, investors pay attention and start voting with their feet—moving their money into the well-performing fund and boosting its AUM. This is known as the *return-flow* dynamic (and there are also hints of a *flow-return* dynamic, discussed shortly). However, the larger a fund becomes, the less likely it is to outperform; put another way, the more successful a fund is at attracting assets, the less successful it is generating returns on them. This is known as the *size-return* dynamic. The size-return dynamic is also evident on a strategy and market level—a phenomenon called "crowding."

The Return-Flow Dynamic

The relationship of prior period returns and current period inflows has been demonstrated academically (see Sirri and Tufano, 1998) in what some people call "chasing returns." Chasing returns is supposed to be something that only unsophisticated retail investors do, but in fact, we will see just how smart the "smart money" is a little later in this section.

Before you make fun of investors chasing returns by piling into last year's winners, consider the logic underlying the choice. If you are an investor looking at a long list of fund names on your computer monitor and you need to decide on one, how would you distinguish among them? A simple and cheap way to figure out where to start is simply to hit the "Sort Descending" command on the returns column. To me, this screening process is simply a function of the natural human desire to reduce search costs.

This idea that fund flows are driven by consistently biased humans trying to drive down the cost of finding information about good performing funds is backed up by the Sirri-Tufano study, which also shows that high-fee funds—which plow some of those high fees into large marketing budgets—enjoy much stronger performance-flow relationships than do their rivals. Indeed, Prem Jain and Joanna Wu find that funds that are widely advertised attract significantly more money (Jain and Wu, 20000).

Whether an effect of returns chasing or that of the psychological impact of a glossy magazine advert, the data strongly suggests that fund flows are positively and persistently correlated with prior period performance.

This relationship might be the result of low financial literacy (which is also evident, on average, in other studies), but it also might be a result of investors closely monitoring the market for evidence of managerial skill using performance as a proxy. This latter, optimistic view posits that when investors observe evidence of skill, they shift assets into the well-performing funds to try to capture the benefits of the skillful manager.

In 2022, Itzhak Ben-David and his colleagues looked at these competing explanations of return-flow (Ben-David et al., 2022) and found that the pessimistic view is more likely. In other words, investors really are like cats chasing laser pointers. The fact that was most striking from the study was that simple performance-chasing patterns of similar magnitude hold for passive index funds. Since there is no skill involved in selecting assets for a passive fund, it seems most likely that the performance-flow relationship is based on a simple low information strategy.

Long story short: retail investors are not playing three-dimensional chess. They are simply following selection strategies that are, in the formal words of the financial economist, "suboptimal." So it looks like the boilerplate warning that "past performance does not guarantee future results" found in every prospectus and advertising brochure used in the industry is there for a reason.

If the conclusion is that retail investors are using the same strategy to generate returns as my cat is to catch the laser pointer dot, perhaps institutional investors are doing something different and hopefully better. Let's see.

The most thorough analysis of the behavior of institutional investors was made by Amit Goyal and Sunil Wahal in a paper entitled "The Selection and Termination of Investment Management Firms by Plan Sponsors" (Goyal and Wahal, 2008). Goyal and Wahal's magisterial study combs through 8,755 hiring decisions by 3,417 plan sponsors between 1994 and 2003. The monetary value of these many decisions was the allocation of $627 billions of client assets.

A *plan sponsor* is usually an employer that sets up a retirement plan—like a 401(k) in the United States—for the benefit of the company's employees. Sponsors are responsible for making the decision to hire and fire external managers when new inflows require more hands on the investing job or when underperforming managers need to be replaced by (hopefully) better performing ones.

The first notable finding is that the number of terminations is substantially smaller than that of hiring decisions. "Substantially" means that 869 managers got fired for nearly 10 times that number of managers hired during the years between 1996 and 2003. These firings led to a reallocation of roughly $105 billion in client assets during this period.

In something that might sound a bit familiar, Goyal and Wahal found that plan sponsors hire investment managers after superior performance but that on average, excess returns earned by the sponsors after switching were zero. In other words, sponsors chased performance and got none.

The study found that plan sponsors fire investment managers for many reasons, including, but not exclusively, investment underperformance. However, in a grand karmic twist, Goyal and Wahal found that the returns of the fired managers after they were fired were frequently positive and sometimes statistically significantly so. In other words, if the plan sponsors had sat tight with the managers they fired, they would have done at least as well with them as they did with their new managers.

Long story short, just like the retail investors, institutional investors are not playing three-dimensional chess either.

I hate to say this, but I think that part of sponsors' decisions to fire managers has to do with the "principal-agent" problem. The employees of the sponsors in charge of picking managers are paid handsome salaries. The last thing that one of these employees would want to do is to kill that golden goose of their salary by being blamed for hiring a manager whose fund performed poorly for a year or two.

"Who hired that moron manager that lost 25 percent last year?" bellows the CFO. This is not a good look for someone trying to make a name for themselves at the sponsor company.

From the previous evidence, there is a linkage between returns and flows into funds (return-flow)—showing that investors can recognize good performance when they see it.

However, it is also worth asking if the opposite relationship is also true. Namely, could flows into funds affect the funds' ability to generate returns (flow-return)? There are two ways that this relationship might come about:

1. Inflows trigger additional costs that lower returns.
2. Inflows boost the price of all assets that boosts returns.

Looking at the first factor (additional costs lowering returns), when a fund receives money, it must incur costs to transact in securities. These costs—the cost of providing liquidity to the market as well as to one's investors—may seem trivial on first inspection but are in fact sizable.

A study by Roger Edelen entitled "Investor Flows and the Assessed Performance of Open-end Mutual Funds" shows that the cost borne by the funds related to cash inflows total a not insignificant 1 percent per year in lagging performance (Edelen, 1999). Hedge funds—unlike mutual funds, which basically promise virtually unrestricted liquidity to investors—limit client redemptions by imposing lock-up restrictions, and in so doing can attenuate these costs somewhat.

The second factor is often linked to the "hot hands" phenomenon, which describes a certain fund with which managers consistently deliver superior performance over a sustained short-term period, thus attracting positive flows. Carhart's 1997 paper shows that a good part of the hot-hands phenomenon is caused simply by riding the wave of momentum in certain hot stocks. Carhart's argument is that hot-handed funds hold, by sheer luck, stocks that are also hot. As long as the momentum behind those hot stocks is strong, the returns of the fund are naturally strong as well. More money gets plowed into the hot-handed fund, and the allocation of that money into the hot stocks pushes up the price of the hot stocks even more.

I was able to follow this classical mechanic of the flow-return relationship in 2007. Back then, I performed due diligence on an event-driven hedge fund based in New York. Over the months prior to 2007, the hedge fund built up a position of almost 15 percent of a US fitness club chain with a market capitalization well below half a billion. In the buildup process, the share price of the micro-cap more than doubled. Supported by the performance, the hedge fund attracted additional assets—from roughly $200 million at the beginning of 2006 to almost $3 billion mid-2007—which partly was poured again into the microcap US fitness club chain. The share price got inflated but did not hold for long. The US fitness club chain went into Chapter 11 at the end of 2007, indicating that the root cause of the increasing share price in the prior months was obviously not the company's fundamentals, but the hedge fund's asset flow.

The "Size-Return" Dynamic

One of the problems with managing a large fund is that as the manager controls more and more money, it becomes harder and harder to find investment assets that have a good chance of generating above-market returns.

For example, let's assume a certain manager has made her reputation as a skillful investor by focusing on small capitalization stocks. As the manager's reputation increases, more clients will hear about her fund and want to invest. When enough new money flows into the fund, the manager has essentially two choices: (1) invest more in her favorite stocks or (2) spread some of the incoming money out over second and third favorite stocks.

If the manager chooses to do the former, soon she bumps up against the problem that her fund owns a significant portion—perhaps even a majority—of the shares outstanding and available for trading (the "float" or "free float") of one of her investment companies. If enough new money flows in and the manager sticks to this strategy, she may end up owning all the publicly available shares outstanding, which would make her the owner of one or more private companies—something that is definitely outside her investment mandate.[1]

If the manager chooses to do the latter (i.e., invests new money in stocks that aren't her favorites) and has true investing skill (i.e., she can reliably pick winners from losers), she is essentially making a conscious choice to underperform.

An example that I read about in a 2022 article in the *Financial Times* regarding Tiger Global, for a long time one of the world's most prestigious hedge funds, illustrates this point perfectly. The headline was "Tiger Global Blames Inflation After 50% Drop in Flagship Hedge Fund" (Gara, 2022).

Quoting from the article: "The losses have chipped into Tiger's enviable record. Its flagship fund, launched in 2001, has now recorded net annual returns below 15 per cent, while the long-only fund launched in 2013 has returned an annual average of less than 4 per cent."

Note from the preceding quote that the "oldest" investor in the long-only fund initiated in 2013 has been invested in very risky assets but has realized essentially a risk-free rate of return. Certainly, someone investing in Tiger in 2017 returned less than risk free— likely negative.

Quoting further from the same article: "The firm has been trimming holdings in groups in which it has 'low conviction', it said, and increasing its positions in businesses it deems 'the best companies at interesting prices.'"

Perhaps it is a bit of *schadenfreude* on my part, but I loved the preceding quote since it speaks directly to the inherent problem of size. Note the mention that Tiger has "low conviction" investments in its portfolio. Simply holding low conviction bets is not unusual— it is sensible to have a portion of one's portfolio invested in what amounts to cheap lottery tickets if these bets are sensibly sized and the proportion of lottery tickets to reasoned, high-conviction bets is relatively small. The *Financial Times* article suggests that Tiger had so large a proportion of low-conviction bets in its portfolios that closing these positions and shifting them into their managers' (now discounted) best ideas makes a material difference. To me, this is a sign that Tiger's managers were essentially throwing new investment money into low-conviction lottery tickets because they couldn't find any other compelling, high-conviction investment ideas.

Another issue with managing a large portfolio is one of simple logistics. Let's say that I want to take a bold, 5 percent position[2] in a certain stock, which works out to my fund buying 1,000,000 shares. Let's say that this stock usually trades only around 100,000 shares per day. In order to buy all the shares I want (aka "build my position"), my purchase volume would equal 10 days' worth of normal trading. Not wanting to drive up the market price with my own purchases nor to alert other market participants to my position, however, I would probably try to stay at no more than around 20 percent of average daily volume. That suggests that it would take around 50 days to fully build my position. Even if I have that much time to build my position, in the back of my mind will always be the question, "What if I need to unwind this position quickly in the future?" Spending over two trading months to enter and exit a position is too much of a risk to even entertain taking a position in the first place, at least for a lot of managers.

The following real-life example of quantity-related issues illustrates the challenge of an asset manager perfectly.

A hedge fund manager I met once structured a trade where the fund bought (i.e., "went long") Brazilian pulp and paper companies while short selling (i.e., "went short") North American pulp and paper firms. The trade was a brilliant one—the Brazilian firms had a natural cost advantage and shipping costs were low, so cutting down swathes of the Amazon rainforest, shaving it down, and turning it into paper to be shipped to the North American market was cheaper than harvesting trees in the Pacific Northwest of North America and processing the pulp there. The Brazilian firms thus easily outcompeted their North American rivals in the pulp and paper commodity market, and the trade generated returns very consistently day after day, week after week with a continuous outperformance of around 10 percentage points a year.

The manager's challenge with this trade was not the return potential—this has been perfectly spotted, reasoned, and executed—but much more the lack of capacity. Pulp and paper companies didn't (and don't) have a large market capitalization, so the hedge fund manager could allocate only a very small proportion of his roughly $1 billion AUM portfolio to both sides of the trade.

The illustration shows that trading ideas need to be weighted in proportion to their capacity when actively managing money. An asset manager would therefore always opt for an idea involving large cap rather than small cap stocks given that both ideas have the same return potential—unfortunately, they seldom do.

I should point out that even if an asset manager could invest successfully in large cap stocks, trading enormous volumes daily can run into problems related to a different sort of capacity constraint.

Namely, there is a limit to the amount of information a single human being can process. A good analyst, who has had a few years covering an industry can probably keep track of a few dozen stocks and really know the details of a handful of them. Let's say that at some point, an investment fund is properly staffed with the best analysts in the world.

As the fund outperforms, more money comes in and the manager is forced to expand the number of investments in the portfolio due to worries about liquidity or risk concentration.

As the number of investments in the fund increases, the analysts—who we have assumed are the best in the world—must know the details of more and more companies. Eventually, the information will become too voluminous for the analysts to processes effectively. Either the manager will keep staffing as is (in which case, the analysts' investing acuity will drop due to overwork) or the fund manager will be forced to hire new analysts (in which case, the new analysts must not be as talented or experienced as the incumbents).

Again, the influx of client capital has created a capacity constraint—this time based on the limitations of the fund's investment talent.

The academic evidence for the size-return dynamic is unequivocal.

In 2004, Joseph Chen, Harrison Hong, Ming Huang, and Jeffrey Kubik published a seminal paper entitled "Does Fund

Size Erode Mutual Fund Performance? The Role of Liquidity and Organization" (Chen et al., 2004). This paper statistically demonstrates that, indeed, fund returns decline as the funds become larger, even if one backs out the effects of managers charging higher fees.

They find that the size-related underperformance is most pronounced in funds with mandates to invest in small capitalization, low liquidity stocks, but that organizational issues—the capacity constraints enforced by limitations on investment talent—also have a performance-dampening effect.

Between the logistical difficulties involved in transacting on a market and the constraints imposed by inherent capacity constraints for humans to process information, it's clear that fund size represents a double-edged sword for a Rolls-Royce-style asset manager trying to charge higher fees for promised outperformance.

The size-return effect is so strong and persistent that in their model of investor behavior, Jonathan Berk and Richard Green (see Box 6.1) hold one assumption as axiomatic: asset management suffers decreasing returns to scale (Berk and Green, 2004).

The Industry's Capacity

As anyone in the business knows from being invested in too popular of a trade—a crowded trade—it is not only one's own fund size that creates limitations on returns.

If you were an asset manager in Japan in the 1980s or one investing in Russia in the 1990s, for example, your biggest job liability was being injured by tripping over large bundles of cash that seemed to be strewn everywhere. To borrow the words of Tom Cruise's character, Maverick, in the movie *Top Gun*, these were "target-rich environments." However, just in the same way that one is not supposed to be able to find a $100 bill lying on the sidewalk on Wall Street, as soon as low-risk profits are to be made in a certain market, geography, or specialty, everyone, and their uncle, piles into the trade and before one knows it, the easy money disappears.

Academics like Ľuboš Pástor and Robert Stambaugh argue that the growth of the active-management industry strains all funds' performance, as growing competition eats away at any profitable strategies (Pástor and Stambaugh, 2012). They even think that industry growth is an even more significant contributor to scale diseconomies of individual mutual funds than the growth of the funds themselves (Pástor et al., 2015).[3]

Even more than academics, practitioners like me feel the effect of crowding very acutely. I read an interesting book recently called *Damsel in Distressed: My Life in the Golden Age of Hedge Funds* by French-born, California-based distressed debt investor Dominique Mielle, who was a director at a fund in which I had an investment. Not only is Mielle's book a terrific read—terrifically funny in places and wonderfully informative throughout—she takes a sharp look at the tidal wave of fund flows moving into hedge funds in the early 2000s and draws a very interesting conclusion. She argues—convincingly to me—that the sheer amount of money flowing into hedge funds during that "Golden Age" period referenced in her title meant that hedge fund investors could, on average, expect absolutely zero performance boosts from investing in them after around 2012 or so.

A Fund's Capacity

Whether it is fund-level diseconomies of scale or those at the industry level (or probably a little bit of both) does not really matter. What matters—especially from the standpoint of a manager trying to succeed or an investor trying to generate wealth—is that the concept of "capacity" is a crucial factor to understand. Unfortunately, capacity is also an issue that is too often underappreciated by investors and academically underresearched.

Marco Vangelisti defines a fund's *threshold capacity* as the AUM at which a given target for excess returns is no longer achievable and *terminal capacity* as the level of AUM at which net excess returns are reduced to zero (Vangelisti, 2006). These seem like excellent definitions to me and ones that resonate with what I have seen in the market.

Any fund that is below threshold capacity can deliver the promised results (on average over time) at a given cost. A fund that grows larger than threshold capacity will still outperform on average, but its outperformance will be eaten away by costs—it will simply be too expensive for what the asset owner receives in return. A fund that grows larger than terminal capacity is clearly destroying asset owner value.

It would be nice if asset managers routinely thought about the level of AUM they could manage that would simultaneously create the greatest value (or "utility" if you're an economist) for the system as a whole—both on the manager side and on the investor side. The manager and investor split the excess returns, so both wind up being happy. As costs of outperforming rise, the fund's profit margins decrease, but if the amount of inflows offsets the margin compression, the absolute profits to the fund will increase. Eventually, though—at the point at which the fund reaches terminal capacity—the additional inflows can no longer offset the decreasing margins, so excess returns to the manager cease, as does her capacity to produce excess investment returns for the new clients. Using this argument, the point at which wealth is maximized for both manager and owner is the threshold capacity.

There are three main diseconomies of scale to a manager:

1. Implementation
2. Crowding (discussed previously)
3. Organization

Implementation simply means that logistically, certain AUMs do not work in certain situations. One cannot stuff $100 billion into a small cap fund without taking all the small cap companies private, for instance. Even if one is not trading in small cap stocks, logistical costs of transacting swamp the opportunity costs of not transacting (Perold and Solomon, 1991).

In terms of organizational issues, Florencio Lopez-de-Silanes and colleagues looked at returns of PE firms. They find that during periods of a large number of simultaneous investments, all investments tend to underperform badly (Lopez-de-Silanes et al., 2015). This suggests that the PE organizations themselves cannot handle large volumes of deal flow—perhaps because of too few experienced personnel involved in each deal or because the personnel involved in the deals are operating above their optimal capacity to analyze, make decisions, and size risk positions. From this observation, Lopez-de-Silanes et al. conclude: "Private equity firms' actions do not appear to be . . . easily scalable."

On the other hand, there are also positives created by increasingly large inflows, such as scope and strategy flexibility.

As for scope, it goes without saying that if asset owners that are relatively less skillful or less able to find the best asset managers to invest their assets send their money to a fund family whose executives are able to assess and hire skillful managers, the owners are relatively better off. Jonathan Berk and colleagues argue that as funds are directed into a particular manager's funds, the productivity—as measured by value added—also increases (Berk et al., 2017). These academics estimate that at least 30 percent of the value created by the manager is created because of an executive's decision to direct more funds to that particular manager.

In terms of flexibility, Joshua Pollet and Mungo Wilson found that as fund flows increased, the fund managers look hard for new securities in which to invest; this dynamic caused funds to become more diversified, thus improving the risk-return balance (Pollet and Wilson, 2008). They note that a fund family that has many "sister funds" show less diversification in any one fund. In other words, a manager in a fund family that has a lot of small, specialized funds cannot diversify in her own fund as much—that is, she does not have the flexibility—because to do so, she would be invading the mandate of one of her fellow asset managers.

Weighing the economies and diseconomies of scale and giving an exact, clear-cut and numeric definition of when a fund is too large is a difficult and dynamic calculation. Managers should be looking at factors like portfolio concentration (e.g., number of stocks), portfolio liquidity (e.g., days to liquidate), number of support staff, and so on. A careful, methodical, and—if one's fund is a certain size— periodic reassessment of capacity is necessary.

NEW FUND DYNAMICS

A portfolio manager's first fund launch is like one's first kiss—not easily forgotten, very exciting, extremely uncertain, and perhaps a bit overenthusiastic.

Indeed, my first mandate to start a fund from scratch had elements of all those characteristics. It was exciting, uncertain, and definitely overenthusiastic. With help and guidance from others, I was able to shift out of my environmental chemist and ecologist's mindset into the mindset of an asset manager and line all my ducks in a row. The fund had a focus on what we would now call the "E" of ESG—large capitalization companies that were focused on sustainability issues.

One becomes wise through various life experiences, but these experiences also usually wind up being painful. In my case, I can say that we were ahead of my time by about a generation. The sustainability fund was my brainchild in the late-1990s, and at that time, investors were much more interested in nutty "Tie-Your-Shoes.com" businesses that tech maven Mary Meeker was valuing based on how many "eyeballs" they attracted. Much of my blood, sweat, and tears were poured into that first fund, but after a few years, we just couldn't make a go of it anymore and closed our doors.

As thrilling as starting a new fund is, asset management's chief aim is not to thrill portfolio managers. Asset management is, for better or worse, a scale business, and if your idea will not reach the scale at which revenues exceed costs plus a reasonable return, it does not make any sense to open a new fund (see the previous section about the dangers of staying too small). Instead, the more efficient route is to channel money into an existing fund.

Considering those hard facts, it is amazing that the number of funds has risen by 10 to 20 percent per year (see Figure 6.1), offset by an attrition rate that Martin Rohleder and colleagues calculated as roughly half of the opening rate (Roheleder et al., 2011). Hedge funds have an even higher attrition rate—probably somewhere closer to 20 percent per year (Joenväärä et al., 2021).

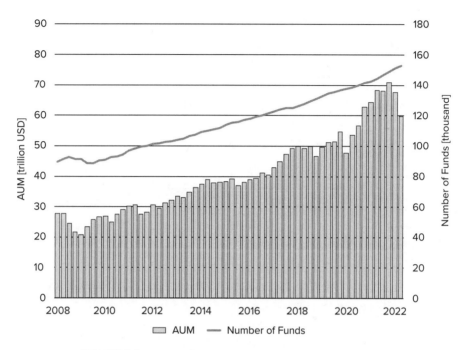

FIGURE 6.1 AUM and number of worldwide open-end funds
(excluding fund of funds)

Source: Data from International Investment Funds Association.

Despite the daunting statistics, there are good reasons why start-ing new funds is popular, especially when a manager sets up a new fund within a large fund company rather than trying to set out her own shingle.

From an investor perspective, asset owners believe that older funds tend to have lower performance, so they tend to be attracted to newer ones. The thinking behind this attraction is that young funds will be more nimble and highly motivated to outperform. Clearly, from what we know about size and performance, if "older" means "larger," we have seen that asset owners are right in believing that older funds will likely perform worse than newer (meaning "smaller").

However, what investors may not fully appreciate is how much costlier it is to run a new fund (due to lack of scale) and that new funds are often run by less experienced managers, with all the attendant problems that inexperience can bring. Academics, however, fail to establish a significant negative relationship between fund age and performance.

An interesting technique to start a new fund and tackle the performance challenge that has become popular in recent years is that of incubation. In the incubation process, several funds are seeded with the fund company's own capital, but not opened to public investment. The most successful private funds at the end of an evaluation period are brought to the public and marketed as the next hot thing. The performance in the incubation period is publicized, and those incubated funds seem to perform much better—according to Richard Evans (Evans, 2010) by around 3.5 percent on a risk-adjusted basis—than nonincubated funds. Here's the kicker: the relative outperformance of incubated funds does not persist after the funds go public.

BOX 6.1 Clients Aren't Stupid and Managers Aren't Evil

In a paper published in 2004 entitled "Mutual Fund Flows and Performance in Rational Markets" (Berk and Green, 2004), Jonathan Berk and Richard Green (BG henceforth) investigated the "central mystery" of asset management: why active asset managers receive such outsized economic rewards despite lackluster average performance.

This is the question screamed from the choir of the church of passive investing: Why do investors persist in investing in active managers if the empirical facts are very clear about their consistent underperformance vis-à-vis passive strategies?

Equally as puzzling is why investors insist on chasing performance given that it is almost impossible to tell good from bad managers? After all, it is a well-established fact that if an active manager outperforms his benchmark in one year, he will likely not repeat the outperformance next year (i.e., returns are not serially correlated). Indeed, the performance of active managers seems to be simply an artifact repro-ducible with a coin-flipping simulation.

Academics and those in the industry have long struggled to recon-cile the discrepancy between manager pay and performance, and it is tempting to think that investors are simply deceived by shiny brochures and smooth-talking managers and marketers.

Indeed, conventional wisdom assumes that the pay versus perfor-mance mismatch is rooted in the irrational, return-chasing behavior of investors (i.e., clients are stupid).

However, according to BG's analysis, which is based on a supply-and-demand model of the asset management industry, the real answer the "central mystery" eludes this conventional wisdom while also simultaneously casting doubt on efficient market hypothesis (EMH) adherents' beliefs.

The BG model is based on three axioms:

1. Asset managers have differing abilities to generate above-average returns. This ability is scarce and attenuates as the scale of operations increases (i.e., performance decreases as AUM increases).
2. Asset managers are utility maximizers (i.e., they do what they can to further their own interests).
3. Investors learn about the ability of asset managers mainly by observing past returns, and allocate their capital while considering various alternatives, (i.e., the market for investment advice is competitive).

Using only these three axioms, BG created a model that describes the salient features of the asset management industry as well as or better than the EMH without assuming flawed decision-making by investors (i.e., clients aren't stupid) or gamesmanship by asset manag-ers (i.e., managers aren't evil).

Note that the first of the BG axioms is that managers do differ in levels of skill, measured by the capacity to generate above-market returns, whereas the axiom underpinning the EMH is that they do not.

Considering that differences in skill are apparent in every other human pursuit—whether that is ballet dancing, dog training, topiary arts, or whatever—in my opinion, it is more sensible to believe that such skill differences exist in investing as well. Because the BG model seems, as we shall see, to have the same explanatory power as the EMH while more closely conforming to what we observe about humans in the real world, in my mind, BG has the advantage over EMH already.

BG's next assumption is that asset managers are utility maximizers. As such, an asset manager that is skillful enough to earn economic rents based on the investing decisions they make will also figure out how to structure his payment incentives such that those rents accrue preferentially to himself rather than to his clients.

Again, I find BG's modeling of managers as utility maximizers as intuitively attractive and probably correct based on what I've observed in my own professional life. BG emphasizes that the fall in economic rents results from investors pursuing past returns and unintentionally reducing their profits. This suggests that asset managers might not be solely to blame for optimizing these rents. Yet, from my professional perspective, I've witnessed asset managers significantly profiting from such rents, especially when investors' attention to incentive structures diminishes.

Given these three axioms, let's look at the intuition behind the BG model.

Assume there are two asset managers—Manager A and Manager B—with different levels of investing skill: Manager A is more skillful than Manager B. Further, let's assume that both managers, as well as prospective clients, can perceive the differential skill levels.

If prospective clients can readily ascertain the relative quality differences, they will obviously preferentially place money with Manager A. Manager's A portfolio will increase in size until some point at which the diseconomies of scale already discussed in this chapter kick in. Once this happens, a utility-maximizing Manager A will begin to invest excess capital into the market using an index-hugging strategy.

Employing a passive strategy for some portion of the portfolio will bring down the average return for Manager A's entire portfolio (because we have assumed that Manager A has skill, so the returns on her high-conviction investments will be above those of the market at large). Even though the returns of Manager A's portfolio will decrease, she will persist in the strategy because she is a utility-maximizer, and each additional dollar of AUM equates to a larger inflow of management fees.

At some point, diseconomies of scale will provide enough of a drag on Manager A's performance that Manager B's skills will be sufficient to generate portfolio returns that are at least equal to the attenuated returns of Manager A's portfolio. At this point, clients will observe that there has ceased to be a difference between Manager A and Manager B's returns, so they will become manager-agnostic. Manager B's portfolio AUM will grow as a response.

Eventually, as Manager B's portfolio reaches a size at which diseconomies of scale kick in, Manager B will also employ the index-hugging strategy in the attempt to maximize utility.

Whereas we originally had two skillful managers and a baseline index return, using BG's model, we now have an index and two active portfolios that generate positive or negative returns randomly based on idiosyncratic asset selection and time horizon factors.

Using an assumption diametrically opposed to the cornerstone of the EMH, BG were able to model outcomes that look like the world we see today.

Obviously, this setup is a bit stilted, since we are assuming that clients can instantly recognize the skill differential between Manager A and Manager B. However, BG allow for a more realistic model by building in a training function that allows participants to ascertain the relevant skill levels over time by observing returns and adjusting allocations accordingly.

I think one of the most interesting and important points about the BG model is not initially obvious to those not used to working in the business: the costs of managing money.

Period performance—being an external and observable factor—is easy to track, but costs—being internal to the asset management organization and thus unobservable to external parties—are much more difficult to get a hold of for a prospective investor.

To achieve outperformance, the manager must find and transact in under- and overvalued assets; the ability to do both gets progressively more expensive as more low-hanging fruit is plucked and as the fund size grows larger. Some of the problems related to AUM have to do with purely logistical problems:

- **Paying bid-ask spreads.** This can add up for managers running strategies that transact frequently.
- **Time and effort it takes to leg-into positions while trying to minimize market impact.** This influences especially investors in small cap stocks and other illiquid assets, of course, but also impacts most other investors (currency might be an exception) to a certain extent.

As discussed in this chapter, these logistical costs are nontrivial and increase exponentially as AUM increases. Even in the period before which our theoretical skillful Manager A realizes that the only utility maximizing strategy left to her is to keep accepting new money and stuff that into the index, she will be running into increased costs to transact in names in which she has conviction. These costs degrade client performance in a way that is quite opaque to the client.

The BG model assumes that fees are fixed (i.e., that there are no performance fees, only management fees), and while this might seem unrealistic, considering the impact of hurdle rates, I believe it is in line with the majority of contractual agreements in the global asset management industry.

In lieu of performance fees, the only way for an asset manager to increase one's wealth in a utility-maximizing way is to collect more assets to try to boost monies received from management fees (i.e., the "become the bank" strategy).

A Closer Look at
Interplay Between Fees
and Investing Talent

This chapter delves into the driving force that is one of the hardest to capture but most critically important—investment talent. Like the previous chapter, this chapter draws heavily from academic literature on the topic.

Investing talent is the currency that active asset managers use to "buy" the ability to charge higher fees. It is the key differentiator among active managers, and thus the discussion of investing talent invariably ties into a discussion of fees.

THE CONFOUNDING RELATIONSHIP
BETWEEN FEES AND RETURNS

Recall from Chapter 5 that I concluded the section introducing the driving force of investing talent with a discussion about a confounding relationship between fees and returns, namely that rather than signaling good performance, higher fees generally signal poor performance. In other words, asset owners who entrust their capital to high-fee managers lose two ways: returns are poor and fees are high.

The impression that high fees are generally inversely proportional to returns is supported by multiple performance studies. Why there should be such an inverse relationship between fees and returns is, however, not at all clear. To attempt to explain the confounding fact, academics have posed two possible hypotheses that I will name *insufficient skill* and *strategic fee setting*.

The Insufficient Skill Hypotheses

Mark Carhart's study of the insufficient skill hypothesis is the seminal analysis of this topic (Carhart, 1997). In short, Carhart found that investment managers do display skill in asset selection—in other words, raw fund returns outperform a broad index—but the fee that they charge for this outperformance, on average, exceeds the outperformance itself. Carhart's work builds off the important work of Martin Gruber and Russ Wermers, which both shaped the public active-versus-passive debate as we know it today. Martin Gruber found that the average alpha for actively managed US equity mutual funds is negative after fees are deducted and that investors can get a better deal by investing in index-tracking funds (Gruber, 1996). Russ Wermers takes the analysis of actively managed mutual funds one important step further: The stock holdings of actively managed mutual fund managers outperform the market by 1.3 percent each year, mainly due to a "talent in picking stocks" in the 20-year period from 1975 to 1994. Despite the average superior skill, the result in the investor's account delivered in average −1 percent, much to the consternation of many investors. The large difference of 2.3 percent is explained mainly by fees and transactions costs and to a lower extent, to precautionary portfolio holdings to accommodate investor's out- and inflows (Wermers, 2000).

After everything is said and done, these facts suggest that active managers are the only ones to be rewarded for their skill (i.e., investors are not only not rewarded, but are also penalized for investing in the fund of a skillful manager) and that *fee setting* is key driver for that.

The Strategic Fee-Setting Hypothesis

A 2009 academic study (Gil-Bazo and Ruiz-Verdú, 2009) suggested that the confounding relationship between fees and returns could be explained as the effect of mutual fund companies accounting for investors with different degrees of sensitivity to performance. From an economic perspective, the mutual funds seemed to be setting fees by observing the inelasticity of demand displayed by their clients rather than by focusing on the performance of their managers' funds.

From my perspective, the strategic fee setting resonates strongly with my experience in the industry. Different types of managers serve different investor groups with different strategies and are quite savvy to the fee-related sensitivities of the groups they serve. In short, less financially literate investors pay a higher price for the services they receive.

A separate point of evidence for the strategic fee-setting hypothesis comes from the 2013 work of Janis Berzins, Crocker Liu, and Charles Trzcinka, who found that asset managers in the United States owned by banks underperform the funds of independent asset managers by almost 0.5 percent per year during the 1990–2008 period (Berzins et al., 2013).

In 2018, Miguel Ferreira, Pedro Matos, and Pedro Pires extended Berzins et al.'s findings after analyzing a data set of global funds. Ferreira et al. found that over the period from 1997 to 2010, funds managed by banks underperformed independent funds by almost 1 percent per year (Ferreira et al., 2018).

In trying to explain this dynamic, both teams hypothesized that the underperformance, despite the fees charged, is driven by a conflict of interest between the banking business and the asset management business. In my experience, though, I think several issues affect this dynamic and all of these are complicated by the comingling of services and, consequently, capturing the banking clients' different degrees of sensitivity to performance.

The unfortunate fact is that whether it is due to insufficient skill or strategic fee setting, it is the client—the asset owner—who suffers from the effect. A few managers out there might indeed be able to consistently outperform a benchmark by a wide enough margin to more than offset their fees, and in so doing offer the client true value.

THE DIFFICULTY IN DISTINGUISHING LUCK FROM SKILL

One thing I know well as someone who spent years trying to pick managers that would dependably outperform some benchmark is that it is hard to unambiguously distinguish luck from skill in investing, given that the professional history of any given manager is short compared to the number of observations required for the science of statistics to tell the difference.

To understand why, let's look at the results of a coin toss created by the random number function in Excel. We'll take a sample of 10 years and say tails (T) represents a year when an investor's portfolio underperforms some index and heads (H) shows a year when the portfolio outperforms: T, H, H, H, T, T, H, H, H, H.

We know that this series was created by Excel's rand function, but it still looks like there are several runs of "wins." An observer seeing performance like this might be forgiven thinking that the manager had genuine stock-picking skill. To make things more complicated, humans do not usually just look at statistics but rather tend to be highly susceptible to being swayed by narratives supplied by managers' marketing departments or by the charisma of the manager him- or herself.

One of investment fund managers' main client-facing duties is to write periodic letters to their investors laying out a narrative about the current investment environment, elucidating their analysis of the dynamics of the moment, and explaining away any poorly performing assets or asset classes. (In fact, managers usually leave the communication of their quarterly letter to a large, specialized team.)

In these letters, a client might hear a story about how "Fed tightening" had an unforeseen deleterious effect on some of the stocks that underperformed (while strangely not affecting the ones that outperformed) or that an unexpected "macroeconomic shock" had created a "dislocation" in the markets.

Through the manager's compelling, insightful, and perhaps in parts humorous account of the portfolio's performance, a client might be swayed to believe that even though the portfolio underperformed during a certain period, the manager retains a special skill that will shine forth in future periods.

The difficulty in statistically differentiating between random happenstance and skill, coupled with humankind's weakness for an entertaining yarn, gives rise to an investment strategy known in the business as "closet indexing."

Whatever dynamics interact to underlie the disconnect between fees and performance, the ultimate reason that Rolls-Royce-style managers tend to underperform over time is perfectly obvious to Kia-style managers. Namely, the price changes of assets traded on modern, data-driven, and largely efficient financial markets look random. No matter how intelligent and skilled you are as a manager, trying to squeeze alpha out of financial forecasting is perilously difficult.

As one would expect from a fair coin toss, about half the managers are lucky in any given year and buy assets that increase in value; the other half are unlucky and invest in assets that decrease in value. Subtracting fees leads to a negative outcome simply because half the sample is already underwater and some of the lucky cohorts were not lucky enough to generate greater returns on their portfolios than the fees they charge. This observation is the essence of William Sharpe's "Arithmetic of Active Management" (Sharpe, 1991) and a topic we will dig into further in Box 7.1.

BOX 7.1 A Delusive Arithmetic of Active Management

In 1991, one of the giants of the academic investing world, William Sharpe, applied a simple argument to explicate the performance potential of active managers (Sharpe, 1991). The logic of his argument was brilliant in its elegance, relying only on simple mathematical operations such as addition and subtraction.

Here is the argument in a nutshell:

A passive investor always holds every security available in the market in the same proportion to the securities' proportional capitalization to the market. An active investor will differ from that passive portfolio some or all the time. Because active managers usually transact when they perceive the mispricing of a security and because these mispricing perceptions tend to change relatively frequently, they also tend to trade relatively frequently.

Let's start by assuming that half the managers are passive and half are active. Of course, this means that the passive half of the managers will perform exactly as the market (assuming zero cost, which is not a bad assumption for passive index funds these days).

The active manager's returns will also be in line with the market before fees because the active managers cannot help but hold market assets. A single active manager might not hold all securities, but all active managers in aggregate *must* hold all securities. The only difference between the passive and active managers is the proportion in which all the assets are held. Since active managers can only hold the market on average, they are bound to perform by the only factor that they display and that passive managers don't—charging a fee.

For Sharpe, it was clear that active managers on average would never be able to generate positive returns. But is asset management so simple? Maybe not.

Building off Sharpe's work nearly 30 years later, another financial economist decided to take his own stab at the arithmetic of asset management (Pedersen, 2018). Pedersen criticizes Sharpe's argument by pointing out that his conclusion ("before costs, the return on the average actively managed dollar will equal the return on the average passively managed dollar") implicitly assumes that the market portfolio never changes.

Here is Pedersen's take on the argument:

Let's again assume a world with two types of managers: active and passive. In this world, there are only two stocks, stock A and stock B. Both A and B have the same market capitalization, so the passive managers hold equal amounts of each stock. According to Sharpe's logic, the average active manager holds the same portfolio.

Now let's assume that a new, tiny stock C IPOs, and after the CEO rings the opening bell of the exchange, it is listed there. Given the very small size of stock C, the index trackers will hold essentially nothing of the stock.

In this case, the average active managers' market portfolios deviate from the passive managers' market portfolio, simply because now active managers can invest in a stock in which passive managers effectively cannot.

If stock C fares better than the market (likely, considering how bored the traders must be only placing orders to buy stocks A and B), active managers may be able to beat the passive market, depending on how large their fees are versus the outperformance of stock C to the rest of the market.

Sharpe's argument that the precost equality of performance between active and passive is based on the implicit assumption that the market portfolio never changes. As Pedersen points out this assumption obviously does not hold true in the real world—new shares are issued, existing shares are repurchased into corporate treasuries, firms acquire other firms, and so on. As such, even passive investors must regularly trade to keep up with the changing constitution of the market.

The real question is how much the market portfolio changes due to new share issuance, repurchases, and all of that. In a broad equity market replication, the turnover can be substantial. According to Pedersen, the turnover when tracking the Russell 2000—an index representing a large portion of the smallest capitalization US stocks—can be in the range of 40 percent! Furthermore, the average historical "one-way turnover"[1] of the granddaddy of all indices—the S&P 500—is a not unsubstantial 4.4 percent due to additions, deletions, and rebalancing actions.

These numbers alone and Pedersen's fundamental argument suggest that the trading activities of passive investment funds allow an ample playground on which active managers can outperform. The examples given here relate to equities, but this effect holds especially true in the bond market, where there is little action in the secondary market.

I don't want to steal my own thunder, but Pedersen's argument provides the fodder for a point I will make later in the book: the question "Is active or passive better?" is completely misplaced. Active managers—I will argue—can be worth positive fees in aggregate as they play an important role in the economy by trying to allocate capital resources efficiently. Passive managers also play a useful economic role—namely, by creating low-cost access to the broader market portfolio.

A cynical manager who understands statistics and the profound difficulty in consistently outperforming an index but who is charismatic, literate, and convincing in his narratives might select a basket of stocks for his portfolio that essentially replicate the index except for a few changes in the weightings of the allocations and/or the stocks purchased.

The cynical manager's portfolio will closely replicate the returns of the index but will sometimes do a bit better thanks to the differences in holdings and the glory of randomness. If the manager happens to catch a lucky break, happenstance might work to his benefit a few years in a row and the underperforming years will not be so drastic. In this case, he might be able to charge higher fees, be feted in the *Wall Street Journal* and *Financial Times*, be asked to speak at influential investing conferences, and in general, live a comfortable life, basking in the admiration of peers and the investing public alike.

This is but one example of the way in which the incentives inherent in the asset management business can drive value-destructive actions.

Is this to say that all active managers are closet indexers? No, of course not. But the temptation to effect a closet indexing strategy can be strong.

IDENTIFYING TRUE INVESTMENT TALENT

Given the data we have looked at so far in this chapter, it is worth asking if there really is something that might be recognized as true investment talent. If so, how can that talent be recognized and measured?

Working in the fund-of-fund world for years in the aughts, selecting talent was one of my main interests and it has continued to be one of my main focuses now for over 20 years of my professional life. While the topic of identifying talent is not nearly as cut and dried as the discussion of fees or size, I believe it is crucial.

In a 1984 article written by Warren Buffett entitled "The Superinvestors of Graham-and-Doddsville." (Buffett, 1984), Buffet points out that it is interesting that a group of investors that have consistently outperformed the market—something that academic theorists say should happen only randomly—all follow a similar strategy to do so. If markets were simply collections of randomly returning assets, one would not expect that following one strategy over another would consistently provide outperformance.

While Buffett's argument can be nitpicked from a statistical perspective, in my opinion, his point is valid. True investment skill does indeed exist, and there is a small set of investors that genuinely have an investing edge.

Obviously, education is important—Warren Buffett got an A+ in Ben Graham's value investing class at Columbia in 1951 after all. Judith Chevalier and Glenn Ellison published a seminal analysis about this in 1999 with the title "Are Some Mutual Fund Managers Better Than Others? Cross-Sectional Patterns in Behavior and Performance" (Chevalier and Ellison, 1999). They found that managers who attended higher-SAT undergraduate institutions have systematically higher risk-adjusted excess returns.

But education is not everything. Once, I was at an influential investing conference in Rome, held at one of the Eternal City's most exclusive hotels, situated on a hill and with an amazing view of Rome's skyline. I and a group of financiers were standing on a patio outside the hotel during a break. In our group of 15 people, I noticed that 14 were looking out over the breathtaking views, while one was staring back at the hotel as if he was assessing how much he might be able to make off a transaction involving the hotel's real estate. The man looking the other way was John Paulson, the hedge fund manager who the *Guardian* newspaper reported as earning around $3 billion in 2007.

This single-minded focus is one thing that sets a great investor apart from a merely good one, in my opinion. In addition to this peculiar form of tunnel vision, the best investors I have met share two characteristics: the ability to bring a real-life perspective when analyzing numbers and the fortitude to be able to commit to expressing an investment opinion contrary to the crowd, on what is often limited information.

Let's look at the "real-life perspective" point first. A lot of people are well-trained in math and finance. Not only are people well-trained, but anyone with a modern laptop (or even just a Raspberry Pi device) has orders of magnitude more computing power than NASA had when it was sending astronauts to the moon in the late 1960s and early 1970s. Put simply, there is simply no lack of talent or computing power. Even still, these superbly trained, exquisitely equipped professionals have developed sophisticated models that would have, without central bank intervention, crashed global financial markets twice in 10 years (long-term capital management [LTCM] and the mortgage crisis).

As Michael Lewis's book *The Big Short* points out, a group of investors profited from the mortgage market fall. One of them, Michael Burry, an ex-medical resident turned hedge fund manager, generated over 400 percent profits in his fund by shorting the mortgage market. In a 2010 op-ed in the *New York Times*, he explains exactly what his reasoning was: the market was structurally incentivized to extend more and more credit to borrowers who did not have the resources to repay loans (Burry, 2010). This real-life analysis did not need sophisticated mathematical calculations or access to investment banks' proprietary models for creating tranches of collateralized debt obligations (CDOs). Burry's insight was simply that a lot of people who couldn't possibly repay loans were receiving loans.

I have seen this dynamic several times in my career. Highly skillful people are trained to calculate according to a certain theory or set of assumptions, and they carry out their duties admirably. Someone on the other side of the trade may not have the computing power or the mathematical background to work out the calculations but instead questions the very theoretical foundations on which those calculations are based. Doing so, they sometimes realize that the theory does not jibe with reality. These iconoclasts take the other side of the trade—buying from or selling to the army of well-trained people busily calculating the "right answer"—and are roundly ridiculed (and often vilified) . . . until the trade works out.

While it is hard to quantify this ability, I believe the skill to think about abstract calculations in terms of what is happening in the real world is one that only a very few people possess.

This distinctive skill ties in closely to the last quality I have seen in the best investors: the ability to express a committed investment opinion that runs contrary to the crowd and for which one may not have complete data or information.

Robert Arnott, the founder and chairman of Newport Beach, California–based asset manager Research Affiliates, makes the point that investing requires something that is psychologically difficult to do (Swolfs, 2017):

> We all want less of whatever has given us pain and losses, but if you want to buy low, you have to buy something that's caused pain and losses. And it goes against human nature. We didn't survive on the African plains by running toward a lion. It goes against human nature.

The fact that investing well is the equivalent of our prehistoric ancestors running toward the lions on the African savannah is one that sticks with me. Arnott's illustration brings home the point that the only way to stand out from a crowd in terms of performance is to invest in something in which others are not investing. Going against the crowd and investing in assets that have caused other investors (and perhaps oneself) pain is difficult to do, and the ability to do it is not distributed among many people.

Considering how difficult it is to find people who meet all these criteria—having investing tunnel vision, being able to think about complex mathematical relationships in a real-world way, and having the psychological makeup that allows one to run toward the lions—it is no wonder why competition for investment talent is so fierce.

ASSET MANAGEMENT'S DEPLORABLE LACK OF GENDER DIVERSITY

If finding and nurturing investment talent is so important and the number of people with true talent so small, I will ask a very straightforward question: Why does the financial services industry routinely shut out half the population from more meaningful participation?

Looking at how few women rise to top positions in the financial services industry, one might think that a prerequisite to success in the business is having a Y-chromosome. In a 2017 *New York Times* article entitled "A Trillion-Dollar Question: Why Don't More

Women Run Mutual Funds?," the author points to industry research from Morningstar suggesting that only around 10 percent of US portfolio managers are women (Dunleavey, 2017). Funds in the rest of the world have roughly twice the representation of women in top positions in fund management, but even that rate falls far below female representation among other professional fields like medicine and law.[2]

This industry research was followed up with careful academic research that the low level of female leadership for US funds was extremely persistent as well, being nearly constant for the nearly 20 years covered by the study (Niessen-Ruenzi and Ruenzi, 2019).

A free-market absolutist might look at those statistics and say that there is an inherent difference that make males more suited to a career in asset management or perhaps more qualified for the role. A free-market absolutist would be wrong.

Studies comparing performance between male and female mutual fund managers fail to find much of a difference (e.g., Atkinson et al., 2003) and a study of differences between male and female hedge fund and fund-of-fund managers (Aggarwal and Boyson, 2016) note that "funds with all female managers perform no differently than all male-managed funds and have similar risk profiles." And for me, this is a fact. After a quarter of a century's worth of research, it doesn't look like the excuse that performance drives the representation disparity holds up. Why are women so underrepresented in the asset management business, then?

From what I have seen there are a few factors contributing to this outcome, some of which are within the power of asset management firms to correct, but some of which will require a much broader (and likely slower) cultural change.

The one piece of evidence that stands out when looking at representation is the difficulty that female managers have in attracting and maintaining assets. Keep in mind that we know that performance does not differ on average between male and female managers. Despite this, Niessen-Ruenzi and Ruenzi's study found evidence that investors simply place less money with funds managed by women. In a depressing commentary of our times, they conclude that

> subjects with the strongest gender bias (according to [a standardized test of gender bias]) invest the least in female-managed funds. Overall, our findings show that gender bias of investors can have a strong impact on financial markets and help to clarify why female-managed funds receive much lower inflows than male-managed funds. Furthermore, as managers generating low inflows are not attractive for fund companies to hire, our results also suggest customer-based discrimination as a possible new explanation for the low fraction of female managers in the mutual fund industry.

The paper from Aggarwal and Boyson also found that "[hedge] funds with at least one female manager fail at higher rates, driven by difficulty in raising capital." They note that female-managed hedge funds that do survive generate higher return than male-managed fund survivors, "consistent with the idea that female managers need to perform better for their funds to survive."

These observations about bias are not unique to the job of a portfolio manager, but also extend to perceptions of analysts' forecast accuracy. A paper by Pu Gu—"The Effects of Social Bias Against Female Analysts on Markets"—finds that despite the forecasts of female analysts being more accurate and timelier than those of males, market reaction to female forecasts tends to be weaker and more delayed (Gu, 2020). Put simply, the opinions of female analysts are systematically underestimated.

All these studies point to a wider social bias that perceives men as being more capable to make decisions and take risks than women, despite the surfeit of data showing no performance-affecting gender-based differences.

Another factor contributing to low female participation in the asset management business, and one that is possible to be changed rather more easily than convincing societies to drop their gender biases, is that of financial literacy.

There is a well-established and commonsensical link between financial literacy and stock market participation: people with low financial literacy (e.g., those with limited understanding of fundamental concepts such as compounding, the differences between stocks and bonds, and diversification-based risk management) are much less likely to invest in stocks. (e.g., van Rooij et al., 2011).

In 2017, Annamaria Lusardi and her research colleagues published a study entitled "How Financially Literate Are Women? An Overview and New Insights" (Bucher-Koenen et al., 2017). They found that women of all age groups were much less likely to understand important fundamental concepts in financial literacy than men and were more likely to respond they did not know an answer.

In 2021, the same team published another study entitled "Fearless Woman: Financial Literacy and Stock Market Participation"[3] that looked again at gender differences (Bucher-Koenen et al., 2021). This study again showed that women would disproportionately choose the "Do Not Know" option if it was proffered; intriguingly, when that choice was removed, women often chose the correct answer. The authors suggest that this dynamic displays a pervasive lack of confidence in most women that accounts for about one-third of the total financial literacy gap. This result about confidence is important because of the huge role self-confidence plays in stock market participation. Between a lack of confidence and a low degree of financial literacy, women are, on average, reluctant to participate in financial decision-making—everything from stock market participation to retirement planning to selecting funds to wealth accumulation and debt management.

The conclusion the academics reach is encouraging: it all comes down to education. Low financial literacy and stock market participation are problems that can be educated out of, not problems that require a massive shift in societal biases.

Indeed, in the classes I teach at the University of St. Gallen in finance and asset management, I am continually tempted to boost the grades of working groups with women by half a grade point, just to encourage more gender participation in the industry. Before you get your hackles up at this statement and start whining about "reverse discrimination," realize that since I'm teaching upper-level classes for people majoring in finance and thinking about going into the asset management business, only about 10 percent of my class is composed of female students. I could probably boost grades by a full grade point and statistically it would not be able for my university's administrators to pick up the bias!

In the end, I agree with the *New York Times* that the lack of gender diversity in the asset management business is a trillion-dollar problem. Think back to the earlier discussion of what I see are the three characteristics of truly skillful investors. There is absolutely no reason to believe that these characteristics are dispersed among the general population along gender lines. If a large percentage of the population who have the characteristics to be truly skillful investors are not even in the business, civilization is shooting itself in the foot in a big way.

The Active-Passive Dichotomy

As we saw in Chapter 5, the concept of asset management as either active and passive developed naturally as asset managers attempted to maximize revenue generation by (1) scaling up size and reducing fees or (2) boosting fees by promising access to exceptional investing talent.

While this active-passive dichotomy is by far the common way of conceptualizing and operationalizing asset management, I am going to swim against the stream and offer my belief that this dichotomy provides absolutely no value to either asset owners or to society at large.

In the next chapter, I lay out a model for conceiving of the tools available to an investor thinking about how to allocate capital that are superior to this active-passive dichotomy, but before delving into that, let me convince you why clinging to this twentieth-century conception of asset management is valueless and should be discarded.

THE ROLE OF INFORMATION IN ACTIVE AND PASSIVE STRATEGIES

Let's start with an important principle when talking about the active-passive dichotomy: informational efficiency. This frightening phrase simply means that a company's stock price reflects the best, most up-to-date information about the present operations of that company that incorporates market participants' aggregate best estimate about what the future holds.

Since the late 1950s, the world of financial economics, the academic branch that concerns itself with investment decisions, has been shaped by the idea of information efficiency.

Information efficiency assumes that everyone is (1) rational and (2) always trying to do what will be the most beneficial to themselves. Or to word it more formally, all market participants are "rational utility maximizers." In this context, being rational means gathering all the necessary information before deciding.

While the capacity of a single person to gather and process all the information needed to make a good decision is limited, the theory goes that as a group, the smartest, most insightful participants whose ideas are closest to being correct will be most handsomely rewarded. To be the handsomely rewarded one, everyone works like a dog to make sure they have all the information necessary to make the best possible decisions.

If everyone is competing for meaningful information to make the best decisions, and the best decisions are most rewarded, the best returns that an investor should be able to get is a decision based on the aggregate best ideas of the assembled market.

This reasoning led to the idea that the returns of the market as a whole will always be better than the returns of any individual participant trying to assemble a basket of stocks. In other words, it would be best to simply own a basket of investments that represented the market, rather than trying to create a custom basket of "special" assets.[1]

Reading between the lines of the preceding description, you can see that active managers are all engaged in a battle to acquire the best information and make the best decisions, while passive managers are essentially riding on the coattails of the active managers.

From this description, two things are clear:

1. Passive managers are basically free riders (i.e., they receive the benefit of a common good paid for by someone else— in this case they receive the benefit of an efficient market made by active managers competing to generate the highest returns).

2. In equilibrium, a passive strategy will not be effective if active managers do not exist.

These observations lie at the heart of what is known as the Grossman-Stiglitz Paradox (Grossman and Stiglitz, 1980; see Box 8.1). In the Grossman-Stiglitz world, one would expect passive and active funds to coexist in equilibrium with their relative market shares depending on information costs and overall market efficiency. The higher the cost of information, the less active management would be practiced; the lower the market efficiency, the less passive management would be practiced.

The insight behind the Grossman-Stiglitz Paradox is that passive strategies simply could not exist without active investors. Active investors find the mispricings and economic impossibilities existing in the market, then put their reputations and the capital of their clients at risk to invest with the expectation that those mispricings and impossibilities will correct themselves in a timeframe that matters to their investors.

Or to put it in different terms, to the extent that markets are efficient, they are so because there are armies of well-paid, well-resourced geniuses looking for any slight inefficiency to exploit in exchange for an elevated fee. Passive strategies "work" as well as they do because markets are efficient; markets are efficient because there are so many people looking for and immediately exploiting any inefficiencies they find.

While one might quibble with the form of Grossman and Stiglitz's argument, I believe that the basic interdependency of active and passive managers is underscored by this famous paradox. Rather than talking about active versus passive (as everyone seems to do in the asset management business), one should always conceive of active and passive strategies being inextricably intertwined.

The predictions made by Grossman and Stiglitz—meaning the interdependent relationship between information costs and market efficiency—is interesting in the context of where we find ourselves in the asset management world today. With so much data available and with so much computer power at anyone's fingertips, the cost for one manager to get an informational advantage over another is going to continue to increase. Just considering the reasoning behind the Grossman-Stiglitz Paradox for a moment, it is clear that the present artificial intelligence (AI) race is going to push more money into passive investment structures at roughly the pace that AI is continuing to develop and improve (i.e., at a rapidly expanding rate). This dynamic I will discuss a bit later in the book.

BOX 8.1 If It Is a Market, It Is Inefficient

The insight that efficient markets are a logical impossibility was formalized by economists Sanford Grossman and Joseph Stiglitz (henceforth GS) in a paper entitled "On the Impossibility of Informationally Efficient Markets" (Grossman and Stiglitz, 1980).

GS's elegant argument runs like this:

- If markets were informationally efficient, investors would be unable to exploit inefficiencies.
- Without inefficiencies that are large enough to exploit in a cost-efficient way, investors will start to generate negative returns. Realizing that searching for inefficiencies is fruitless and value-destructive, investors would stop searching.
- As investors stopped looking for market inefficiencies, information would not be fully processed by market

participants. The longer investors stopped searching for market inefficiencies, the more inefficient the markets would become.

- As markets became increasingly inefficient, investors would soon discover they could find and exploit inefficiencies to generate excess returns. This realization would prompt the restarting of expensive efforts to exploit inefficiencies in the attempt to generate excess returns.

In GS's view, the fact that active investors exist in a market is proof that markets are inefficient. In the world of finance, this is known as the Grossman-Stiglitz Paradox.

In the view of GS, market inefficiencies are inextricably tied to the cost of gathering and processing information. Inefficiencies will exist to the extent that information is expensive to gather and analyze. As more participants look for inefficiencies in the attempt to generate excess returns, those inefficiencies that are cheapest to find, analyze, and exploit are found, analyzed, and exploited—leading to them disappearing. (This leads to the famous conclusion that you will never find a $100 bill on Wall Street. If someone had dropped one, someone else would have picked it up already.) Any "excess" returns are, in GS's conceptualization, simply reflections of the costs associated with finding the inefficiencies in the first place.

As the relatively cheaply exploited inefficiencies disappear, it becomes more expensive to exploit the remaining inefficiencies. Eventually, the cost of exploiting efficiencies will become so great that it will not make sense to attempt to find, analyze, and exploit them any longer. Any market without exploitable inefficiencies will eventually collapse because it loses its ability to perform its main function: process information related to securities prices and optimal allocation of resources. The equilibrium point, GS argue, is a market that has inefficiencies that are expensive to find and exploit. Or to put it another way, if a market exists, it must be inefficient.

Considering GS's findings, it is worth asking whether a large proportion of passive investors in a market decrease the efficiency of the market to an unacceptable level. Some asset managers even argue that an economy with substantial passive investing is worse at efficiently allocating capital to the best ideas than a centrally planned economy. Adi Libson and Gideon Parchomovsky even argue that regulators should impose a tax on passive investment funds to help decrease the active-passive fee differential (Libson and Parchomovsky, 2021).

A very recent paper, published in the fall of 2022, entitled "On Index Investing" looks precisely at this question (Coles et al., 2022) and concludes that a large proportion of money invested in passive instruments does have an influence on information creation (e.g., fewer search engine queries, analyst reports, and the like) but does not affect the information content of security prices (i.e., security prices reflect available information).

According to Coles and colleagues, inclusion in an index changes the composition of the company's investors—active investors sell to passive investors—but does not decrease the overall effectiveness of the market in processing economic information to price securities.

THE JOYS AND STRUGGLES OF ACTIVE MANAGERS

Those of you who are golfers should appreciate the power of a good drive early on in one's golf-playing career. Maybe you hook the ball into the woods on the left or the pond on the right 9 times out of 10 when you're learning how to swing. However, on that tenth drive— when the ball sails straight and high down the fairway—suddenly, one's brain is washed with a wave of dopamine that can be very addictive. Driving well as a beginner can be dangerous, since years can be spent on the course trying to replicate that initial dopamine hit one received as a newbie.

Asset management is just like that.

It is hard to imagine anything in this world that is as addictive as investing the $1,000 one has saved up from a summer job in high school in a penny stock and seeing the value of that $1,000 position swelling to $10,000 in a matter of a few days.

This dynamic is true not only for individuals, but for the entire industry too.

After the stock market crash of 1929 and the market carnage of the Great Depression that followed it, reputable investors considered any investments other than government or blue-chip corporate bonds to be speculative and unbefitting to the fiduciary responsibilities that asset managers were bound to.

This lack of investor attention on equity markets meant that opportunities existed for quick, well-informed managers to outperform, simply because there were so few players trying to do so.

Aside from the lack of meaningful and rational equity market participation, there were simple logistical issues related to the availability of high-quality information. Asset price information was available intraday, but in general, financial and company information took longer to be published and propagated.

The data company Bloomberg—today, a ubiquitous presence on trading desks the world over—was not founded until 1981, and the financial data for nonprofessionals was not widely available for years after that. Yale economics professor Robert Shiller wrote a working paper in 1987 that surveyed individual and institutional investors about their reactions to the October 1987 Black Monday crash (Shiller, 1987). He found that individual investors learned of the market's extreme price drops at an average time of 1:56 p.m. on Black Monday, just two hours before the close. Nearly one-fifth of individual investors only learned of the extreme price drops after 5 p.m. that day. In this day of smart phones and virtually free financial market data, imagine not knowing about a 20+-standard-deviation price event until two hours before the market close!

Moving from price information to company-specific data, the SEC only began mandating electronic filing of financial statement information in 1993, and until the 2002 passage of Sarbanes-Oxley regulations, company managers could (and did) provide tips to favored analysts and investors.

Information is power in the financial markets, so during these environments displaying relatively low investment competition and relatively difficult-to-acquire financial data, investors that could assemble important information and analyze it better than others might have plausibly maintained that they could consistently perform better than an index benchmark.

However, as more money flowed into investment funds, more aspiring fund managers were attracted to the industry; these managers began demanding more and more timely information and data providers stepped in to fulfill that demand. The result was that the information efficiency taken as axiomatic by academics like Eugene Fama and Burton Malkiel moved closer to what was happening in the markets.

Active managers were (then as now) forced into an informational arms race. As informational efficiency improved in the markets, each marginal dollar invested by a portfolio manager to acquire better, faster information or better information processors had less and less effect on performance, while reducing asset managers' profit margins.

The immediate effect of this dynamic was that asset managers began to attempt to maintain AUM by competing on price—in other words, by lowering fees (see Figure 8.1).

When lowering fees started to eat too much into asset managers' profitability, they began looking for ways to maintain or expand AUM levels other than by cutting fees. The easiest ways to do this were through slick marketing and by building effective distribution channels.

Think about it. If you are a client of J.P. Morgan, for example, all the funds available for you to choose from would be those managed by J.P. Morgan's asset management arm. This is what I mean by a distribution network, and the fact that they exist and are so powerful is incredibly important, especially in countries where the end client is paying high fees, like in Italy.

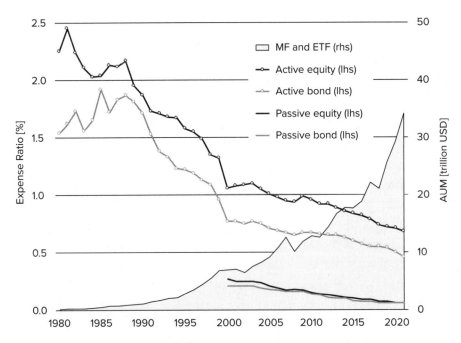

FIGURE 8.1 Expense ratios and AUM of active and passive US mutual funds (including ETF)

Source: Data from Investment Company Institute.

The pricing wars gradually died down as marketing power and strong distribution networks allowed managers to retain some semblance of pricing power. Managers understood that clients were usually insensitive to small and/or temporary underperformance versus the reference indices but fled from extreme underperformance. The rational choice for a manager in this situation was to cling as close to the index as possible and come up with compelling narratives to convince clients to maintain or increase the amount of capital placed within the funds.

If "clinging as close to the index as possible" sounds like the closet indexing discussed in prior chapters, that's because it is.

This "closet indexing + slick marketing = asset management success" formula helped asset management companies' bottom lines in the short term, but in 2011, a paper from influential Yale scholar

Martijn Cremers and others (Cremers et al., 2011) found evidence of widespread closet indexing in markets across the globe and showed that "'closet indexing' is positively associated with fees and negatively with performance." In other words, closet indexers charge more for poor returns.

This effect was about three times more prevalent in markets outside the United States than within, with more than 50 percent of funds in Poland and Sweden showing evidence of levels of closet indexing. More than 40 percent of funds in "enlightened" markets such as Canada, Finland, and Spain also displayed evidence of closet indexing.

As these data became apparent to influential shareholder groups, it is only natural that clients began to feel hoodwinked. "Hoodwinked investors" is a trigger phrase for lawyers, and indeed, class action lawsuits started to pop up globally, asking asset managers to refund capital to make up for excess fees and underperformance.

In 2014, the Swedish Shareholders Association (SSA) brought a suit against the second largest fund company in that country, Swedbank Robur; around 2,500 other plaintiffs also joined the suit as a class action. The *Financial Times* quoted Carl Rosén, the CEO of the SSA, as saying that it was unsurprising that Sweden appeared so prominently in the academic research. The reason he offered was that the Swedish market is "dominated by large banks with a strong distribution capacity" (Norman, 2016).

In the wake of lawyers swim the regulators, and indeed, in 2016, the ESMA published a statement on its supervisory considerations regarding closet indexing strategies. From ESMA's press release at the time:

> Closet indexing, also known as index hugging, refers to the practice of fund managers claiming to manage portfolios actively when in reality the fund stays close to a benchmark. ESMA is concerned the practice may harm investors as they are not receiving the service or risk/return profile they expect based on the fund's disclosure documents while potentially

paying higher fees compared to those typically charged for passive management.

After that time, national regulators began to get involved in studying this issue as well. As recently as 2019, the United Kingdom's Financial Conduct Authority fined Henderson Investment Funds Ltd £1.9 million for overcharging investors in two of its funds. Specifically, according to *Investment Executive* magazine, Henderson managers "had decided to reduce the level of active management in its Japan and North American sector funds" (Langton, 2019).

Indeed, Henderson informed institutional investors about the change and offered to cut the management fees institutions were paying, but somehow neglected to give retail investors the heads-up or to cut their fees.

At present, active funds make up something like 60 to 70 percent (Wigglesworth, 2022) of global assets under management, and considering the likelihood that some of these active funds are index hugging, the costs of this problem to asset owners are estimated to be extremely high.

A simple calculation shows the magnitude of the costs of closet indexing. Let's assume active managers have in aggregate AUM of $40 trillion under management. Furthermore, assume that 10 percent of these assets ($4 trillion) are allocated to closet indexers earning 0.5 percent more than they should. This results in $20 billion per year in extra costs! To put that fee number into perspective, it is equivalent to roughly a quarter of the yearly management fee of the hedge fund industry.

If my assumption that 1 out of 10 active managers are closet indexers, the value destruction stemming from this problem is enormous. Think of it, that is a quarter of all AUM being charged as if the clients were gaining exposure to the most sophisticated, bespoke active management strategies, while in fact they are exposed to nothing more than the underlying index. Ouch.

While some might question the degree to which active managers are successful at creating value for their clients, most active managers pour a tremendous amount of time and energy into researching investments and understanding the operations and strategy of the underlying companies well. These managers often use their positions as shareholders to affect the future of the companies in which they are invested, whether they are considered "activist" investors or not. This active involvement offers, I would argue, a real net benefit to society—sharpening the focus and competitive capacity of companies and/or encouraging them to focus on strategic and governance issues.[2]

Clearly, a closet indexer is going to be much less interested in or able to positively influence strategy at companies in which they hold investments—they are tagging along for the ride, not trying to influence direction. This free-riding should also be counted as among the costs of closet indexing, in my mind.

We will explore engagement, a true advantage of active management versus passive later in this chapter, but now let us look at the challenges associated with the opposite end of the active-passive continuum.

THE JOYS AND STRUGGLES OF PASSIVE MANAGERS

What a life to be a passive investment manager! Most days—except for special times like the annual "Russell Rebalance"—you can go home early and sleep soundly without having to worry about things like that large position in Greek banks or Turkish lira you took a few months ago that is starting to give you heartburn now.

As a passive manager, you have no responsibility to select assets or stick your neck out regarding a call on the relative performance of one market or one asset over another. Sure, you are not going to become a billionaire from your compensation as a passive fund manager, but you will have a very comfortable, upper-middle-class life; send your kids to good schools; and enjoy a genteel, elegant retirement, all thanks to the fact that if you are a passive investment manager, you are managing a truly eye-watering amount of client capital. A four-basis-point fee on a portfolio of $1.3 trillion (AUM of the Vanguard Total Stock Market Index Fund Admiral Shares) is $520 million. That is enough to maintain a nice head office, well-educated, efficient staff and still have enough left over to pay the manager a handsome salary.

So what's the problem?

The problem is that passive funds, while serving their clients better than active funds, on average, are still not serving their clients well. And while it is more difficult to assess the cost to clients for investing in passive strategies when compared to active ones, we try to quantify the economic costs in the next section of this chapter.

To understand why passive funds ill-serve their investors, let's look at a few concrete examples, then turn to financial theory.

The first thing to grasp about a market index is that it reflects human choices, especially as to weighting. There are three meaningful ways to weight an index, and all carry with them unintended consequences that can harm investors:

1. **Equal weighting.** This is the method used to calculate the Indian Nifty 50 Index. This is a confusing weighting methodology because the index must be reweighted often to maintain an equal weight of each component. The Nifty 50 are the largest stocks in the Indian market, but a broader equal-weighted index that includes many more stocks of smaller companies would clearly ridiculously underweight the most important stocks in an economy. Imagine, for example, an equally weighted oil and gas industry index. This index would give investors equal exposure to both a global behemoth like ExxonMobil and a tiny independent fracking company operating in only West Texas.

2. **Fundamental weighting.** This method is not used to calculate any major index. "Fundamental" is defined as some feature that is a derivative of price and some balance sheet or income statement value—for example, price-to-book (PB)

and price-to-earnings (PE) ratios. The weighting of each stock is a function of the fundamental value used. Like equal-weighted indices, fundamentally weighted indices tend to have a fairly high turnover, but the weakness for a global investor is that different markets tend to have different average fundamental ratios that are "typical" for that particular market. So an index that aimed to be a fundamentally weighted global index might only contain Japanese and a few German stocks—hardly a representative selection of the global economy. Indices based on "fundamental" criteria are, in my mind, closer to being hybrid funds midway along the active-passive spectrum (aka factor investing). Essentially, by investing in a fundamentally weighted index, the investor is choosing to invest in a systematic small cap-value fund.

3. **Market capitalization weighting.** "Cap" weighting in one form or another is, by far, the most common weighting scheme for index construction, used for all the most important indices: S&P 500, NASDAQ, Russell 1000, Wilshire 5000, Toronto TSE 300, FTSE 100, CAC 40, and so on.

Because cap weighting is so widely used in industry and is also the most widely accepted weighting scheme used by academics, I will proceed with my comments regarding passive investment costs focusing only on this weighting scheme.

Whereas the equal-weight scheme puts a disproportionate weighting on small, unimportant companies, cap weighting puts a disproportionate weighting on the largest, most overvalued ones. This scheme, in other words, provides investors an allocation to *yesterday's* best ideas without a thought of what *tomorrow's* best ideas are likely to be. During times of technological or societal transitions this rearview mirror emphasis turns out to be enormously risky.

Great examples of this abound. For instance, at its peak during the millennial dot.com runup ending, Nortel represented more than 36 percent of the Toronto TSE 300 index. In other words, a passive Canadian investor in 2000 was allocating over one-third of his portfolio to a single dot.com name. In that same year a passive investor in Helsinki would have been sinking over two-thirds of her investment in Nokia. Needless to say, neither of those allocations worked very well over the 10 years that followed.

Even in less extreme cases than these, the overweighting of index components based on market capitalization can cause problems. For example, Apple, Microsoft, Amazon, Alphabet, Facebook, and Tesla accounted for almost 50 percent of the NASDAQ 100 index in 2020, which was designed to be composed of the 100 largest publicly traded nonfinancial institutions. Obviously, having this much of an index's market capitalization tied to only six stocks creates an element of idiosyncratic risk, which determines the index performance substantially.

These examples have been taken from the practitioner's perspective, but from a formal, academic perspective, capitalization weighted indices clearly have this problem as well.

Jack Treynor (Treynor, 2005) shows this in his article "Why Market-Valuation-Indifferent Indexing Works." The intuition is simple: an allocation to a stock in a portfolio that is positively correlated to its valuation has a cost.

For example, a market capitalization weighting allocates more money to high market capitalization stocks—those that are most likely to be overvalued—suggesting that they make up more of the index than they should. If the stock then reverts to the fair value, the index loses. The same holds true the other way round. If done systematically this could have a large effect.

A comparison provided by Bob Arnott and his colleagues (Arnott, 2005) gives an indication of how large the cost of passive investing can be. Arnott constructed an index of companies running from 1962 to 2004; his index, however, was weighted by the number of employees working for a company rather than its market capitalization. They found the employee count-weighted index delivered a return of 12.8 percent compared to only 10.6 percent per year for the market capitalization weighted index. In other words, the gross cost of the decision to passively index based on market capitalization was more than 2.0 percent per year and just short of 2.0 percent after adjusting for trading costs.

It is difficult to justify this finding using conventional economic intuition. Why should a company with many employees have a better return? In my mind, using the number of employees as a weighting method is, in fact, a red herring and the reason for the outperformance lies elsewhere. The crucial statistical feature of employee numbers is that they change only very slowly, making any weighting scheme based on this number essentially equivalent to maintaining a constant weight—one that is relatively insensitive to changes in value of individual stocks. The elegance of equal weighting schemes is attractive to me—they are simple ways to diversify while avoiding the trap of estimation risk.

My contention is that both active and passive methodologies carry with them an economic cost to the owner of capital. These costs will become an extremely important factor in my mental model of the imperatives that will shape the asset management industry in the next century.

WHY PASSIVE VERSUS ACTIVE DOES NOT WORK?

The efficient market hypothesis (EMH) is such an elegant theorem about how the financial markets work that it quickly gained almost unquestionable orthodoxy among academics. The students of those academics like me, who went on to become practitioners, had the EMH drilled into us for so long that it seems natural for us to buy into it as well.

Because of the ubiquity of the EMH, it is no wonder that people consider passive investing to be the most cost-efficient way to invest. For years, studies have estimated the cost of active management, implicitly or explicitly comparing the cost of investing in an active strategy to the base cost of passive. Costs of active management are easy to tease out. Active managers charge high fees; these high fees provide a performance headwind that almost always makes it harder for investors to do as well as passive investing counterparts. What's more, the proportion of active managers that have the capacity to repeatably, materially beat their benchmarks is certainly south of 10 percent.

No matter how easy it is to calculate active costs and to make comparisons to passive as the "base," I believe that passive investing also has a cost—albeit one that is lower than that of active management most of the time and much trickier to calculate.

The costs of passive management stem from a structurally poor portfolio construction methodology that forces passive managers to invest most of their capital in the most overvalued securities and less (or nothing) in ideas that have the potential to change civilization for the better in the future. There is no other way to put it: passive investments do not shape the future; they only reflect what happened in the past.[3]

This is not to say that passive funds do not exert some influence on companies whose stocks they hold. Passive strategies now make up a majority of AUM, and this means passively managed portfolios hold enormous proportions of many companies. If a portfolio manager for Vanguard wants to talk with the CEO of an S&P 500-component company, all she has to do is pick up the phone. Because the proportional holdings are so large, passive investors have a potentially very loud voice regarding governance and other strategic matters.

William McNabb III, the chairman and CEO of the vanguard of the passive fund movement, Vanguard Funds, once underscored this point better than I could ever hope to do (McNabb, 2015):

> We're going to hold your stock when you hit your quarterly earnings target. And we'll hold it when you don't. We're going to hold your stock if we like you. And if we don't. We're going to hold your stock when everyone else is piling in. And when everyone else is running for the exits. That is precisely why we care so much about good governance.

An academic paper entitled "Passive Investors, Not Passive Owners" studied this question and tested McNabb's anecdotal comment with statistical data (Appel et al., 2016). The paper found that passive mutual funds influence firms' strategic choices, especially those related to corporate governance. Ownership by passive funds, the academics found, resulted in more independent directors, the removal of (management-centric) takeover defenses, and more equal voting rights. What's more, the paper tied these governance improvements to improvements in firms' long-term stock performance as well.

The influence granted by large holdings allows passive investors to tackle important issues such as carbon footprints. A recent paper entitled "The Big Three and Corporate Carbon Emissions Around the World" (Azar et al., 2021) found evidence that the "Big Three" passive investment fund families—BlackRock, Vanguard, and State Street Global Advisors—had exerted influence on large firms with high CO_2 emissions in which they held significant stakes. The academics found that engagement regarding decarbonization from the Big Three led to "strong and robust negative association between Big Three ownership and subsequent carbon emissions" and that this relationship strengthened the longer the study ran.

While it seems that the managers of passive funds have some influence over corporate decision-making, one crucial bit of leverage that the passive manager does not possess, that the active manager has in spades, is that of the threat of exiting an investment.

No matter how uncomfortable a meeting between a passive portfolio manager and a CEO might become, when the meeting ends and the portfolio manager gets back in her limo, the CEO has the absolute certainty that as long as the Standard & Poor's index team does not remove the company from the index, the passive manager must be invested in the company's stock. A passive manager simply does not have the prerogative to allocate resources differently than to reflect outcomes of the past as reflected in the proportional value of the company's stock in the target index.

Because the active manager holds the power over portfolio construction decisions, the active manager can allocate capital to the brightest ideas of the future—to the companies that society needs the most to become better, fairer, and more sustainable. The passive manager, on the other hand, cannot.

It is my view that the relative inability for passive managers to proactively guide capital toward tomorrow's best ideas ends up imposing a high cost on society as a whole, even if the costs to any single investor in a passive fund may be small.

Let's look at an actual example from the world of investing to illustrate the costs to asset owners of allocating using a rearview mirror, passive strategy. Examples are endless, but I will use the sad story of the Eastman Kodak company.

In January 1997, Kodak released its fiscal year 1996 earnings and announced it was raising its dividends for the first time in eight years. The stock soared on the news, eventually hitting $93 soon after earnings were released. The company had the fourth most valuable brand in the United States and was a member of both the Dow Jones Industrials and the S&P 500 index.

Given its market capitalization of $31 billion in February 1997, when the stock was at a record high of $94.75, a passive manager running an S&P 500 tracking fund would have invested somewhere around $0.01 of every new dollar flowing into her fund into the stock of Eastman Kodak.

The problem was that everything good about Kodak had already happened sometime in the prior 118 years. The company started missing their own announced earnings targets, restructuring operations, cutting staff, and issuing revenue and profit warnings later in 1997. By the end of the year, the stock was trading for $60.56 per share, about a third lower than its peak earlier in the year.

Eastman Kodak had enjoyed over 100 years of amazing success, during which time it saw profit margins peak in the 80 percent range. The company's strategy was based on selling cameras as a loss-leader and relying upon sales of film to generate profits. An engineer at the company had invented solid-state image sensors that converted light to digital images in the mid-1970s. Because digital photography would have killed the cash cow of Kodak's film business, the engineer responsible for the advances in solid-state image sensing was discouraged from pushing ahead with the project by Kodak managers.

The strategic decision to toss Kodak's solid-state image sensor technology into a broom closet is terrible when viewed from the perspective of hindsight, but managers at the time were concerned with their own positions at the company and with the thought that they could not afford to be perceived as the ones who are upsetting a very profitable apple cart.

Essentially, by allocating capital to Kodak in 1997, a passive portfolio manager was allocating capital to yesterday's good idea and the vested interests of shortsighted corporate agents, while turning a blind eye to the realities of the present and the potential of the future.

The first mass market digital cameras began being marketed in 1994–1995 (one of the earliest manufacturers was none other than Apple with the Apple QuickTake 100). Kodak also began adjusting to the realty of the oncoming wave of digital photography by marketing its own digital camera in the mid-1990s, but its business model was too dependent on the "cheap camera-expensive film" business model for it to adjust appropriately.

The first digital camera incorporated into the body of a mobile phone was in 2000, just three years after Kodak's final blowout earnings report (Hill, 2013). Just over 10 years after Kodak's great report, Apple released the iPhone, complete with a 2-megapixel solid-state image sensor-powered camera.

Kodak was dropped from the Dow Jones Industrials Average after the first quarter of 2004—on April 8—when its stock was trading in the upper $20 range. And after 53 years, Kodak was dropped from the S&P 500 in December 2010 when it was trading in the $5 range—Kodak was an original constituent of the S&P 500 in 1957.

In 2012, Kodak filed for bankruptcy protection—a perfectly natural outcome of what has been called the "iPhone moment."

The tracking fund's portfolio manager would have simply ridden the stock down all this way (a loss of around 95 percent) from 1997 (and before) to 2010, clipping dividend coupons to partially offset the stock price losses but taking a capital loss bath in the process.

Active investors, on the other hand, profited mightily from this stock price fall, as long as they and their investors had the fortitude to buck the trend when Kodak had hit its peak and the foresight to open a short position in advance of Kodak's stock price decline.

For a single investor in a passive fund holding Kodak stock at its peak, the loss was slight—around $0.01 for every one dollar invested. However, if we look now at investments in passive funds, something like $0.05 of every dollar invested is flowing through to companies involved in the mining, refining, or burning of fossil fuels. I write much more about sustainability and climate change investing later in the book, but let me steal a little of my own thunder now by stating that however fossil-fuel-related stocks perform in the near term, in the long term, investing in them is putting our very civilization at risk. The thought that $0.05 of every passive dollar invested today is going to enterprises that are provably destroying the ability of our biosphere to support human life is one that should give you pause.

Put simply, a focus on active versus passive doesn't work. Explicit costs and fees associated with active management are provably value-destructive to investors. The implicit costs associated with backward-looking portfolio construction associated with passive management does not allow society to allocate capital in a way that it should be—toward tomorrow's best ideas.

Any successful investment strategy needs elements of both. Part III of this book sets forth a model for the asset management industry that will work. Let's turn our attention to that.

PART III

A First Principle Model

A Financial Intermediation Perspective on the Asset Management Industry

After the last chapter, we know that both active and passive styles have their strengths and weaknesses, and we understand better the costs that are associated with both.

As we enter the second quarter of the twenty-first century, it is clear to me that the dichotomy between active and passive styles of fund management will not help our civilization during a critical and pivotal time in human history. However, it is also clear to me that the concept of "passive versus active" would not have had as much staying power as it has if active and passive were not getting some things right.

To serve our asset owner clients and society at large, I strongly believe that we must discard the active-passive dichotomy and move to a first principle model that allows us to use the strengths of both active and passive while discarding their weaknesses.

My thinking about this has been influenced by Frederic Mishkin and Stanley Eakins (Mishkin and Eakins, 2018), who highlight critical outcomes of successful financial intermediation related to lowering of transaction costs, enabling risk sharing, and lowering the level of information asymmetry.

Every type of financial intermediary provides these advantages in different shapes and sizes. For the asset management industry, I slightly rephrase these critical outcomes:

- Lowering investing cost
- Transforming investing risk
- Lowering information asymmetries (between asset owner and asset manager)

To the three outcomes, I add one of my own—the responsiveness to savers' needs and societal imperatives—which I call *meeting societal preferences*. The reason I believe this last role of intermediation is key is because I have seen the overwhelmingly powerful role that capital markets play in the shaping of a society and believe that asset management—to act successfully as an intermediary in this pivotal twenty-first century—must address the challenges facing our civilization.

The model for building a better, more responsive asset management industry attempts to balance each of these key elements. Before we dig deeper into that model, however, let's look at how passive and active strategies appear when viewed from the perspective of successful financial intermediation.

ACTIVE AND PASSIVE THROUGH THE FINANCIAL INTERMEDIATION LENS

Over the past generation, there has been a shift of savers directing their money toward passive funds and this trend has a very good reason: passive funds outperform active funds over time on both a pre- and post-fee basis.

Clearly, passive managers are doing some things right. Let's look at what these things are.

What Passive Gets Right

First, passive funds charge extremely low management fees—significantly lower than those of active mutual fund managers and an order of magnitude lower than those of hedge funds. Unlike hedge funds, performance fees are not charged (as index trackers, the funds would not and should not have any performance excess of the index, of course).

Not only are some passive funds' management fees very low, one prominent US-based investment company has begun waiving fees and minimum investment amounts for several of the company's passive funds.

Considering what an enormous drag on performance fees are, lessening them goes a long way to improving savers' realized investment returns.

But recall that passive funds also beat most active funds on a pre-fee basis. As such, lowering of fees cannot be the only element leading to passive strategies' relative outperformance to active ones. I have a view of the advantage afforded by passive vehicles that allows them to outperform active vehicles on average over time,[1] but let's continue looking at what passive funds are doing right.

The second thing that passive funds do well is to share risk across a pool of investors. The easiest way to explain this in nontechnical terms is to offer the example of a corporate bond fund.

Let's say that you are a saver with a small portfolio, of which you want to allocate $10,000 to corporate bonds. Looking through a list of corporate bonds available, you notice that the smallest denomination you can purchase is exactly $10,000. In other words, if you want to allocate that amount to corporate bonds, you will be able to buy exactly one bond. Let's say that you are buying this bond in February 1997, so you decide you want to buy 20-year bonds issued by Eastman Kodak Company. Knowing the history of Eastman Kodak from last chapter, we know that those bonds are extremely risky on an ex post basis (in other words, we know from the benefit of hindsight that the company will go bankrupt in 2012 and that holders of the company's bonds will be paid back only pennies on the dollar).

A corporate bond fund, on the other hand, uses the capital pooled from many investors and holds those bonds as assets, then issues its own liabilities—shares of its own bond fund—to its investors. These liabilities are designed to be able to be finely denominated such that every bond fundholder receives the blended return of the entire portfolio. In other words, the saver with only $10,000 to invest in corporate bonds receives not only the coupon payments and returns of one company—the former Eastman Kodak Company in this instance—but the blended returns of a large number of companies that fit some criteria (e.g., a bond rating of a certain level or above).

This risk-sharing function is essential to performance in that it radically decreases the possibility of an extreme negative return, due to the diversification effect. The diversification effect also limits upside returns, but the truncation of the downside risk is obviously the more important point related to risk sharing.

The last thing is that passive funds remove all information asymmetry, as it is known in the academic financial literature. What do I mean by information asymmetry in this case? It is simply a condition in which one party involved in a transaction knows something that the other party does not. Residential real estate transactions typically have a very high level of information asymmetry, for example. The seller of a home knows that the downstairs drain tends to back up during heavy rain, that the neighbor across the street has a drinking problem and is often visited by the local police squad, and so on.

In the context we are discussing now, information asymmetry means that a saver knows what assets into which the portfolio manager will invest and what the outcome of the investment will be. If you buy an S&P 500 fund, you can easily look up exactly what 500 names the fund will hold and in what proportion. If you wanted to, you could create an S&P 500 tracking portfolio on your own; that would not be a cost- or time-efficient choice, of course, but the information asymmetry is so low that it is indeed possible!

Lowering information asymmetry is, I will argue, an important duty of an asset manager, but it certainly does not affect returns. I'll discuss this dynamic more later in this chapter.

What Passive Gets Wrong

As we saw in the example of Eastman Kodak, the biggest weakness of passive strategies in my mind is the fact that they are essentially ones that focus on past glories—they are rearview mirror instruments, in other words.

From a philosophical and societal perspective, passive investing's backward-looking focus is also questionable. The purpose of capital markets is to allocate money to the best ideas, and the definition of *best* must include, in my mind, products and services that are best for the advancement of society. Investing in a company that generates arguably excessive economic rents due to historical circumstances hardly fits the bill for the condition that an investment helps society become more just, equitable, and wealthy.

This focus on forward-looking investment allocations is so important, I believe it is a worthy measure on which to judge the success of a financial intermediate's operations. With this reasoning, I have included responding to savers' preferences and societal needs as my fourth criteria of successful financial intermediation.

What Active Gets Right

The thing that passive gets most wrong is the thing that active gets most right. Active managers are always looking to the future—whether that future brings with it the collapse of a century-old blue chip or the arrival of the next industry-defining trailblazer.

The other facet of successful intermediation that active managers generally get right is risk sharing, though the degree active managers focus on this differs on the type of fund.

On a spectrum of *risk sharing*, mutual funds with a broad mandate tend to be on the high side and some hedge funds—especially those focused on *activist investing*—are on the low.

Mutual fund managers understand that while most investors want good returns, they are scared away by excessive volatility. Large drawdowns tend to be associated with overconcentration in particular assets, and large drawdowns are the bane of any asset manager who does not have the security of a lock-up agreement with fund investors. Mutual funds, then, tend to spread investment risk out of a wide range of sectors and industries, to the extent that the composition of their portfolios start to look a lot like that of broad-based indices—hence the lawsuits regarding closet indexing described in the last chapter.

Many equity hedge funds do tend to have greater concentration and thus higher return volatility. Activist hedge funds, especially, are focused on building positions in a single stock that are large enough so the portfolio managers can select one or more board members and thus have some indirect control on the operations of the company. Some hedge funds are little more than special purpose vehicles dedicated to investing in the assets of a single company. An excellent example of this was Bill Ackman's doomed activist campaign with his investment in US retailer Target. Ackman created several funds, all of which were invested solely in Target's equity, options, and swaps.

Viewed from the four criteria of successful intermediation, active managers are responding well to society's changing preferences and demands. Risk sharing is a mixed bag, with some active managers doing a better job with it than others.

What Active Gets Wrong

First and foremost, active managers are on the wrong side of the fee debate. Hedge fund managers are especially so, and it is not hard to see that the hedge fund industry has already hit a wall. For the past few years, it has been struggling to figure out how to transform their businesses in such a way to continue to charge high fees for the services and expertise they provide. My conviction is that they will fail.

The normal fee structure for a hedge fund is 2-and-20. Two percent management fee and 20 percent performance fee (usually performance relative to a benchmark or a high-water mark).

Let's say that a hedge fund is benchmarked to the S&P 500 and take the S&P 500's average return in the postwar period to be about 10 percent to be our example one-year return. Let's further say that a hedge fund outperforms its benchmark by a respectable 20 percent, generating 12 percent returns from its investments.

What does the hedge fund take home at the end of the year? It takes two percentage points of the asset value in management fees—dropping the savers' returns to 10 percent for the year, equivalent to the benchmark—then takes another 20 percent of the two percentage points (i.e., 40 basis points) in excess of the benchmark's return in performance fees.[2]

In other words, in a year in which the hedge fund exceeded the benchmark by a healthy margin, the saver whose capital the hedge fund invested ended up lagging the benchmark's returns by 40 basis points.

If we look at active management from the information asymmetry perspective, active managers also fall behind their passive colleagues. Active managers must maintain compliance with their investment mandates; so for instance, if a manager is running a global long-short equity portfolio, the investors in the fund know that their capital will not be invested in Turkish government bonds (because bonds are not within the "equity" part of the mandate), but other than knowing what asset class their capital will be invested in, they will not have a clue.

Reduction of information asymmetry is usually done after the fact, in quarterly letters by the portfolio manager. The portfolio manager provides a narrative about the assets in which the fund is invested, as well as his or her thoughts about why the position has worked out or not worked out, and perhaps some indication of what assets might be attractive candidates for future investment.

As the hedge fund business became more competitive, portfolio managers increasingly narrowed their mandates to certain industries or geographies in the attempt to achieve economies of scale on the research side. Also, because performance fees are often benchmarked against a passive index, one might say that there is a reasonable expectation that fund returns will be something like those of the underlying index. Of course, this harkens back to the discussion of closet indexing in the previous chapter.

A FIRST PRINCIPLE MODEL THAT WORKS

Rather than talking about active versus passive, I believe a better mental model for us to approach asset management is using the four-scale framework that I discussed earlier in this chapter.

When I teach students about this, I talk about the framework in terms of a house (Figure 9.1).

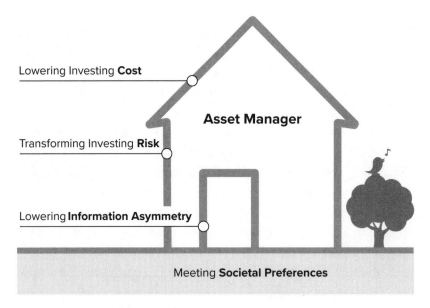

FIGURE 9.1 House of asset management

The asset management house is created by a structure of *walls* that improves risk sharing. The structure is protected by the *roof*, the capacity of the manager to scale up operations, which reduces investing costs. The greater the degree to which asset selection is made transparent and the quality of the manager revealed is represented by the *door*. The entire structure is based on the *bedrock* of changing societal preferences.

The four scales on which we judge asset managers and funds might look like Figure 9.2 for a typical equity index ETF, an active equity impact mutual fund, and an equity long/short hedge fund.

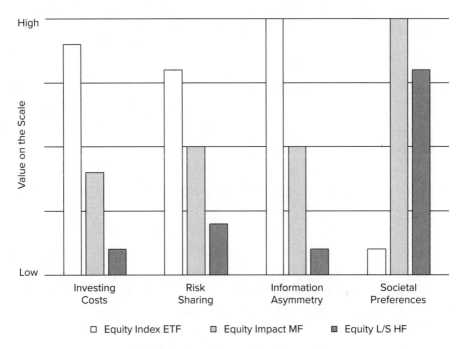

FIGURE 9.2 Intermediation fingerprint

An equity index ETF scores high on investing cost, risk sharing, and information asymmetry and lower on societal preference (because it is essentially a rearview mirror instrument). Obviously, these ratings are subjective—ask someone else and they might come back with slightly different impressions—but the graphs in Figure 9.2 illustrate the nature of the discrepancies if not necessarily its exact magnitude.

An impact-oriented equity mutual fund has much higher costs than our index tracker, but the fees are still modest compared to the hedge fund. Information asymmetry is relatively higher with this fund—an investor does not necessarily understand the outcome of his investment. Furthermore, he understands what sector and what market capitalization range of the companies in which the mutual fund will invest but does not have any idea of how weighting is accomplished. More important, the investor likely only has a vague understanding of what the actual impact of his investment is. Even accounting for this uncertainty, however, it is clear to see that an impact-oriented fund will score high on the axis related to reflecting societal preferences.

The hedge fund scores high on its response to societal preferences but carries with it a very high monetary cost and the nonmonetary cost of uncertainty—the portfolio manager is going to offer her investors minimal foreknowledge of what assets might be bought or sold by the portfolio during the investor's holding period. It might well be that the overall market ends a year positive and the hedge fund delivers a negative return.

From an industry perspective, I believe our job for the next 80 years will be to try to maximize scores for our funds over all the categories. The best funds will create vehicles that allow asset owners to effectively share risk while reducing investing costs. The portfolio compositions will reflect societal preferences while limiting, to the extent possible, all sorts of information asymmetry between the asset owner and the asset manager.

Lowering Investing Cost

T he first thing that the asset management must focus on is reducing costs.

When you read that sentence, what is the first thing you think? Reducing fees? But the fees that a fund manager charges to its client represent only one cost to asset owners.

Talking about costs in investing is tricky, and different specialists think about costs from different perspectives—economists look at investing costs in a different way from business executives, who in turn may think about it in different terms from accountants or regulators.[1]

In this chapter, I offer my thoughts on the true cost of investing, then create a taxonomy of those costs and offer examples of each. Last, I look at the dynamics between each cost category and offer my perspective on where there is the most potential for cost reduction in the future.

It is worth remembering that what an asset manager calls revenues an asset owner calls costs. Asset managers use those revenues to cover their own, separate costs of production. Obviously, the goal from an asset manager's business perspective is to maximize revenues while minimizing production costs. The goal of an asset owner is to find asset managers whose services offer good value for the money spent in fees.

Technology and its effects loom large over this discussion, and we will look at how technology is likely to affect investment costs in the future. My conclusion—that more technology does not automatically mean lower costs—may surprise you, but when you see my reasoning, I think you will be convinced.

A HOLISTIC VIEW OF INVESTING COSTS

First, let's agree what we mean when we are talking about the cost of investing. I define it as costs an asset owner incurs while carrying out the investing process. By "investing process," I am looking not only at the cost one incurs in exchange fees when trading a listed security, for example, but at the total economic burden of deciding what asset to invest in and how much, then in implementing and maintaining that investment over time.

The first element incurred in the investing process is the time and expense associated with formulating an objective. For retail investors, formulating an investing objective usually just means sitting down to think about it for a while and/or discussing possible objectives with an advisor. For institutional investors, however, there is a fairly high monetary cost in formulating an objective, because consultants are usually hired to help with this task and consultants are never shy about charging fees for their services.

Once the objective is determined, one needs to consider what assets can be invested in or which asset managers can be hired whose characteristics (in the case of assets) or strategies (in the case of managers) will match one's objectives. Obviously, picking the wrong asset or the wrong manager can have terrible consequences for one's portfolio—even including a total loss of one's investment. Realizing what's at stake, it should be clear that this step of the investing process is important and should carry with it a fairly high cost.

Once the appropriate asset or manager is identified, the costs incurred next relate to the initiation of the investment (a onetime setup cost) and its maintenance (which is ongoing). For a mutual fund, the original setup cost is termed a "load" and the ongoing maintenance costs are known as management fees.[2] Obviously, both costs will depend on the characteristics of the managers and the funds and strategies they use.

In this chapter, we will talk about four types of managers: passive, faux-active (i.e., closet indexers), true active, and alternative (PE, VC, and hedge funds). Passive and both flavors of active strategies invest in listed instruments, and alternative managers can invest in either listed or unlisted assets (usually, VCs invest in private, PE firms in both public and private, and hedge funds mainly invest in public). In general, the more complex the strategies used by the managers, the higher the cost to asset owners on the theory that more complex strategies offer the potential for higher returns. From lowest to highest, fees charged by asset managers run from passive on the low end to alternative on the high.

Finally, as you will see, how investors manage their exposure once invested might also incur costs. For those investors who do not eventually forget about their investment, potential costs of managing their investment can be very large. Emotions can be a big enemy when investing.

Considering these steps along the investing process, I identify four different costs to investing, each of which affect asset owners. They are:

1. Opportunity costs
2. Search costs
3. Management costs
4. Behavioral costs

Opportunity Costs

Opportunity costs arise from deciding. The Latin root of the word *decide* means "to cut off," and indeed, when one decides, one cuts off all other choices in favor of one, which the outcomes of the decision-making process will depend on.

For example, an asset manager might decide to invest in a low-fee index-tracking domestic mutual fund. This choice minimizes the direct costs associated with the investment but carries a large opportunity cost, because by deciding on a domestic fund, one has cut off the ability to invest in a foreign market that might end up performing better (either on a risk or return perspective) than the domestic market.

Since hindsight is 20/20 and we can always find room to kick ourselves—even for decisions that turned out to be profitable but not "perfect" once the future becomes the past and is perfectly known—opportunity costs are hard to measure. In fact, in an environment characterized by random interactions, one might say that everything is pure luck anyway, but I do not believe this is completely true. The act of (skillful) decision-making is predicated on the formulation of objectives, and these objectives offer guidance as to how to invest. This process, I contend, has value, whether the decisions stemming from the process are proven right or wrong.

Let us look at a few cases to identify the opportunity costs involved.

If you run a tactical asset allocation mandate, it means you are legally bound to allocate assets either to the stock or the bond market, depending on your perception of each market's outlook. In this case, the opportunity cost is well defined: the strategy has either zero opportunity cost (in the case your projections are proven right) or the return difference between the two markets in absolute terms (in the case your projections are proven wrong).

A more complicated example is a pension plan, which typically invests with the goal of generating future cash flows that offset its future liabilities. In this case, the yearly withdrawals of the retirees dictate how to invest, while taking lumpy spending patterns and inflation into consideration. In this case, the investments a manager can make cease to be a random choice; a specific goal is set, and the manager must plan such that all investments serve that goal.

Long-term deviations from the goal become opportunity costs or gains.

Formulating objectives precisely reflecting the goal and needs is paramount. Setting the wrong objectives can cause large opportunity costs, since asset owners might not get what they want or need when they want or need it. Advisors and consultants can help institutions with thinking through this goal-setting process and in a perfect world, can reduce opportunity costs arising from fuzzy or incorrectly set objectives.

Search Costs

Search costs are inextricably linked to opportunity costs.

One portion of search costs can be estimated by looking at the opportunity cost of searching for excess returns. In his presidential address to the American Finance Association in 2008, Kenneth French mentioned that he had found that from 1980 through 2006, investors had spent 0.67 percent of the aggregate value of the market each year just "searching for superior returns" (French, 2008). He concluded that given the relative success of passive strategies over this period, the average investor would increase his or her average annual return by 0.67 percent per year by switching to a passive market portfolio. In hindsight, this simple calculation can indeed be considered a good approximation of search costs.

However, a better definition of search costs includes the time that it takes for an owner or manager to look for investment opportunities, analyze them, decide how much capital to allocate to the investment, and finally figure out how best to execute the investment strategy. The mental and monetary resources, to say nothing of the time expenditure, that go into this process of analysis and decision-making represent a difficult to measure but very real component of search costs.

For a typical retail asset owner, search costs usually consist of comparing the explicit fees associated with a given investment. For instance, answering questions like: "What is the management fee?" or "Is there a withdrawal fee?" Even if this sounds simple, it is not.

Ali Hortaçsu and Chad Syverson performed a fascinating case study concerning the cost to find an S&P 500 index fund (Hortaçsu and Syverson, 2004).

"Wait a moment!" you are probably saying, "They are all the same, right?" Of course, that's true—they are all tracking the same index, and given that they are or should be perfectly fungible, the expectation would be that there is only one large index fund. Even still, there were 85 S&P index tracking funds in operation in the year 2000. The large number of these funds and the sizable dispersion in fees charged suggests the existence of market frictions in the form of search costs. In fact, the researchers found that the implied search costs necessary to sustain the price dispersion was recorded to be around 10 basis points. A similar analysis for mutual funds in general conducted by Nikolai Roussanov and his colleagues estimate search costs in the ballpark of 40 basis points overall (Roussanov et al., 2020).

With advancing technology and the emergence of various financial service platforms, a typical observer's intuition would be that the frictions shaping search costs decline over time. Let's look at the case of NFTs—blockchain ownership records of digital assets—to test that intuition.

NFTs provide an interesting illustration of how technology innovation can cause search costs to climb quickly and drastically.

Any digital asset—JPEG file, digital movie, and so on—can be tokenized and sold as an NFT. Potentially this ubiquity would allow NFTs to slice and dice almost everything into transactable digital assets. If this were the case, however, the explosion in the number of digital assets an owner would have to choose from would simply make it impossible to find the right one.

For example, let's say that you are interested in owning a work by Beeple, the artist whose digital work (a JPEG file) entitled *Everydays: the First 5000 Days* sold for $69 million at a Christie's auction in 2021. Mind you, this is a JPEG file—right now, you can go onto your favorite internet search engine and download the JPEG in question onto your laptop's drive. You will not have the $69 million version of the work, because the original's data has an ownership record on an Ethereum blockchain. However, a clever person, determined to show how spurious ownership claims of NFTs were and how easily they could be gamed, created an exact replica of Beeple's work with an ownership record that appears to show authorship by Beeple himself—in other words, to a nonexpert buyer, there is nothing to distinguish one Beeple "masterpiece" from an exact replica that has a fraudulent ownership provenance.

What is an exact digital replica of *Everydays: the First 5000 Days* worth? $10? $100? $1,000? In September 2021, a few months after the Christie's auction, the fraudulent replica was selling for $232.54 (Kim and Sinclair, 2021).

With the ability to easily replicate a digital asset and replicate a seemingly bona fide digital ownership provenance, the search costs for an NFT (or any asset whose ownership records are stored on blockchain) naturally increase. If and when the ubiquity of digital ownership tracking increases, finding the asset one wants to buy will be one element of search cost, and verifying that you own what you think you own will be yet another.

As global markets deepen and as the financialization of assets through technological innovations such as blockchain increases, I expect investing search costs will do nothing but increase.

Management Costs

We already talked about fees in Part I, so we will not go into detail about them again. Suffice it to say that because asset management fees are explicit, they are the investing costs that most often come to asset owners' minds.

From the perspective of an asset manager, asset management fees do not represent pure profit, of course, but rather must be allocated to pay the day-to-day "plumbing" expenses, that most of us don't give much thought to: salary and bonuses, data and research cost, office space rental, computer maintenance and management, transaction costs, legal costs, and the like. Because the only "asset" with which an asset management firm can generate cash flows is the knowledge and insight of people that work for the firm, it makes sense that employee salaries are by far the biggest part of these plumbing expenses.

While the dependence of asset management firms on the skills of their employees is an obvious fact, the remuneration of portfolio managers might surprise you.

Markus Ibert and his colleagues analyzed the relationship between asset managers and their key employees in Sweden (Ibert et al., 2018). Portfolio managers' pay depends crucially on the company for whom they work, but the relationship between salary and performance is weak. Furthermore, the relationship between salary and revenues (i.e., the AUM of the fund being managed) is 10 times higher than that of salary and performance. In economic terms, the elasticity of salary to revenues generated by a portfolio manager is on the order of 0.15, meaning an increase in revenues generated at a fund of 1 percent increases the manager's compensation by 0.15 percent. In other words, the bargaining power of a portfolio manager increases with the share of revenues generated, presuming that the asset manager is perceived as responsible for the attraction of new assets under management. Put simply, the asset management business is a business like any other, and just as in every business, the person that can retain and boost revenues gets a larger share of the pie.

While I think that it is possible that increasing costs associated with other plumbing functions—especially the cost of information processing—will put pressure on asset management firms, I think it is safer to assume that an increase of these expenses will simply create an additional tailwind for consolidation and the further buildup of scale in the industry. If AUM increases at a quick enough pace, the change in direct costs per dollar of AUM will turn negative. This industry dynamic will also be reflected in a downward pressure on asset management fees paid by asset owners.

Behavioral Costs

Asset owners wishing to avoid behavioral costs would do well by using dollar cost averaging[3] into low-cost indexing funds. This is not to say that it is the best investment strategy, just that it minimizes behavioral costs.

Behavioral costs arise from human nature. When considering their own happiness, humans typically compare their own state to that of others. If my neighbor is making 10 percent per year investing in a low-cost index fund, chances are that I will naturally want to invest in an investment vehicle that offers the promise to generate at least the same—or preferably, more than 10 percent.[4]

Because my neighbor is investing in a passive instrument, my only route to greater relative happiness is to invest in an actively managed fund. I voluntarily incur some search costs to find an actively managed fund that has, according to my analysis, a good chance of outperforming the passive strategy. Indeed, the active fund I select might outperform a passive fund over time. However, market volatility makes sure that the outperformance is anything but steady. Companies that can be expected to generate better-than-market returns tend to be those that are riskier—either due to a short operating history, a corporate event, or whatever. If the fund I have invested in has invested in assets that have increased risk, it is distinctly possible that the risky fund will underperform the passive investment in any given period.

Recall that humans tend to be happiest when their own situation can be favorably compared to that of others'. If my neighbor's passive investment is outperforming my active investment in a certain period, chances are that I will be unhappy. And if I am unhappy, I might start to incur additional search costs to find another active manager who will outperform both my present active asset manager as well as my neighbor's passive fund. If and when I find an active manager that fits the bill, I may well pay some extra costs to move my investment money from my prior active asset manager to my new, favored active asset manager. This behavior, called "chasing returns" and mentioned in Part I, exerts an enormous cost on asset owners (see Box 10.1).

BOX 10.1 Enormous Behavioral Costs When Investing in
Hedge Funds

In 2020, Itzhak Ben-David and his colleagues studied long-run outcomes associated with hedge fund compensation structures (Ben-David et al., 2020). They found that over a 22-year period, the actual performance fee was closer to 50 percent of profits rather than the 20 percent nominally advertised in a 2-and-20 structure. The cause for this 2.5 times delta was twofold.

First, there was the problem of a hedge fund that had initially performed well—thus was able to charge a 20 percent fee—but hit a rough performance patch and opted to close its doors and return its clients' money. Clients were presumably happy about their excess returns during the good years but lost a considerable slice of their investment during down years. It is hard to say that this effect is a result of investors' behavior, though I don't think it is too bold of a suggestion to mention that some hedge fund managers might suffer from something known as *overconfidence bias*, which leads to this pattern.

The other reason for clients' high fees does, however, relate directly to investors' behavioral issues. Clients cannot control when a prima donna hedge fund manager is going to throw in the towel, but they can control whether they redeem their funds after a bad year. In fact, this action ended up accounting for a significant proportion of the 30 percent higher-than-notional performance fees.

Humans do not like pain. They wish to always be happy. This primal drive ends up leading to performance chasing—moving money from a manager who has had a losing year to one that had a winning year. So in addition to the search costs incurred when owners are searching for outperforming managers, tack on another substantial cost due to hyperactive searching and the realization of losses to which such behavior leads.

Another reason that asset owners tend to bear behavioral investing costs is due to a tendency to try to time the markets. Market timing requires human decision makers to make two decisions—when to exit the market and when to reenter it. Unfortunately, thanks to the only two emotions that matter on Wall Street—fear and greed—human decision makers are not terribly good at making either of these decisions. When markets are falling and asset owners feel fear, they tend to try to escape by selling their assets. Selling an asset locks in a return, and that return may be positive or negative; obviously, locking in a negative return is not a path to investment success, but even if an investor locks in a positive return, the ultimate returns on the investor's portfolio will depend on the timing of the reentry decision. This is when greed kicks in. Maintaining a policy of disinvestment is psychologically soothing for as long as the price of the asset is lower than the investor's sale price, but because of the lingering memory of fear, investors are often distrustful of investing at prices lower than that at which they sold. Instead, they watch the price rise above their sell price—expecting "the other shoe to drop." Due to the random nature of markets, the other shoe often fails to drop, and the asset price keeps rising. The investor now sees that other investors are profiting from the asset, and greed kicks in: "I want to make some money too!"

The owner reinvests at a higher price—locking in a transaction in which the sell price was low and the buy price was high. Clearly, selling low and buying high is not a recipe for investment success, but just as clearly, it forms one factor for the high cost of behavioral effects.

Behavioral costs are not only unique to amateur investors; professional investors—asset managers—must also contend with them. One of the main behavioral pitfalls is that analysts and portfolio managers fall in love with investments in their portfolio. "Falling in love" is called by different names in the industry, but generally, some circles acknowledge it as that investing with *conviction* is a good thing. How does one develop conviction in an investment idea? Usually by gathering data, assessing, and analyzing it, speaking with industry insiders and company management, and the like.

An analyst researching a company is processing a huge amount of information about that company—much more than a typical asset owner would process. In a cruel twist of human decision-making fate, it might be the volume of information an analyst is processing that adds risk to a rational assessment.

In 1973, the psychologist Paul Slovic published a study entitled "Behavioral Problems of Adhering to a Decision Policy" (Slovic, 1973). Slovic conducted research with professional horseracing handicappers, giving them anonymized data about horses competing in races that had already taken place. For each group of handicappers, he proffered different amounts of data and let the handicappers select the data points they believed were most important to review. In some of the tests, the handicappers could only use five essential data points (e.g., horses' previous finishes, weight to be carried, weight carried in last race). For other races, the handicappers were allowed to gather 10, 20, and 40 data points. With each prediction, they were asked to predict which horse would place (come in first, second, or third) and what their confidence in their prediction was.

The outcome is frightening for anyone who purports to make a living through data analysis: accuracy was flat no matter how much data the handicappers had, but as the number of data points increased, so did the reported confidence of the handicapper. Handicappers processing 40 data points were twice as confident as handicappers analyzing 5 data points.

In other words, the analysts were no more accurate the more time and energy they spent making their analysis, but the more time and energy they spent on the analysis, the more confident they became (i.e., the greater their "conviction" they were right).

This study has been replicated many times with experts from various fields—doctors, judges, and yes, even stock pickers. Time after time, each set of experts displayed the same overconfidence born from additional data. So asset owners share this love, too.

WAYS OF LOWERING INVESTING COSTS

Now that we understand how to look at investing costs, let us turn our attention to the question of how these costs will likely change in the future. Certainly, the enormous popularity of passive investment funds has shown that asset owners are focused not only on performance but also on management cost. My perspective is that to be a successful asset manager in the twenty-first century, one will have to attempt to lower investing costs—not only management costs—for asset owners, while also figuring out how to deliver the corresponding performance.

In this section, we investigate how asset managers should think about cost dynamics for each class of investing costs moving forward, with a special focus on what costs can be cut or reduced.

Opportunity Costs

Opportunity costs arise because there is simply no way around one's budget constraint: if one invests in one instrument, one cannot invest the same money at the same time in another instrument.

Opportunity costs are the hardest costs to quantify and the hardest for asset owners to avoid. Advisors and consultants can help, but hiring an advisor also carries a fee, and if the advisors and consultants were perfect, they would be billionaires, not worker bees. Be that as it may, the most value-creative role an advisor or a consultant can play is to help reduce opportunity costs.

The right way to quantify these opportunity costs would be the difference between the returns of the advised portfolio and the portfolio that the investor would have held in the absence of advice. In "Money Doctors," Nicola Gennaioli, Andrei Shleifer, and Robert Vishny describe an example where trusted financial advisors move clients' equity allocations from zero to a higher level (Gennaioli et al., 2015). By doing so, the advice seekers are likely to harvest a long-run equity market risk premium of 5 percent.[5] Compared to the portfolio the client would have held without an advisor, the client is still better off in terms of opportunity costs, even if the recommendation is to invest in equity funds paying high commissions.

Obviously, the more financial sophistication a client has, the lower the opportunity cost. However, asking an asset owner to accurately assess their own financial sophistication is a fraught process, since it also requires a great deal of insight and rationality to begin with (recall that somewhere between 70 and 80 percent of all drivers assess their own driving skills as "better than average"). It might be an interesting alternative if there were some ways to bring down opportunity costs by something a little bit more subtle.

The behavior of asset owners has been shown to be easier to affect through the use of what University of Chicago behavioral finance professors Richard Thaler and Cass Sunstein term "nudging" (Thaler and Sunstein, 2008).

Nudging involves some organization—a company or a government—structuring user choices to achieve some specific outcome. It turns out that the way choices are structured makes an enormous difference in what options are eventually selected. Nudging, while subtle by definition, has been shown to significantly impact investing behavior (Cai, 2020).

While the concept of nudging is new—Thaler and Sunstein's book was published in 2008—it garnered great interest from policy makers and quickly became one tool in the regulatory and legislative toolkit. In 2013, the United Kingdom's Financial Conduct Authority published Occasional Paper No. 1, which laid out the three reasons it believed nudging was so effective in the finance and investing context:

1. Financial products are complex.
2. Financial products involve trade-offs between the present and the future.[6]
3. Financial decisions are made infrequently for nonprofessionals, limiting the ability of those making the decisions to learn and improve.

Nudging can occur in various situations in asset management. I'll discuss a few I find the most compelling here.

When a person begins a new job in the United States, they are often asked to select whether they would like to invest in a 401(k) plan and if so, which funds or assets they would like to purchase into the account.

Choice often causes consternation in the chooser, as a surfeit of opportunities immediately brings up the necessity of incurring an opportunity cost. Rather than forcing the new employee to make a positive choice as described previously, Thaler and Sunstein suggest that a better approach would be to allow him or her to *opt out* of some predetermined allocation (e.g., a checkbox saying "Yes, I want to invest 5% of my pretax salary in a low-cost mutual fund that tracks the S&P 500 index. I understand that my employer will match the first 2.5% of my salary dollar-for-dollar in my account.").

Some criticize this nudging strategy as paternalistic, but in fact, it does seem to work as a strategy to aid decision-making and brings with it benefits to the person liberated from making a choice between confusing options that they may not feel qualified or comfortable to make.

Another example involves changing the way investment funds present performance information. Many investors make the mistake of paying high fees based on a fund's past performance. Investment funds are not time machines—one cannot pay more to receive yesterday's investment results. This seems perfectly clear, but the fact is that many investors fall for this mistake due to some basic human psychological wiring.

First, humans have difficulty in comprehending relative charges. For example, when a plumber comes to your house and quotes you for some work, he says, "I will do that work for $240 plus parts," not "I will do that work for 24 percent of the median US weekly salary plus parts." The problem in the financial world is that everything is expressed in relative terms (2-and-20, for instance).

Second, when percentages mentioned are small, people tend to devalue them (the so-called peanut effect). A mutual fund might, for example, charge a 1 percent management fee per year; 1 percent sounds very small, but if the return of the fund that year is 5 percent, the 1 percent management fee has eaten through 20 percent of one's yearly return. Einstein once said: "Compound interest is the eighth wonder of the world. He who understands it, earns it. He who doesn't, pays it." Paying small percentage fees ends up putting an investor in the position of "paying" Professor Einstein's compound interest.

A simple way to solve this, according to Philip Newall and Bradley Love, is to take this difficulty in processing relative costs into account and simply list fees in currency (e.g., dollar, euro, pound) amounts rather than in percentage terms (Newall and Love, 2015). It does not seem a big thing, but when fees are expressed in currency values rather than as percentages, investors have been shown to be much more careful in selecting managers.

The progress made by nudging investors into the right decision is at the beginning. To my opinion, however, it has a big potential not only for private but also for institutional clients to correctly define their objective and reduce the opportunity cost substantially.

Search Costs

Search costs are bound to increase for asset owners and managers alike, and the most successful managers will be those who are most successful in controlling these costs.

For investors in passive funds, the search cost is going up due to the proliferation of new indices being created.[7] Suddenly, it's not enough just to be invested in the market portfolio—fund companies are creating new "flavors" of the market portfolio to entice clients into. For evidence of this, just look at the enormous proliferation of ESG funds and funds using a *smart beta* strategy over the past few years. As the number of flavors goes up, the search costs for the investor will go up. "Should I buy the plain vanilla index product or the sustainability index product?" "Which of these smart beta indices give me the exposure I want at the lowest possible price?" These are some of the questions that investors in passive funds have to answer and answering them drives up the search cost.

Demand for these new flavors of indices has risen due to the changing preferences of investors, a recognition of the obvious shortcomings of passive market capitalization-weighted products, or a combination of both. Supply for this swelling demand has been governed by the implementation of new technologies that allow for more and more elaborate benchmarking methodologies—all of which are attempting to overcome the shortcomings of the market-cap weighted paradigm more elegantly—to be defined and tracked. Therefore, as technology and theory improve, search costs for end customers are bound to go up—more choice is better but also implies that more time is required to make a selection.

The situation is much the same for active managers and the asset owners who invest in active funds.

Active managers traditionally use bespoke methods to find good investment ideas—reviewing financial statements, quarterly presentations, and press articles. Researchers have found that investors in active funds place a high value on unique strategies—funds perceived to have unique investment strategies experience greater inflows of assets than those that do not (Kostovetsky and Warner, 2020).

Modern technology enables active managers to reduce a lot of grunt work that was formerly related to researching a company. For instance, a manager no longer needs to hire a data input analyst to enter 10-key financial statement figures into a spreadsheet when all the numbers in a financial statement are stored in XML-style tags integral to the statements published on a public website. Using a product like FactSet, they can quickly look at comparative financial ratios for all the companies in an industry and run screens for companies that meet some particular criterion.

These data and technology products cut search costs for asset managers and have, in fact, given birth to a new form of active asset management—the type that I know particularly about—which involves quantitative analysis of massive amounts of data and algorithmic asset selection. Thanks to amazing decreases in the cost of computing resources, for me and my quant colleagues around the world, searching for investment ideas now has much greater operating leverage.

Technology is bringing down search costs for asset managers, so it might be reasonable to assume that more asset managers will enter the industry due to lowered barriers to entry. From my perspective, that assumption may be partially true, but it ignores the importance of a marketing and distribution channel to sell financial products. I believe there continues to be opportunities for young, smart asset managers with novel perspectives on investing, but to grow to scale, those young asset managers will need at least to partner with organizations that have greater marketing reach (e.g., through the kind of incubator system mentioned in Part I). At the very least, I think it is safe to say that the reduction of search costs for managers will bring many more funds and products to market, as evidenced by the wave of ETFs over the last few decades.

As the number of new financial products and funds increases, the search costs for asset owners will certainly increase—more products from which to choose means more time and expense must be expended to find the best one.

Management Costs

Over the last half century, the average fees borne by asset owners in the form of management fees have decreased. Burton Malkiel suggests that the active management fees have stayed roughly the same over this period, but the prevalence of low-cost index funds has increased, as has the percentage of owner assets directed into these funds. This change—a higher proportion of funds in low-cost, passive funds—has been greatly responsible for the fall in average management fees paid by asset owners (Malkiel, 2013).

I believe that passive strategies will continue to garner more owner capital and as more assets are managed with passive strategies; in this case, it makes sense that the average direct costs of investing will continue to fall. However, while there is the potential for a "mix shift" into passive investing bringing down average costs, costs to owners of placing capital in passive funds is already very low; in some cases, there is zero cost to owners to place assets in passive strategies. In the absence of funds paying asset owners to place money with their funds (i.e., negative management fees), it seems like the opportunity for further lowering the cost of passive investment is hitting a wall.

While active portfolio management fees have surprisingly resisted decreasing over the past 50 or more years, there is evidence that in markets that have large, influential low-cost index funds, active managers are more active, charge lower fees, and record better investment performance (Cremers et al., 2016). Interestingly, the more faux-active managers (i.e., those that are engaged in closet indexing) are active in a market, the lower the performance of the active managers in that market as well. In short, it is clear that price competition—especially that from passive funds—and product differentiation are both important preconditions for asset managers to capture market share (Khorana and Servaes, 2012). And it is safe to assume that more competitive markets are more efficient.

As the regulatory environment continues to internationalize and focus on investor protections, the plight of the faux-active manager will become more and more perilous. As regulators monitor the performance of funds purporting to be active and prosecute those that clearly are hugging their benchmarks, these faux-active managers will eventually be weeded out. But this process will not occur overnight, and it is contingent upon asset owners allocating more to passive funds.

True active managers, with the competence and structures in place to systematically outperform, will be able to maintain high fees as faux-active competitors are cleared out of the market. Profit margins for these managers will slightly rise as well, since technology will bring down the cost of providing the investment services, but fee structures will likely remain the same.

In addition to a shift toward increased allocation to low-cost passive funds, another factor that has contributed to lower investment fees is the increased ubiquity of data and the reduction in technology costs associated with computing power that follows Moore's

Law.[8] Even as semiconductors start to reach the physical limits of their capacities, changes in business models (e.g., having access to cloud-based computing resources) and in processes (e.g., financial and news data being captured and published much more widely and regularly) have meant that technology-centric cost reductions are still continuing.

While we have mainly looked at the dynamics of fees and their levels to date, I believe that the way fees are implemented is arguably as important as the level of fees themselves. The fee model influences the outcomes of asset owners in three different ways:

1. Influencing the risk-taking behavior of the asset manager
2. Establishing the framework for sharing risk between the asset owner and the asset manager
3. Signaling the quality of the underlying manager

There are two types of fee models, symmetric and asymmetric. Symmetric fees are a system by which the manager charges either fixed amounts for services rendered or something known as fulcrum fees, which I explain more below. They are symmetric to the extent that fees depend on whether performance is good or bad.

Asymmetric fee structures offer economic incentives to managers for performing well but do not penalize bad performance. For example, a hedge fund manager might make 20 percent of any returns over a specified benchmark when returns are strong, but is not due a fee if the fund does not outperform the benchmark. Asymmetric fee structures are illegal for mutual fund managers in the United States, but common for hedge fund and private securities managers and a natural choice for these types of "active" strategies.[9]

To the extent that asymmetric fee arrangements are meant to align managers' interests with the interests of the owners, the ability of the manager to participate in the gains of a successful, outperforming strategy incentivizes managers to look hard to find benchmark-beating investments. The clear advantage of an asymmetric model is exactly this—it encourages managers to outperform, and its application is transparent and fair.

However, the lack of an immediate economic downside to the manager for weak performance tends to force active managers in a dangerous behavioral trap known as the "other people's money" bias. In short, if one is playing poker with someone else's chips— as an asset manager essentially is when using an asymmetric fee arrangement—one has the tendency to make riskier bets. Making risky bets using asset owners' money is good in the short term at least because if the bet works out, the manager gets a share of the winnings, and if it turns pear-shaped, the only pain for the manager is not being paid. Because the manager is not forced to pay an underperformance penalty, downside exposure has a floor, while upside exposure is theoretically limitless—just like a call option.

The typical hedge fund fee arrangement that sets up asymmetric fees separating the management fee from the performance fee further blunts the downside of underperformance. If a manager underperforms the benchmark, it loses the performance fee but can continue to draw the management fee.

Before you get too upset about the injustice of asymmetric fees for hedge fund managers, realize that hedge fund managers justifiably point out that they are also significantly invested in the funds they manage as well, so they feel the pain of underperformance as acutely as the clients do.

If a manager receiving asymmetric payments continues to underperform longer term, obviously, there is the risk that the client will redeem its investment, which will remove the manager's cash inflow from the management fee. However, the fact that the return profile is asymmetric on upside and down and favors the manager in the short term shows the complexity of establishing a fee schedule that appropriately aligns the interests of owners and managers.

Mutual fund fee models contrast sharply with those of hedge funds. Regulated mutual fund investors typically pay a fixed management fee and do not require managers to coinvest in the fund. What's more, mutual funds are closely supervised by regulators who impose position or risk limits on the funds. For example, European funds governed by the Undertakings for the Collective Investment in Transferable Securities (UCITS) framework are not allowed to have a single position whose value is greater than 10 percent of the portfolio's total net asset value (NAV).

In other words, in terms of fee models, hedge fund managers get the performance-based carrot; mutual fund managers get the regulatory stick.

Which is better? Should asset managers align interests with investors in asymmetrical relationships, or should the bets that asset managers make be more controlled, under which arrangement symmetric fees make more sense?

In my view, the answer to this question comes down to the topic of leverage and whether asset managers are free to take levered positions or not. In a world where the use of leverage is unconstrained, an asymmetric incentive fee structure is better; in a world where the use of leverage is restricted, a symmetric, fixed-fee model is best.

Leverage is a tricky thing, and even professionals with vast experience in investing have time and again been shocked by the power of leverage in both good times and bad. Leverage can create fortunes overnight when one is on the right side of it. On the wrong side, losses accrue quickly and sometimes catastrophically, since one can wind up losing more than they own.

For the very wealthy, investing in levered instruments represents a risk but not a catastrophe. Elon Musk borrowed money to buy Twitter. Even if Twitter (now renamed X) becomes a replay of defunct early social media property MySpace, Musk will not have to file for unemployment benefits or figure out how to feed his family with food stamps.

For those who are less well off—the vast majority of workers who are invested as a way to provide for a comfortable retirement—investing in levered instruments can lead to catastrophic outcomes. For investors for whom a levered loss would be catastrophic—investors in retail mutual funds, for instance—regulators are right to place guard rails on the amount of leverage a fund uses, in my opinion.

This is exactly why Congress created the Investment Advisers Act of 1940 and banned most financial advisors from charging performance-based fees to retail investors. Congress understood, from the devastating example of Black Monday and the subsequent Great Depression, that establishing a structure that incentivized investment advisor risk-taking on behalf of retail clients could cause very negative consequences. It was only in 1970—two generations after Black Monday—that Congress partially relented and created a carve-out to allow registered investment advisors to charge performance-based "fulcrum fees." This structure allows the advisor to participate in both the upside when the advisor outperforms and (at least some of) the downside when the advisor underperforms.

Why is leverage the key to fee structures? To understand this, let's carry out a thought experiment contrasting two fund managers.

Both Managers A and B passively invest in the market. Let's assume that only Manager A uses leverage and understand that by using leverage, both the positive and negative returns from the passive portfolio will be amplified vis-à-vis Manager B's returns.

In this case, rational investors would allocate assets to Managers A and B in a way that appropriately expresses their personal degree of risk aversion/seeking. Consequently, Manager A would end up with a lower asset base providing the same investment profile to investors.

If both Managers A and B are compensated with a flat fee, Manager A would earn less than Manager B, given that the fund sizes are equivalent. The reason is that Manager A can charge a flat fee on only the equity portion of the fund, and the equity portion of a levered fund is necessarily smaller than the equity portion of an unlevered one.

Sooner or later, Manager A is going to tire of making less money for doing the same work and cease to use leverage. In other words, the fact that the fee is a flat one incentivizes managers away from levered structures.[10]

The contrary is easy to show as well. If an asset manager can generate large returns by using leverage, an asset manager compensated with an incentive structure will be more likely to use that leverage. To do otherwise would limit the compensation the asset manager would earn.

Now we understand the perspectives of asset managers under different fee/leverage arrangements, but we should take a step back and ask which fee structure is better for society at large.

In my view, both incentive-based and fixed fee structures are important to allow society to progress. In general, asymmetric incentive fees combined with a manager's ability to take levered bets helps push the envelope of innovation and allow capital to flow to innovative new ideas. This class of investment is risky and carries with it the real possibility of a complete loss of capital. As such, limiting investment into these risky bets—whether at a portfolio level and/or a regulatory framework that protects less wealthy people from catastrophic loss—makes good sense.

Fixed-fee arrangements also make sense from the standpoint of consumer protection and from the perspective of simple logistics. Consider the challenges of executing an incentive fee structure for the millions of individual retail investors in mutual funds, for instance. The billing process would be onerous to calculate, and the results would be tough for many clients to understand; the fund's revenues would be volatile, making managing an asset management business even more challenging. It would also, in my opinion, introduce a dependency on distributors and the producers of financial products, which the industry does not want.

In short, the current state seems likely to persist—riskier, levered instruments available to high-net-worth investors and flat fees applied to mass market mutual funds that are restricted from making risky bets.

That said, while it is hard to imagine a shift to incentive fees being applied to retail accounts, the same cannot be said for institutional investors. Given the rise of passive strategies, institutional investors have a vested interest in finding which managers are truly active and which among them can generate alpha. Given these conditions, it is sensible for asset managers to signal investing skill to allocators by implementing fulcrum fees—allowing skillful managers to share in both the upside and the downside.

In the final analysis, I see the direct costs of index tracking funds falling to zero and the average direct costs of investing going down due to a continued mix shift toward index tracking funds. The faux-active chaff will slowly separate from the skilled-active grain with the help of regulatory oversight. Fees for skilled active managers will stay stable and any cost savings from technology will be captured by the asset management companies, increasing the profitability of successful active managers.

Behavioral Costs

The instincts and behaviors described in the section about behavioral costs are difficult to tame. More often than not, one is not even aware when one is caught in a behavioral trap, and predicting how behavioral costs are likely to change going forward is therefore almost impossible. Reducing behavioral costs implies that one is able to not only perceive the existence of behavioral pitfalls but also to change something fundamental in one's own natural instincts—something that is close to impossible to do.

The first, best chance we have in taming our animal instincts is to better understand them. The last few decades witnessed the rise of a discipline called "behavioral finance," which exists at the intersection of the Venn diagrams of finance and psychology. The Slovic study quoted earlier is a perfect example of the overlap between these two fields, for example. The focus of behavioral finance is usually on individual-level cognitive biases and their effects on financial market, but Thaler and Sunstein's work on nudging is one systemic example.

In much the same way that the concept of the EMH took the world of economics and finance by storm, behavioral finance was (and is still to a certain extent) a favorite academic flavor-of-the-month. Motivated by academics such as Robert Shiller, the Nobel Laureate in Economics in 2013, asset managers started to embrace behavioral finance to justify their sometimes hand-knitted investment processes. In essence, they worked hard to figure out how to justify their gut feelings and instincts as insights into behavioral finance, while failing to recognize that their gut instincts were influenced by the very same behavioral biases as everyone else's.

For a time, it seemed like everything in finance and investing could be explained by various biases. While this explanatory power may sound nice, to me it seems like the ever-growing list of potential behavioral biases is simply a way of categorizing how someone else screwed something up, rather than as a tool for helping us not to screw something up in the future. Just how many behavioral biases are there, anyway?

According to David Hirshleifer (Hirshleifer, 2015), three psychological structures explain most of the biases studied in behavioral finance:

1. Limited attention and processing power resulting in heuristic simplification
2. Emotional reactions short-circuiting rational analyses
3. Overconfidence born from self-deception

Hirshleifer's structures seem to be very resilient with respect to learning from past errors. The studies looking at different questions concerning the asset management industry is vast, and interested readers are encouraged to read through other summaries.[11]

Observing investors, colleagues around me, and myself, I have a strong sense that behavioral biases are ubiquitous. Only a handful of people are able to shut out emotions in the way that algorithmic strategies do. However, to perform the art and science of decision-making a little better, I believe investors may be able to use formal tools and exercises to help guard against the danger of behavioral biases (e.g., checklists, pre-mortem analysis). There are plenty of examples out there, but do not expect miracles—human beings (thankfully) are not and never will be machines.

Transforming Investment Risk

R isk is one of the key concerns of the field of financial economics, the branch of economics that studies the economic choices made by corporations and investors. Over the years, financial economists have spent enormous amounts of energy and time thinking about risk and attempting to model it.

It is funny, then, to realize that—despite all the academic and industry time, ink, and computational power dedicated to the question of risk—the fundamental mechanism to reduce risk is so simple as to be trivial: diversification.

In a cosmic coincidence born from the relationship of risk and return, diversification not only limits risk but also boosts an investor's long-term sustainable returns. I will delve into this lucky coincidence more in the upcoming section "The Good Risk."

I don't want to leave the mistaken impression that all an asset manager needs to consider when thinking about risk is diversification, though. The more I thought about this chapter while I was writing it, the more I realized that there is another risk born of timidity. This risk is related to the concept of opportunity costs I discussed previously—it is the risk of diminishing growth due to a lack of innovation. This is a risk for asset management firms, but much more for society in general; as I discuss later, societies that seek to increase the well-being of their citizens spend a nontrivial amount of tax revenues attempting to spur innovation in their economies. I believe that in addition to government money, private capital is key to building successful innovation economies. We are seeing a shift to more private funding, but more can and should be done, in my opinion, to create structures that allow for wider funding of innovative projects. In my mind, innovation expenditures represent the "other good risk"; I firmly believe this is another essential risk for the asset management industry to embrace.

Much of the discussion of risk in this chapter harkens back to the discussion of fiduciary responsibility I brought up in the very first chapter of this book. Certainly, sharing the risk of investing in innovative projects directly relates to the responsibility of a fiduciary to "transform risk."

THE MAGIC OF DIVERSIFICATION

People might take diversification for granted, but in my opinion, it is one of the most magical features of nature—sort of like how so many diverse natural processes can be mathematically modeled by e and the natural logarithm.

Diversification is often considered the only free lunch in investing. During periods of (moderate) market stress, diversification reduces losses, though it also often attenuates returns during boom times.

Recall from Chapter 1 that four of the main purposes of financial intermediaries are to (1) transform notional size, (2) transform liquidity, (3) reduce costs, and (4) transform the risk of an investment. Miraculously, diversification is key for mutual fund managers to accomplish all these purposes at once—I think this is, in fact, the main reason for the development and continuing popularity of mutual funds to retail and institutional investors alike.

Because mutual funds pool large amounts of capital and act as intermediaries, even owners with less assets to invest can hold a well-diversified portfolio. For example, if an individual were to try to buy one share of every stock in the S&P 500 index, they would have to shell out almost $100,000 and would get an equal-weighted, rather than market cap weighted basket. The amount to buy this 500-share basket is roughly twice of the median holdings in individual retirement accounts for a US citizen in their fifties (Brandon, 2015). Also, buying a mutual fund allows investors the opportunity to hold a portfolio containing securities they might not otherwise be able to buy—those with high per-share values or—for US citizens—securities from foreign countries, for instance.

Over the past few years, mutual funds have also pioneered a new diversification product called "fractional shares." Fractional shares allow an investor to spend a small amount of money to buy a claim on a proportion of a single high-priced share. For example, the American brokerage, Charles Schwab, allows clients to select any 10 stocks in the S&P 500 index and invest as little as $5 in those companies. Here is the explanation Schwab offers on its website (Charles Schwab, n.d.):

> Let's say you want to invest in a company, but its stock price may be higher than what you want to pay. Instead of buying a whole share of stock, you can buy a fractional share, which is a "slice" of stock that represents a partial share, for as little as $5. For example, if a company's stock is selling at $1,000 a share and you were buying $200 worth of it, you would own 0.2 (20%) of a share. With stock slices [N.B. Schwab's term for its fractional share product], investing has never been more accessible.

This type of product has been so popular that in 2021, transactions in fractional shares of the most expensive stock in the United States, Berkshire Hathaway, Class A, by the discount brokerage popular with Gen Zers, Robinhood, has boosted Berkshire's daily trading by a phenomenal amount, creating "phantom volume" totaling roughly 80 percent of Berkshire's daily aggregate transaction value (Bartlett et al., 2022).[1]

It is likely that fractional shares will further grow going forward. An interesting enabler of this growth could be the next frontier of the asset management industry: mass customization.

Separately managed accounts (SMA) for active strategies and *direct indexing*, which represents bespoke, passive-equivalent strategies, are the two techniques spearheading mass customization in money management. There also may be some new technologies involving so-called factor investing, which will allow investors to segregate and compartmentalize risk even better and achieve diversification more accurately, as well as to adapt indices to individual investor taste.

After diversifying private customized accounts in a similar way as collective investment accounts (i.e., mutual funds), it is, however, hard to see how the asset management industry can squeeze more juice out of the orange of diversification.

That said, the tendency when anyone finds something good is to try to do more to move from good to great. "If a little diversification is good, a lot of diversification is better," is the attitude.

It turns out this is not the case. In Burton Malkiel's classic investing book, *A Random Walk Down Wall Street* (Malkiel, 2003), Malkiel points out that increasing the number of stocks in a portfolio past a certain point has limited effect on reducing risk. To quote Malkiel:

> By the time the portfolio contains close to 20 equal-sized and well-diversified issues, the total risk (standard deviation of returns) of the portfolio is reduced by 70 percent. Further increase in the number of holdings does not produce any significant further risk reduction.

According to Malkiel's calculations, by the time the number of shares in one's portfolio approaches 50, one has a portfolio that is little different in the classic definition of risk—standard deviation of returns—than the total market portfolio.

This decreasing efficacy of increasing the number of assets in a portfolio also applies to the diversification of investment funds. An analysis entitled "Hedge Fund Diversification: How Much Is Enough?" (Lhabitant and Learned, 2002) found that the volatility in the return of a portfolio of hedge funds was reduced by approximately 75 percent with an equal-weighted allocation to just five managers. However, the researchers also found that allocating to 15 or more managers ended up *increasing* correlation to the overall market. In other words, assembling an overdiversified portfolio of hedge fund investments gave allocators both market returns and horrendous fees of 2-and-20.

Diversification is magical, but clearly we are reaching a limit to the degree to which additional diversification benefits are easily imaginable.

THE GOOD RISK

The word *risk* has bad connotations, but the fact is that every economic choice a person makes carries risk with it. Even if you take your savings and bury it in your back yard—the pinnacle of "safety" because you are then beholden to no institution or other person to care for your savings for you—you have made a risky choice. Namely, you risk the opportunity to invest your money in an instrument with a positive return, and by the time you dig up your money again, it will have much less purchasing power than when you left it there.

Everyone knows there is a relationship between risk and return, but a lot of people misunderstand that relationship. For instance, if you invest all your life savings into a privately held, high-tech startup, your investment can easily turn sour if the promise of the startup does not materialize.

Clearly, both approaches to risk—burying your shekels in the backyard or performing the investment world's equivalent of betting one's entire net worth on a roulette wheel's number 18—have problems.

In the finance world, however, there exists good risks and bad.

One is consistently (though unevenly) rewarded for taking good risks and inconsistently (and equally unevenly) rewarded for taking bad ones. If one continually exposes oneself to good risk, over time one will become wealthier. If one continually exposes oneself to bad risk, over time one will become poorer. In other words, we are only rewarded for taking good risks, not for taking bad ones.

In the parlance of high finance, good risk is called *systematic risk*. It is basically the risk that human civilization will continue to improve the quality of life for more people through technological, social, and political progress.

Bad risk is *idiosyncratic risk*—the risk that one particular investment in the universe of all possible investments will succeed. Idiosyncratic risk is always a gamble—sometimes it works out and sometimes it does not.

Asset owners and their managers can expose themselves to systematic risk by investing in the market as a whole—essentially betting on the success of Team Humanity. When economists talk about "investing in the market," they mean investing in every asset across all asset classes. Investing in this, the broadest of all concepts of the market portfolio, eliminates idiosyncratic risk and perfectly exposes an owner to systematic risk. The magic of diversification at work.

Luckily, the mathematics of diversification are generous enough to allow owners to eliminate idiosyncratic risk without owning every investment asset under the sun. As we saw in the previous section, if one combines many different investments in a portfolio—let's arbitrarily say 50—one essentially can diversify away idiosyncratic risk as long as one chooses those 50 assets in a sensible way.

Allowing one's capital to be exposed to the systematic risk of the market through holding a diversified portfolio eliminates idiosyncratic risk and offers the asset owner a premium—the equity market risk premium—in return for financing the activities of society. In essence, this is both the fundamental insight to the capital asset pricing model (CAPM[2]) and the impetus for the growth of passive investments.

The bad news is that typically private investors usually do not appear to know about or utilize the natural advantages of diversification—a much noticed study in 2000 by Brad Barber and Terrance Odean (Barber and Odean, 2000) found that private investors' portfolios typically hold only four stocks. Four stocks, even if in different sectors or industries, does not provide much diversification benefit at all, and (especially thinking about when that survey was done) if all the stocks in the portfolio are in similar businesses (like dot.com companies), the portfolio essentially displays zero diversification benefits.

One reason for this pattern of private investment in stocks is simply that investors do not have enough capital to invest in more stocks—think about my earlier comments about Berkshire Hathaway and the attraction of fractional shares, for instance. Of course, the answer to the quandary of how a private investor with limited means can diversify is easy: work through a financial intermediary whose raison d'être is to diversify and repackage risk: for instance, a mutual fund or ETF.

THE OTHER GOOD RISK

Financial economists assume the manufacture of goods and provision of services as a given and build the bulk of their models on the assumption that goods and services will naturally be produced by an economy. This simplified setup is sometimes labelled as "exchange economy" or "endowment economy." The economy is endowed with goods and services, and financial economics provides theories as to what are reasonable prices at which those goods and services will be exchanged.

For example, the classical exchange economy designed by Robert Lucas (Lucas, 1978), 1995 Nobel laureate, models the output of the economy as fruits—probably coconuts—dropping from trees. The crop depends on the weather, and the price for trees is determined by balancing out the production of fruits and their demand by consumers.

Innovation—for example, the introduction of fertilizer to grow more and better coconuts—is not considered in such an endowment economy; rather, technological improvements are a given.

A more realistic model for an economy would be to internalize innovation by, for example, letting tree owners decide how many coconuts they want to put aside to invest in the development of fertilizer. Investments to innovative technologies are often neither explicitly studied nor factored into our understanding of capital market risk, nor is the *displacement risk*[3] that existing companies face due to innovation.

In reality, capital markets are not just used to allow investors to price the assets of companies with well-defined product and service offerings. The ultimate purpose of capital markets is to allow companies to raise capital for new projects—channeling money into a society's best ideas. The much-vaunted free market system's greatest strength, in fact, is that it allows asset owners to allocate investment capital toward the development of innovative and beneficial technologies that will yield societal benefits and drive economic growth.

It is probably not an overstatement to say that human civilization's biggest challenge is to finance innovation and manage the risks posed by those innovations. One mechanism by which civilization may do this is through global, well-oiled capital markets. There is clear evidence that liberalized stock markets—that allow for enhanced risk sharing between domestic and global investors—promote innovation (Moshirian et al., 2021). Looked at from this perspective, it is clear what an important role the global asset management industry plays in enabling innovation.

One asset management tool that has developed to enable innovation is something known as thematic (or trend) investing. Thematic investing finds current technological (e.g., AI) or business process (e.g., cloud computing) trends that the manager believes will shape the future and provides capital to the most promising companies working in those target areas by building a portfolio of those securities. Note that a thematic fund is different from a sector fund, since thematic funds can cross industry or sector borders.[4]

You might be rightfully skeptical that purchasing a company's shares on the secondary market helps innovation. After all, the company received funds upon its IPO, so the money from making a speculative purchase of the stock goes to another secondary market investor rather than the company itself.

Allow me to retort.

A company's common shares are an important potential currency that can be used for acquisitions, partnership arrangements, and the like. As investors demand more shares of a company, prices react by going higher, and thus the currency a company has to undertake corporate actions also increases in value. This is a very direct way that asset managers investing in public securities can aid in innovation (Brown et al., 2009). Also, if the company issues bonds, demand for those issuances can drive down further borrowing costs and allow corporate activities to be funded through tax-sheltered capital sources. In general, a liquid, in-demand share issuance increasing in value or bonds that are likewise sought after by investors relieve a management team from financial constraints. It's easier for companies like this to float more stock, receive revolving bank credit, or issue debt with superior terms to the debt it is retiring. There is strong evidence that the removal of financial constraints makes a big impact on the funding of research and development. In fact, an analysis entitled "Do Financing Constraints Matter for R&D?" (Brown et al., 2012) found evidence that equity funding of research and development projects promotes economic growth by increasing innovation at the firm level.

INVESTING FOR PROGRESS

If an asset owner wishes to leave the safe harbor of systematic risk and exercise a more direct role in allocating capital in a way that directly funds innovation—either through a company or perhaps even an individual project—such a concentrated strategy is also possible. Some hedge funds concentrate in certain thematic areas to invest in (mostly) public companies and venture capital, and private equity firms also often specialize in certain innovative corners of the private markets.

The important thing to remember in investments such as this is that innovation is an uncertain process with uncertain outcomes— the quintessential "long shot" as explored in Box 11.1. Depending on the field, investments in innovative projects can be quite large and may have payback times that are quite far in the future (if they happen at all) compared to the typical quarterly time frame of many financial analysts. A perfect example of this is Bill Gates's Breakthrough Energy Ventures fund, which was investing (and investing heavily) in technologies such as direct air capture and synthetic proteins well before the commercialization path for these technologies was even known.

BOX 11.1 Exploring the Potential to Fund Long Shots

Long-shot investments have four features:

1. A low probability of success
2. Long gestation periods before any cash flows are realized
3. Large required up-front investments
4. Very large potential payouts in the unlikely event of success

If the first three elements of the definition do not make you a little queasy, you should go back and reread them. Essentially, what the definition describes is a lottery ticket that costs several times one's annual salary and will take years before you know if you're holding a winning ticket or not.

Funding long-shot investments is becoming increasingly difficult— even for high-risk investment vehicles like hedge funds and venture funds. Human civilization and technology have solved many problems to date, but many of those that remain—nuclear fusion, climate change,

Alzheimer's disease, and cancer—are in a class of problems that we have little experience in dealing with to date, are extremely expensive to develop and operationalize, and/or have been resistant to our best attempts at solving them so far.

A paper by John Hull, Andrew Lo, and Roger Stein (Hull et al., 2019) suggests that rather than conceiving of investments in long-shot investments from an individual asset perspective, some mechanism might be developed such that long-shot assets be pooled, then divided up into risk-based tranches. These tranches could be sold off as securitized debt securities, with some buyers selecting less-risky tranches and others more risky ones with much higher implied rates.

This may sound familiar to you if you ever traded in or read about collateralized debt obligations (CDOs) during the 2008–2009 kerfuffle, and the authors of the paper admit that the conceptual similarity to CDOs might limit the initial popularity of these innovation instruments.

If you can get past the CDO similarity, the idea makes a lot of sense. Being able to slice a pool of assets into risk tranches would allow for a new class of investors—not just hedge or venture funds but mutual funds as well—to allocate capital to these low probability of success tranches.

I believe that however outlandish this might seem, some aspects of financial engineering are necessary to allow for more capital to flow into high-impact, low-probability of success bets.

The economist John Maynard Keynes (Keynes, 1937) described technological innovation as an example of true uncertainty:

> By "uncertain" knowledge, let me explain, I do not mean merely to distinguish what is known for certain from what is only probable. The game of roulette is not subject, in this sense, to uncertainty; nor is the prospect of Victory bond being drawn. Or, again, the expectation of life is only slightly uncertain. Even the weather is only moderately uncertain. The sense in which I am using the term is that

in which the prospect of a European war is uncertain, or the price of copper and the rate of interest twenty years hence, or the obsolescence of an invention, or the position of private wealth-owners in the social system in 1970. About these matters there is no scientific basis on which to form any calculable probability whatever. We simply do not know!

The risk in financing innovation is, according to Keynes, "simply not known" and so by nature difficult to assess. At the same time, there is risk of not funding innovation. The risk of not funding innovation is the same risk I described at the beginning of this chapter when I discussed burying money in one's backyard. Without innovation, the world stands still. The status quo is maintained, and the rich grow richer while the poor lose comparative ground.

Without innovation, we would go back to an age when an infected scratch could be fatal, the quickest way to transmit a complex message would be through a handwritten letter, and most human activity ended when the sun went down.

Asset management has an enormously important role to play in supporting progress because it alone can spur innovation by allocating transformative amounts of capital to innovative companies. This role is, in fact, a central tenet to Schumpeter's argument in *Capitalism, Socialism, and Democracy* (Schumpeter, 1942). Schumpeter's notion of "creative destruction" describes a process whereby the free market allocates capital to innovative ideas, which in turn replace stagnant legacy ideas, which are eventually rendered obsolete.

For established companies, the support of investors focused on future-oriented innovation research is essential, especially as government support for basic research has often lost out to the more immediate "kitchen table" issues that may resonate more with political constituencies. William Kerr and Ramana Nanda suggest in a worthwhile overview, "Financing Innovation" (Kerr and Nanda, 2015), that the share of private sector expenditures on R&D has doubled in comparison to public sector expenditures; according to their research, private sector expenditures account for two-thirds, versus one-third for public sector ones.

An example of financing innovation from my own investing career was an allocation I made back in 2000 to a hedge fund specializing in event-driven, distressed debt and special situation investment opportunities. The fund was particularly involved in what was at the time cutting-edge communications technology—cable, wireless, and satellite telecommunications. One of this fund's investments was a position in a satellite company that had yet to launch its first telecom satellite. While this investment might seem run-of-the-mill today considering such literal moon shots such as Elon Musk's SpaceX, at the time it was a risky venture with a high level of uncertainty. Prior satellite networks had been launched by governments, but the company the hedge fund had invested in was on the avant-garde of private investments in satellite telecommunications. Technical risk, operational risk, financing risk—each of these elements were layered on top of one another, making it difficult for traditional funds to take a position. To make matters worse, it was not clear how much demand there might be for private satellite networks at the time, so there were many questions as to whether the company would be able to find clients after the satellite launch.

Every time I FaceTime my friends overseas and realize that I have access to an unlimited number of such conversations for the price of my present monthly mobile phone contract, I think about that early satellite investment.

Linking hedge funds to innovation is also confirmed by academic research. In a brilliant paper by Alon Brav and colleagues entitled "How Does Hedge Fund Activism Reshape Corporate Innovation?" (Brav et al., 2018), the researchers showed that a company targeted by activist investors improved their innovation efficiency over the five-year period after the activist involvement. According to Brav and colleagues, target firms increase both patent counts and citations despite a simultaneous lowering of R&D as a percentage of revenues. These effects became stronger for targeted companies that held more diversified innovation portfolios to begin with. It appeared that these effects were due to a reallocation of human resources and a redeployment of human capital, paired with a shuffling of board members to include people with greater innovation expertise at that level. Put simply, both the strategic posture and the tactical posture of the firms targeted by activists changed to promote a healthier, more robust innovation environment.

The push for innovation by asset managers is not wholly (or mostly) confined to hedge funds. Institutional investors in general enable and support innovation.

This dynamic is analyzed by Philippe Aghion, John Van Reenen, and Luigi Zingales in an article entitled "Innovation and Institutional Ownership" (Aghion et al., 2013). Their analysis shows that there is a causal link between institutional ownership and greater innovation. Given the importance of innovation for society, it is interesting to understand the incentives for management teams to innovate.

In contrast to the "lazy manager hypothesis" (Bertrand and Mullainathan, 2003)—that managers prefer to do little while raking in a high salary—it seems that career risk is a major motivator for management teams. This motivation is reflected in the fact that institutional investors are more important for innovation when management teams are less entrenched and run the risk of losing their jobs for underperformance. The takeaway, I guess, is that innovation requires a stick rather than a carrot.

Another area, and probably the most important one, that shows even more clearly the importance of asset management to innovations is the financing of startups by venture capital funds. An increase in VC activity in a given market leads to higher patenting rates and to a larger number of innovative commercial projects based on that intellectual property. Politicians and bureaucrats around the world have gotten hip to this dynamic and have initiated policies providing public support for private investing networks. One example of this type of government money priming the pump of private sector investment is that of Israel's Yozma Group.[5] In the mid-1990s, Yozma invested around $80 million for a 40 percent stake in 10 new VC funds. Yozma also subsidized the funds with a valuable put option, insuring 80 percent of the downside risk, and offered them a five-year call option on Yozma's stakes if the funds wanted to buy the government out within that period. Yozma forced the funds to coordinate their investing activities as a further way to backstop risk and provide better due diligence and postfunding support. In addition to this "indirect" venture investment (i.e., subsidizing and nurturing the VC environment itself), it also invested $20 million directly in startups; of an initial 15 portfolio companies, 9 eventually exited via IPO or acquisition.

The value of Yozma's holdings more than doubled in value from 1993 to 1996, but more important, from the Israeli government's perspective, VC investments in Israel jumped sixtyfold from $58 million to $3.3 billion. By 1999, the only country with a higher ratio of private equity capital to GDP than Israel was the United States. Thanks to Yozma and related agencies such as the Israel Innovation Authority, many high-tech names familiar the world over have roots in Israel, and the number of multinational companies with R&D hubs in Israel is huge.

Similar initiatives have taken hold in the United States with the Small Business Investment Company (SBIC) program, in the European Union with the Venture Enterprise Center, and in Japan with initiatives sponsored by the Ministry of International Trade and Industry (MITI). In general, these types of programs allow experienced managers and engineers to enjoy financial incentives large enough to induce them to leave cushy corporate positions, for scientists and researchers to commercialize laboratory research, and for young up-and-coming technologists to start potentially lucrative careers.

From a theoretical perspective, academics believe that one way the VC industry incentivizes innovation is by providing financial rewards for investing in what would normally be an underinvested area of the market—small, immature firms with business models that may still not be fully baked (Hall, 2002). Another theory is that VCs, through their connections, industry knowledge, and access to talented prospective employees, help new firms grow quickly and quickly cross the chasm from "good idea" to "commercial idea that at least breaks even" (Sahlman, 1990). Indeed, I think that both perspectives are true—certainly VCs take meetings with companies that a mutual fund manager would not even think about making space on her calendar for, and the extent to which VCs become involved in providing operational and moral support in addition to financing capital must be one key to many startups' success.

This is a bit of a dated paper by now, but Samuel Kortum and Josh Lerner found (Kortnum and Lerner, 2000) that patents granted to VC-backed companies were cited more often than other patents. This suggests that either VCs are more reliably finding company with strong and valuable patentable innovations (i.e., investing in a normally uninvested portion of the market) or they are advising their investees to spend money to protect intellectual property (i.e., helping companies become commercially successful). In general, Kortum and Lerner found that VC investments signal a higher likelihood of high patent counts.

At the end of the day, it is obvious that among the mutual funds allocating capital to listed companies that show technical prowess, the activist hedge funds that needle companies into making better and more efficacious R&D investments, and the increasingly sophisticated world of VC backing young, promising thoroughbreds whose legs are still shaky, asset management plays an enormous role in attenuating the risk that civilization will stagnate. Hopefully, with a large crop of climate tech entrepreneurs coming up with innovative ways to maintain the quality of life in developed countries, improve the quality of life in developing ones, and simultaneously allow the earth's environment to support it all, asset management will again step up to the plate.

Lowering Information Asymmetries

While not talked about much by practitioners, frictions related to information asymmetries are a problem that the asset management industry needs to solve to create optimal outcomes for investors, the industry, and society in general.

This is because information asymmetries are aggravated by conflicts of interest arising from the fact that participants along the asset management value chain have different objectives and different incentives.[1] Because of their limited expertise, asset owners delegate many tasks and decisions to consultants, investment advisors, and asset managers. But it does not stop there. Financial intermediaries may be guided by other institutions such as rating agencies, investment banks, or other specialists. With every new relationship link, there is the potential for increased information asymmetries and conflicts of interest.

A simple but important example of such a conflict of interest is what asset managers call *trade allocation*. If asset managers are responsible for different mandates, they will need to decide at a certain point if they need to allocate a trade to mandate A or B. Asset managers for private clients prefer to allocate trades to clients who pay higher fees. Asset managers for institutional clients that are investing through separately managed accounts prefer to allocate trades to their mutual funds with a similar strategy. Obviously, this is a conflict of interest, since asset managers have a fiduciary responsibility to allocate trades in a fair manner.

Typically, fair allocation is defined by the manager's internal policy. However, once an investment opportunity is limited in size, such as the IPO of a hot tech stock or an undervalued bond, it starts to get tricky.

The most important relationship in the asset management industry is that between an asset owner and an asset manager. Asset owners and asset managers that serve them form a classical principal-agent relationship. There are problems related to the principal-agent relationship in the best of times, but the fact of information asymmetry between the two parties makes the relationship a particularly tricky one.

Not only are asset owner-manager relationships characterized by information asymmetry in general, but different flavors of asymmetry exist before the contract is signed and persist after the manager is hired. Economists classify the first sort as *adverse selection* and the latter as *moral hazard*.

ADVERSE SELECTION

Before an asset owner hires a manager, a clear information asymmetry exists because the asset owner cannot tell whether the manager is truly skillful or if they are an index-hugging faux-active poser. There are plenty of faux-active managers, and they are difficult to distinguish from the very few alpha-generating true-active managers. Often, it takes years of observations before an asset owner can tell whether the manager is faux or true active. In fact, only by asking the right questions throughout an asset owner's collaboration with an asset manager will an asset owner finally receive a dependable answer.

What is the best approach when selecting a portfolio manager? Let's follow the advice of professional forecasters. Professional forecasters always start their prediction with unconditional expectations about the quantity they want to forecast (Tetlock and Gardner, 2015). To start with an "objective" hypothesis about the manager's quality, therefore, sounds like good advice. In the context of manager selection, the quantity that needs to be predicted is the probability of a manager having true skill. What is the probability of true skill for the portfolio manager sitting in front of you or presenting her investment approach on the stage right now? Let's start with unconditional expectations as an optimal reference point or "anchor." How many managers with superior skill would show up in a "lineup" of 100 managers? In other words, what is the percentage of skilled managers one expects to encounter when randomly walking around. Looking at various academic studies it is safe to assume the percentage is between 0 and 10 percent. Owners need to keep these statistics in mind when talking to a manager—if you go to a conference and speak with 10 managers, only one of them *may* be one with true investing skill.

Starting from this low percentage, specific questions can further sharpen the assessment. Unfortunately, asking the right specific questions is not simple.

The information asymmetry that exists before an asset owner invests is well described by George Akerlof—Nobel laureate and husband to Janet Yellen, famous as chairwoman of the Federal Reserve and the US Treasury Secretary—in an article entitled "A Market for Lemons" (Akerlof, 1970).[2] In the case of cars, there is no way for a buyer to tell, before the fact, if a new car will perform well or whether it will be a lemon, riddled with mechanical issues.[3] The fact that it is so hard for asset owners to differentiate between faux-active, true-active, and true-active with exceptional skill, coupled with a very attractive economic incentive in the form of 2-and-20 for hedge funds, makes the environment ripe for faux-active managers to enter the market so they can capture some economic rents from ignorant clients for as long as the ruse holds.

Obviously, passive funds do not suffer from the same problem—there is no asymmetry of information. This fact—completely removing the uncertainty about what assets a passive manager will buy or sell, and the returns of the fund versus the benchmark —is one of the factors I mentioned earlier in the book, which I think accounts for at least some of the popularity of passive funds among both institutional and retail investors.

MORAL HAZARD

Once an asset owner invests with a manager, another information asymmetry again related to the difference between true-active and faux-active managers arises. This topic was covered in an interesting 2017 article by Brown and Davies entitled, "Moral Hazard in Active Asset Management" (Brown and Davies, 2017). In this paper, Brown and Davies assume that faux-active managers know that they do not have a stock-picking or market-timing edge but continue marketing themselves as true-active managers able to generate alpha. Over time, investors can track these faux-active managers' investment records and realize that they are unable to generate returns in excess of the benchmark after fees. Realizing this, rational investors redeem their money, causing the managers' absolute management fee inflows to drop. As faux-managers' cash inflows fall, they have more incentive to continue to market themselves as true-active managers able to produce alpha but less incentive to spend money on the research activities that would allow them to generate alpha.

This situation—in which a manager is essentially obfuscating his or her own capabilities at the expense of principals—is termed *moral hazard.*

The problem with this aspect of moral hazard is that it is very nearly impossible for an asset owner to observe this dynamic directly without expending truly heroic due diligence efforts. In my opinion, asset owners would be well served by focusing on this very topic when they have placed money with a certain manager—attempting constantly to ferret out the truth of the situation. From my experience, one good indicator of a faux-active versus true-active manager is that the former will spend relatively more on marketing than on research activities. This said, while it may be possible for an asset owner to ask an asset manager what the manager is spending on both marketing and research and observe changing ratios over time, there is nothing that says a manager cannot increase research salaries simultaneously to increasing marketing spending and/or hire researchers who, delicately phrased, do not generate value greater than their remuneration.

This is another area in which both passive funds and funds like the ones my colleagues and I like to run, which utilize rule-based strategies, have an advantage. With passive portfolios, obviously, the asset owner knows exactly how much research is going into the portfolio's construction (i.e., none) and exactly what the criteria for selecting assets for the portfolio are. Quantitative, rule-based portfolios can also provide complete transparency related to asset selection criteria, something which discretionary managers cannot. For competitive reasons, however, most quant managers are more or less cagey about the exact algorithms that go into making asset allocation decisions, but general rules of thumb are communicated to clients. For instance, "We buy or sell the S&P 500 when the mid-term price crosses the long-term trendline."

Recently, there has been a lot of talk regarding nonpecuniary goals and objectives for asset management. These are goals related to sustainability, equity, social justice, and the like. Some believe that the moral hazard risk is lowered by setting nonpecuniary objectives, but I disagree. Newly created words such as "greenwashing," meaning "the practice of making unsubstantiated or misleading claims about the company's environmental commitment" (Flammer, 2021) or the general version of it, "ESG-washing" (Candelon et al., 2021), clearly point toward a growing information gap between principals and agents. In my opinion, the establishment of nonpecuniary goals simply adds categories of questions that asset owners need to ask managers and thus increases the already difficult task of seeing whether or not managers are investing money in the way they promised they would before the contract was signed.

I also do not think that moral hazard has to do with honesty, per se. While the end result may strike clients as dishonest (with results backing up their beliefs), moral hazard has much more to do with the natural human inclination for efficiency, with efficiency defined as "maximum efficiency for minimum effort." While that might sound like a cop-out to you, every business on the face of the earth attempts to cut costs to provide the offerings they promise to their customers in a way that maximizes bottom-line results. The asset management business is no different, except for the rule regarding fiduciary responsibility. Fiduciary duties are not carved in stone, and multiple interpretations can be made of the meaning of this rule in different situations. Humans are creatures governed by incentives, and unfortunately, economic incentives exist that lead to faux-active management, overcharging of fees, and this moral hazard born of information asymmetries.

Interestingly, there is some evidence that distribution channels provide a good signaling mechanism for which managers are alpha-generating true-active managers and which are value-destroying faux-active ones. Diane Del Guercio and Jonathan Reuter published an analysis entitled "Mutual Fund Performance and the Incentive to Generate Alpha" (Del Guercio and Reuter, 2014) in which they support my claim about efficiency.

Specifically, according to their research, active managers that market their funds directly to retail customers outperform both passive investments and active investment funds sold through brokerage channels by a significant margin. Del Guercio and Reuter suggest that, far from being a monolith, the retail market for investment services is split between involved, self-directed investors who move their money from fund to fund in search for the best risk-adjusted performance and slow-moving, advisor-directed investors who are uncomfortable with making investment decisions without the help of their broker or advisor.

Fund families that sell indirectly to the latter type of investor through broker distribution channels need not focus as much on generating alpha, because their clientele simply does not demand it. Fund families that sell directly to investors actively searching out good performance, on the other hand, are incentivized to outperform and indeed do so. In other words, this result reflects perfectly on the description I give for faux-active managers' focus on efficiency—these managers and fund families are naturally searching for maximum effectiveness for minimum effort. This dynamic is explained elegantly in Del Guercio and Reuter's paper:

> Our explanation rests on the premise that mutual fund families will expend resources to generate alpha only to the extent that they expect the investments to increase investor flows. The lower the expected benefit associated with investing in active management—because, for example, investor flows are less responsive to alpha—the weaker the incentive to do so.

In combination with the fact that a large proportion of asset owners is not sensitive to alpha provides an optimal setting for "strategic pricing" of investment products such as previously described.

Itzhak Ben-David and his colleagues ask "What Do Mutual Fund Investors Really Care About? "(Ben-David et al., 2022). The researchers show that simple performance-chasing behaviors best explains the investment flows and conclude "mutual fund investors behave like normal *homo sapiens* . . . , that is, they possess limited financial sophistication, are inattentive, extrapolate past performance, and rely on simple signals to do so."

Given the understanding that investors are not "hyperrational alpha-maximizing agents" (Ben-David et al., 2022), moral hazard as well as adverse selection in the asset management industry is probably as much about selling as it is about investing.

OVERCOMING INFORMATION ASYMMETRIES

Active managers often decry the growth of passive investing, but we must admit that passive investing provides a strategy that is 100 percent effective in overcoming information asymmetries. I believe that it is this benefit of passive investing that has contributed most to its rapid adoption by both institutional and retail clients.

The two forms of information asymmetry issues I have mentioned—the adverse selection related to choosing lemons and the moral hazard based on natural human proclivity to value efficiency—are unique manifestations of active management. Passive and, to a lesser extent, rule-based approaches do not manifest this weakness. I believe that over the next few generations, active managers' focus must be on closing this gap between the information available to owners and managers. If this gap is not resolved, we can expect to see active management relegated much more to a niche investment strategy reserved for the wealthiest clients.

The challenge of how to lesson information asymmetries will, I believe, arise from cooperation between owners, managers, and regulators. There are, as I see it, three different possibilities for addressing issues related to information asymmetries:

1. Increased regulation
2. Increased disclosure
3. Alignment of incentives

Some of these are good—meaning they will meet the challenge of closing the information gap between owners and managers—and others are considerably less so. Let's take a look at each.

Increased Regulation

While the most likely and obvious solution to lower information asymmetries and decrease moral hazard is regulation, my experience with recent regulatory action in Europe makes me suspicious whether this answer will end up being a good one for society.

Other examples of the past provide good case studies of the unintended adverse effects of regulation. An interesting example is presented by Yuyan Guan and colleagues in 2019 (Guan et al., 2019), which addresses the brain drain in investment banking after the Global Research Analyst Settlement of the Sarbanes-Oxley Act. The settlement required investment banks to separate investment banking and research in terms of collaboration as well as budgeting. The regulation addressing the conflicts of interest in equity research was implemented from 2002 to 2003.

Over the period from 1995 through 2007, Guan and his colleagues find that percentage of star analyst leaving the sell-side doubled after the regulation took place. The departure of better-performing analysts shows that regulation might alter the career choices of the more skilled part of a profession. This holds particularly true when compensation is affected, as was the case for research analysts.

Regulations are helpful to the extent that if they are not made and imposed, there is a clear cost imposed on society or an increased risk borne by it. Regulations set clear expectations—which can come in the form of restrictions, bans, and rules with which managers must comply—and this clarity is the biggest advantage of a regulatory approach. Regulators should always keep a reminder of this principle written in permanent ink on a sticky note on their desks!

Obviously, the big disadvantage is related to the cost to the asset manager of compliance with the rules and how that increased cost affects manager behavior. Here, I'm using the word "cost," but of course there are monetary, time, and attention costs that come part and parcel with regulatory compliance. Even before the regulations go into effect, organizations spend significant resources lobbying politicians, participating in comment periods, and the like. In total, we should realize that when all these costs are added up, they create a barrier to entry that has the implicit effect of favoring large organizations over smaller ones. This dynamic of regulation favoring the large incumbent can, of course, have substantial adverse effects on future innovation.

Trying to quantify the costs of financial regulation, considering all the factors I've listed previously, is very difficult. Regulators do not have a direct way to assess likely compliance cost, but instead must rely on estimates reported by the regulated entities themselves. Regulated entities have a vested interest in lobbying against the regulations or in getting the regulatory body to grant them regulatory relief. Overall, this process seems to me flawed to begin with.

If regulatory costs are hard to assess, imagine how much harder it is to estimate the benefits of imposing that regulation. With costs, at least you can sort through check stubs and calculate a cost estimate, but how on earth do you figure out the incremental monetary benefit to each asset management client as a result of imposing the regulations?

Back in 2021 here in Europe, the Sustainable Finance Disclosure Regulation (SFDR) illustrated some of the difficulties in assessing costs and benefits of regulatory oversight.

The SFDR forms a fundamental pillar of the European Union's sustainable finance agenda. It was introduced by the European Commission as one of the core sections (along with the Taxonomy Regulation and the Low-Carbon Benchmarks Regulation) of the 2018 Sustainable Finance Action Plan. The SFDR was introduced to improve transparency in the market for sustainable investment products—attempting to prevent greenwashing and increasing visibility into the metrics used by financial market participants regarding sustainability claims. The SFDR regulation is quite comprehensive, imposing disclosure requirements at both the entity (i.e., a fund management complex) and the product (i.e., a particular fund) levels related to ESG metrics.

If I had only one word to characterize the rollout of SFDR, it would be "chaotic." It even triggered raids at the offices of asset managers—typically a death sentence for a company competing in an industry built on trust. It is hard to imagine how many man-hours and headaches and how much legal fees and programing time was spent trying to understand what the regulations meant and what practical steps needed to be taken to implement them.

The very title of an early 2022 analysis reviewing the SFDR implementation speaks volumes: "Regulating Sustainable Finance in the Dark." The authors of this paper point out that the SFDR was implemented before effects of the Taxonomy Regulation (which formally classifies the degree to which investments can be considered "sustainable") had time to be analyzed. In other words, the SFDR was based on legislators' view of what they thought would happen regarding the risk and return of sustainable investments—without actually having any data on which to base that view.

The abstract of the paper, written by Dirk Zetzsche and Linn Anker-Sørensen (Zetzsche & Anker-Sørensen, 2022) is biting but in my view completely on target:

> Analyzing the revised EU Sustainable Finance Strategy disclosed in two steps in April and July 2021, we identify as core issues of any sustainability-oriented financial regulation a lack of data on profitability of sustainable investments, a lack of broadly acknowledged theoretical insights (typically laid down in standard models) into the co-relation and causation of sustainability factors with financial data, and a lack of a consistent application of recently adopted rules and standards. The three factors together are now hindering a rational, calculated approach to allocating funds with a view to sustainability which we usually associate with "finance."

In other words, the regulation *prevents* investors from making an informed investment decision. Ouch.

The SFDR exists now as settled law throughout the entire European Union, so it ends up affecting around 30 trillion euros worth of AUM in Europe. Even if the cost of implementing SFDR is only one basis point of that AUM figure, it still works out to a yearly monetary cost of 3 billion euros. Now, 3 billion euros is not a lot of money to a bigshot like you or me, but keep spending it every year for a few years and it starts to add up.

The problem—aside from the fact that the SFDR might not be well thought-out—is that the cost is high and the regulation may end up having unintended consequences related to manager incentives.

First, higher costs without more revenues means lower profits. Lower profits reduce the incentive of active managers to spend on research. This is the old "guns or butter" dichotomy—a euro spent to implement the SFDR cannot be spent to find good investment opportunities.

Second, it is in the interest of active managers that are skillful and can generate alpha to simply pass the cost of compliance on to clients. As such, the new regulations are a sort of back-door tax on asset owners, pensions, and the like.

Last, if the cost and complexity of compliance are too high, it is conceivable that some alpha-generating true-active managers will simply move over to the hedge fund world where such regulations need not be followed. If alpha-generating managers go from managing more people's money to fewer people's money, it is hard to say that the change was one beneficial for society at large.

I have a hard time imagining that the cost of SFDR compliance will not simply be passed onto the consumer. If we assume there are around 300 million investors in Europe and a 3-billion-euro impact, that translates to a 10-euro-per-year tax on investors, all with no suggestion that the regulation will do what it is designed to do.

Minimizing information asymmetries in asset management is a tricky task and the costs and benefits are difficult to assess. One thing is for sure though: the rarest and most valuable flower in the asset management garden is true investment skill. Regulation can have a lot of benefits, but it can also crush the shoots of that flower if implemented poorly.

Increased Disclosure

If there is an imbalance between what managers and owners know, the most straightforward solution is for managers simply to disclose more information to their asset owner clients.

Theoretically, Bengt Holmström, the Nobel laureate for his work on contracts between principals and agents, has shown that in moral hazard problems more information about the agent does not harm the principal and therefore is simply better (Holmström, 1979). The MIT professor's rigorous mathematical analysis, "Moral Hazard and Observability," however, provides only limited guidance for the asset management industry.

While it is straightforward in theory, in practice, it is very difficult to implement more information disclosure without some regulatory requirement. Investment management is a game of information processing. The manager who can process information most efficiently and intelligently can pick the right assets in which to invest. Managers who lack an information processing advantage are either faux-active or passive.

A successful manager is reluctant to offer more disclosure—the alpha generator does not want his or her informational advantage to be lessened; the faux-active manager does not want to be exposed as such. In both cases, managers end up reducing their own ability to earn economic rents if they provide greater disclosure.

It may sound strange, but limiting transparency serves asset owners as much as it does the asset managers. While it would be technically feasible and probably not too costly to have managers report daily on their portfolio's composition, this kind of disclosure requirement would definitely be the "Wrong Kind of Transparency" (Prat, 2005).[4] It is easy to understand that this level of transparency would eradicate the information advantage of true active managers and level out all managers' returns.

Marcin Kacperczyk and his colleagues estimated the value of the "Unobserved Actions of Mutual Funds" (Kacperczyk et al., 2008). In this paper, the academics discuss the "return gap," the difference between the actual return of a fund during a reporting period and the hypothetical returns of the fund were it to have used a buy-and-hold strategy on its previously disclosed holdings. The difference in return is taken to be the results of unobserved actions of the fund manager.

While on average the mutual funds do not show any added value by their unobserved actions, there is a wide dispersion of the return gap among the funds totaling several percent per annum. This dispersion is not a random result, since managers that add value through their unobservable actions continue to show positive contributions, and vice versa. In other words, the robust persistency of both value creation and value destruction is a clear indication of the presence of skilled and unskilled investment managers. Skilled managers continue to add value, and bad managers continue to destroy value through their unobservable actions. This further suggests that a higher disclosure frequency would be a drag on the performance of truly skilled managers.

In general, asset management is like mushroom farming: it's best to keep one's crop in the dark. Regulators frown on this approach, however, and mandate some standard information be offered to clients so asset owners can make intelligent comparisons between the offerings from different managers.

In Europe, regulators ask managers to provide what is known as the key investor information document (KIID) as part of the UCITS IV Directive framework. The KIID is a two-page document that must be provided to potential clients before the owner signs the investment contract. Other jurisdictions have their own KIIDs—in Hong Kong, they are known as key fact statements (KFS) and in Singapore, as product highlight sheets (PHS). Whatever the jurisdiction, these forms are all designed to protect investors. They are set up on a standard to facilitate a comparison between different fund offerings and typically contain statements regarding investment objectives, risk profiles, costs and fees, and past performance. The SEC makes this goal explicit in the Investment Company Act of 1940: "The focus of this Act is on disclosure to the investing public of information about the fund and its investment objectives, as well as on investment company structure and operations."

Again, this approach sounds very sensible, but one look at an actual statement to be found on one of these forms hints at the difficulty:

> The Fund's current risk category is 4. But this information may not be a reliable indication for the future. Furthermore, the risk category does not take into account certain risks and is not guaranteed and may change over time. Please check the Annex for a full description.

This supposedly clear statement leaves a reader with almost more questions than before they looked at it. Is a fund with a risk category of 3 ten times less risky than 4? What has been the historical performance of funds with a risk category of 4? If this risk category may not be reliable, why are you telling me about it? You say the risk category may change over time; are you obligated to inform me when it changes? Will you know that the risk category changed before something bad happens? And so on.

You can see the problem. These statements are written by lawyers for the sake of regulators—all of whom have a very good understanding of the framework of rules and assumptions that govern risk categories. Mrs. Schwartz, sitting in her kitchen in Frankfurt, is not so lucky.

Clearly, the information presented here would do nigh on to nothing to overcome the challenges of adverse selection (picking a lemon) or moral hazard. If I was a bit more cynical, the information here might even strike me as something equivalent to "strategic obfuscation" (deHaan et al., 2021).

Don't get me wrong. I do think it is important to provide standardized information to help investors make well-informed decisions about managers and funds. I just don't think that "disclosure Kabuki" really helps anyone get the ball across the goal line.

Another shortcoming to this approach to disclosure is that it implicitly assumes that even if the data provided were helpful, the asset owner or the prospective client will know how to analyze and think about it.

This brings us to the topic of financial literacy. Most newspapers are written using words that someone with three years of elementary school training can read, and I think that level is probably about what is safest to expect of the typical reader of a mutual fund prospectus. I have spent a few decades in the financial services business and hold a PhD in finance. After spending all the blood, sweat, and tears, I know very well that trying to tease out whether a manager is a faux-active poser or an alpha-generating star is not a straightforward task. What hope does someone with the financial literacy of a 10-year-old have?

Long story short, I do think that disclosure rules are more useful to society than more intrusive regulatory control over manager behavior, but it is still of dubious benefit in many cases.

Alignment of Incentives

In both approaches mentioned previously, there is an attempt to force managers to act in a certain way. This is the "stick" approach because the force applied acts contrary to the way managers are naturally incentivized—raising costs in the case of regulation and mandating performance-harming disclosure. I think that a better way to decrease the dual facets of information asymmetry—adverse selection and moral hazard—is by designing incentives that will encourage a manager to decrease the information gap. This is the "carrot" approach.

In asset management agreements, economic incentives are structured and set out by the contract between the asset owner principal and the asset manager agent. The trick is to figure out how to structure a contract that encourages the best managers to compete for the business (cutting down on adverse selection by weeding out faux-active managers) and once managing the funds, to focus on working hard to outperform (solving the moral hazard problem).

As I explained in Part II, one of the biggest draws for an asset manager is the management fee. It is easy money that is proportional to the amount invested. The money it takes to find good investment ideas is not generally proportional to the amount invested, so after a certain point, increasing AUM simply means a bigger payday for the manager him or herself.

To cut the attractiveness of this management fee, one possibility is to structure management fees as a flat dollar value rather than as a proportion of AUM. The management fee should be used to cover the operating costs of servicing the clients, so it is reasonable for an asset owner to pay something here, but the manager should not be taking a vacation to Monaco with it.

While this flat fee might seem attractive, there is no doubt that a regulation mandating this framework for active managers would constitute a substantial intrusion into the principle of the freedom of contract, a cornerstone of the free market economy.

Nevertheless, theoretically cutting the attractiveness of a management fee windfall is a good way to prevent faux-active managers from bidding for the contract. But how can we cut the moral hazard aspect of the information gap—in other words, how can we incentivize a manager to continue to work hard to generate alpha?

One of the key risks for a manager is that even if the manager picks good investments, the market as a whole declines, thus removing the possibility of receiving a performance fee. To properly incentivize the manager, an asset owner must be willing to remove the exogenous risk of a general price decline and continue to encourage the manager to search out relatively well-performing securities. The key to that sentence is "relatively." Namely, if the contract determines performance in terms of relative return versus a benchmark, rather than absolute return, the manager no longer needs to worry about a general market decline but instead simply needs to concentrate on finding investments that will generate good performance on a risk-normalized basis.

In economics, a contract that rewards an agent as a linear function of outperformance no matter the environment is termed a *linear* one. Linear contracts provide a good risk-sharing mechanism: the asset owner removes the market risk otherwise borne by the manager; the asset manager is motivated to generate alpha, thus removing (or at least limiting) the moral hazard risk to the client.

While linear contracts are considered a robust solution (Holmström & Milgrom, 1987), if the asset owner places investment restrictions on the manager, the selection of a benchmark can become more complicated. Zhiguo He and Wei Xiong show that there is no "one model fits all" incentive scheme and that the optimal scheme highly depends on the given mandate setting (He & Xiong, 2013).

With all this in mind, it is very likely that the optimal asset management contract has a linear form in which the manager is paid a flat management fee plus a share of the performance (when possible) defined relative to a benchmark. It is, however, hard to figure out how this can be practically implemented since to try to do so by regulatory mandate would impinge upon the concept of freedom of contract.

SUMMING UP INFORMATION ASYMMETRIES

It feels like there is much more work to do to overcome the key information asymmetries in asset management.

In the adverse selection area, it is hard to distinguish the skilled active managers from faux-active ones. Asking right question (e.g., "Why did you perform well/badly in this environment?" "What was your thinking at these points in time?") is important but like Blade Runners trying to find replicants, depending on the sophistication of the counterparty, it might take a lot of the right questions to come to an accurate conclusion.

Once a truly skillful manager is found, the incentive to keep the manager researching and performing according to the stated goals (i.e., the goal to outperform, do significant research regarding environmental impacts of investments) rather than simply cashing the check and taking a nice vacation is the other big topic.

Proper incentive contracts look most promising. But there are practical and perhaps unclearable hurdles that come with them.

As a manager managing funds under various incentive contracts, I felt from a fiduciary responsibility perspective most comfortable with a fulcrum fee. This framework pays well, simply put, if you deliver what you promise and pays poorly if you don't. However, the manager is typically only one link within the whole value chain; this makes it difficult to align all the interests and incentives up and down the asset management food chain.

Long story short, the legendary investor, Charlie Munger's quip to "show me the incentive and I will show you the outcome," is probably easier said than done for vast swaths of the asset management industry.

Meeting Societal
Preferences

When we talk about "societal preference," we need to distinguish between a structurally based, secular economic trend on the one hand and an investment flavor-of-the-week fad on the other. Certainly, catching the first swell of a flavor-of-the-week fad can be phenomenally profitable and can even make someone's investment career if the fad is long and strong enough. However, a secular trend based upon deep shifts in a society's aggregate conception of what is good and proper is a wave that can potentially last through many investing lifetimes.

In thinking about modern investment history—and by "modern," I'm starting in the middle of the nineteenth century, when our present concept of a corporation and intellectual property developed—I see two of these long-cycle societal preference waves occurring. I will elaborate on them in the first section of this chapter.

The swell of the third wave is just beginning and will be what I discuss for most of this chapter: environmental, social, and governance (ESG) investing.

SHIFTING SOCIETAL PREFERENCES IN THE PAST

The first of the two big waves of societal preference are what I call the *nation-building wave*. This wave started in the mid- to late-nineteenth century and started to wind down with the Allied victory during World War II. The second wave, which began to build at the end of World War II and overtook the nation-building wave in the 1970s, and has lasted until more or less today is what I call the *consumer wave*.

Note that these two waves overlap. A lot of the political and social conflicts of the last 50 years has been a result of the frictions between the respective waves' imperatives.

Where There Is Smoke, There's Progress

From the mid- to late-nineteenth century until the early- to mid-twentieth century, "progress" for the nations that we now consider "developed" meant possessing a flourishing industrial base.

This wave was sparked by the Second Industrial Revolution and was characterized politically by the expansion and economic importance of European colonialism and the concept of Manifest Destiny in the United States.

The nation-building phase was literally powered by coal and later by oil—fossil fuels—whose energy density allowed for enormous increases in per-capita productivity. The Second Industrial Revolution changed the temporal and geographical patterns of life—the concepts of centralized production, standardized machining, working hours, and weekends all came about during this period. Conditions for most of society were terrible—overcrowded cities, rampant hygiene-related diseases, lack of education, oppressive working conditions, and early death made up the typical menu for a working-class person.

Nations eager to promote their modernity and industrial might often did so on their bank notes and postage stamps—lithographic representations of sprawling factories, speeding locomotives, industrial steam tractors, and vast ocean liners were commonplace. Another common feature in these representations was the presence of smoke. Nothing seemed to better characterize an economy at full throttle than forests of belching smokestacks (Figure 13.1).

FIGURE 13.1 First $10 Federal Reserve note (1914)
Source: Bureau of Engraving and Printing.

In the United States, Pittsburgh, Pennsylvania, which is situated at the fork of two rivers and sits upon rich coal deposits, heralded the ascendency of the economic power of the nation with air so filled with smoke, it often blotted out the sun. It is no coincidence that one of the wealthiest men in history and the quintessential American industrialist, Andrew Carnegie, made his fortune in Pittsburgh, known at the time as "the City of Smoke."

For an investor, the principle of being "long smokestacks" would have served one very well for long stretches. Today, that is very different.

Keeping Up with the Joneses

After World War II, American GIs returned from Europe and Asia to find a manufacturing sector geared up to produce on behalf of the Allied war effort, but without any war. The relief of the returnees and their waiting families, coupled with an increase in production capacity that companies naturally wanted to fill, layered on top of a very-long-cycle bounce back from the Great Depression of the 1930s ended up creating a phenomenally powerful wave of consumer spending. Part of this spending was in housing, a market that saw significant structural changes due to the founding of the Federal Housing Administration and its sponsorship of home loans that encouraged more buyers to take on mortgage debt (Chambers et al., 2009).

Post–World War II Europe had another final round of nation building in the 1950s as, thanks to the destructive influence from a certain German politician, it was hard to find buildings with two bricks sitting atop one another in many European cities. The strong desire of some of the countries in Western Europe most affected by the destruction of war—Belgium, Germany, France, Italy, Luxembourg, and the Netherlands—to share a flourishing industrial base as a way to promote lasting peace motivated the founding of the European Coal and Steel Community, aka *Montanunion*. The Treaty of Paris, which was signed in 1951, formed the world's first supranational organization and led to first association of European states after World War II. The union is widely considered to be the starting point of the European unification process.

As the industrial capacity of Western Europe began to be rebuilt, American luxury goods flooded into European stores, and American culture permeated the cinemas. US companies were at a significant advantage over their European and Japanese counterparts. No part of the US mainland had suffered an enemy incursion during the war, its productive capacity was at a peak, and wartime research and development contributed to a wave of inventions and products that could be directed at consumers.

In the United States and later in Europe, labor-saving devices such as washing machines and dishwashers became absolute necessities. President Eisenhower initiated the construction of high-speed public highways, which in turn boosted the auto industry. In Germany, the *Autobahn* system, which had been started in the 1930s but was only about one-fifth complete by the end of the war, was also built out. Soon, automobiles were transformed from luxury items to virtual necessities. War production of battle tanks and high explosives found a new market in the manufacture of heavy farm equipment and agricultural chemicals. The United States moved even more quickly after that point from a rural, agricultural society to an urban, professional one. And all those new professionals needed to keep up with the Joneses—buying the newest gadgets and cars.

In Europe, the Marshall Plan, and the rivalry of the United States with the former USSR, made sure that the US consumer lifestyle was exported. The new battlefield was the hearts and minds of European housewives, and US "attacks" concentrated on driving the domestic consumption of products such as kitchen and household goods (Castillo, 2005).

Note that in this period, the focus was on building wealthy citizens within countries rather than on building wealthy nation-states. The one-two punch of World Wars I and II destroyed the reputation and standing of aristocrats and kingly figures. Democratization took hold and democracies rely upon relatively well-off, well-educated citizens who have a stake in the success of the country.

The Cold War was essentially a war between different visions of what constituted providing power to citizens. Communists focused on egalitarianism, central planning, and sharing of the fruits of production; the West focused on democratic process, free market capitalism, and strictly controlled transfer payments from wealthier to poorer citizens in the form of redistributive taxation. As such, the fall of the Berlin Wall on November 9, 1989, could be viewed not only as a deathblow to the Communist system, particularly in the GDR (the German Democratic Republic—a country, which like the Soviet Union, no longer exists), but also to the nation-building wave and as an acceleration of the consumer wave.

I might have called the consumer wave the "American Wave" because the foundation of this age of societal preference had an overwhelmingly American feel to it, thanks to Hollywood movies and later television shows, as well as to years of virtually no overseas competitive pressures for American companies.

The consumer wave has continued to the present day and encompasses the development of all the innovations in technology and communications, the financial engineering that allows for broad home ownership in the United States, and—I would argue—the trend toward passive investing strategies as well. Thanks to communication technology, all nations of the earth now view the markers of "success" as living the life of an American movie star or "influencer"—this is a very individualized concept of success compared to the communal concept of success that ruled during the nation-building wave.

For an asset manager, the principle of supporting the consumer would have served well for the last 70 years.

THE TRIAD REFLECTING TODAY'S SOCIETAL PREFERENCES: E, S, AND G

In the preceding description of the first two waves, you will have noticed that the start of a new wave does not mean the end of the earlier one. Big industrial companies figured out how to get exposure to consumerism, then to a global client base.[1] In addition, sometimes a new wave takes years to build and swell. Such is our world's most recent wave: ESG.

Growing Environmental Concerns in the Seventies

It was 1972 and the three passengers in the command module of the last Apollo mission trained a camera on the majestic figure of the retreating earth. This photograph (Figure 13.2) became one of the most famous in history—a haunting view of diaphanous rivulets of clouds laced across Africa, Madagascar, Egypt, and the Arabian Peninsula, supported by the solid expanse of ice covering Antarctica and framed by the deepest black of empty space.

The photograph underscored the beauty and also the isolation of our little planet—with a paper-thin atmosphere—and kindled interest in ecological matters that had been sparked by counterculture figures of the 1960s.

FIGURE 13.2 *Blue Marble* **(1972)**
Source: NASA.

The overlapping waves of industrialization and consumerism have contributed to severe ecological problems in many industrialized countries. Rivers on fire in the United States, thick smoke in Germany's industrial regions, severe birth defects and health concerns from poisoned waters in Japan—countless cases of terrible ecological damage prompted social outrage, followed by political pressure.

Far from being seen as a symbol of success and wealth as it was during the nation-building wave, since the 1970s, smoke became associated with the destruction of natural spaces and negative health impacts on people and animals. The same year that the *Blue Marble* photo was published, a team at the Massachusetts Institute of Technology, sponsored by a group called the Club of Rome, published a sobering monograph detailing the results of an early effort to apply computing power to economic and social questions, entitled *Limits to Growth* (Meadows et al., 1972).

The monograph's introduction provides an outline of the work's conclusions:

> If the present growth trends in world population, industrialization, pollution, food production, and resource depletion continue unchanged, the limits to growth on this planet will be reached sometime within the next one hundred years. The most probable result will be a rather sudden and uncontrollable decline in both population and industrial capacity.

Considering this conclusion that under a business-as-usual scenario is basically a collapse of human civilization as we know it, it would have been nice if the nations of the earth sprang together to establish sustainable policies, but alas, world leaders were more intent on riding prior waves of industrialization and consumerization to be bothered.

I count the environmental movement as having started at this time in the late 1960s and early 1970s, but like a tidal wave in the open ocean, the swell was barely visible for several generations. Today, however, it is reality. Everyone needs to pay attention, and this is especially true for asset managers.

From Student Protests to Social Movements in the Eighties

In the postwar period, the emergence of a young, egalitarian country whose national identity is wrapped up with the concept of individualism prompted significant cultural and commercial changes across the globe. In the Europe of my birth, there is a sense that hierarchies are good and natural, contributing to stability and societal well-being. In the United States where I finished my PhD, I felt uncomfortable to call my professors by their given names and—gasp—to hear a classmate disagreeing with one of the professor's points. For Americans, I quickly realized, there is a sense that hierarchies are limiting and destructive and contribute to stagnation in society.

In the United States, there is the sense that everyone's opinion is as good as anyone else's and the certainty that if one can gather enough people to one's point of view, the system can be changed. This understanding has led to important mass movements: the environmental movement, and the movements to abolish slavery, extend suffrage to women, enforce food safety regulations, and ban the sale of alcohol—each of which had profound, long-lasting political and commercial impacts.

With an improving standard of living, the growing middle-class baby boomer kids, imbued with the US culture of egalitarianism, began to turn their attention to social matters such as civil rights, women's rights, and—as they came into early adulthood in the 1960s to see the United States take over the colonial duties of the French Empire in Vietnam—the antiwar movement.

This chain of events may explain something about the initiation of social movements in the United States, but why would this local cultural change in the United States have any effect on global commerce? Again, I believe this is an artifact of the state of the world after World War II and the globalization of societal preferences.

Eventually, this social evolution with its focus on individualism and equity bumped up against the technical evolution of improved telecommunications, satellite broadcasts, and 24-hour news networks. With communication deregulation and the introduction of cable television in the 1980s, suddenly Americans could witness instances of deprivation and inequity across the globe.

One of the first set of images that flashed into US homes was that of the radical disparities inherent in the apartheid system in South Africa: the juxtaposition between light-skinned Africans of European descent living in ease and luxury, while dark-skinned Africans of African descent were beaten by police and fired on by paramilitaries in crowded, impoverished shantytowns like Soweto.

In December 1984, a group of students at the University of California–Berkeley marched from their campus walkout to the university administrative offices, demanding to speak with the chancellor and president. Their demand was that the University of California divest nearly five billion dollars from the securities of companies that by doing business in South Africa were tacitly (and sometimes not so tacitly) supporting the status quo (University of California, 2018).

The Berkeley protest was no flash in the pan. Students camped out at the administrative offices for months, turning the area outside of the building into a tent city and harkening back to the heady days of the antiwar protests in the 1960s. Students boycotted classes and joined protest marches, which also attracted celebrity figures and even the 1984 Nobel Peace Prize winner, South African Anglican bishop Desmond Tutu.

In summer of 1985, the administration agreed to divest some of its South African holdings. The half measures (really "quarter measures") were rejected by the student organizers as window dressing, so protests continued for another year. Finally in July 1986, the board of regents voted to divest the remaining $3 billion of holdings in companies doing business in South Africa.

Eventually, the University of California action was followed by other institutions, and four years after Berkeley students forced divestiture, the imprisoned leader of the opposition African National Congress, Nelson Mandela, was released from prison.[2] A year after that and almost exactly five years after the board of regents' vote, the system of apartheid was legally dismantled in South Africa.

While political effects from the international attention and institutional divestment movement were great, evidence from its effects on corporate security prices is much less clear.

In 1999, Ivo Welch and his colleagues published a paper entitled "The Effect of Socially Activist Investment Policies on the Financial Markets: Evidence from the South African Boycott" (Teoh et al., 1999). They examined how securities prices and institutional shareholdings changed in response to activist pressures and concluded that "the announcement of legislative/shareholder pressure or voluntary corporate divestment from South Africa had little discernible effect either on the valuation of banks and corporations with South African operations or on the South African financial markets." In fact, the Johannesburg Stock Exchange reached new highs throughout the period of most intense political pressure.

The year of the Berkeley divestment protests also saw an 89 percent rise in the number of cases of AIDS. The AIDS crisis ended up providing another prominent example of social activism's effects on commercial activity. As the disease spread quickly through the LGBT community and tens of thousands of people died, the US Food and Drug Administration (FDA) sent an urgent request to pharmaceutical companies for compounds that might be effective in slowing the progress of the disease. The winner was a failed cancer drug from British-American pharmaceutical company Wellcome PLC, called zidovudine and known as AZT (its trade name was later changed to Retrovir).

AZT was approved for use in the treatment of AIDS in 1987 after a rapid approval process. Upon announcement of the drug's approval, Wellcome's stock price soared. The drug was expensive—$8,000 per patient per year, not including the cost of the blood transfusions that were required when taking the strongly cytotoxic (toxic to cells) medicine. In addition, there were no alternative treatments (the next drug to be approved for the treatment of AIDS, didanosine, would not receive FDA approval until 1991), meaning that Wellcome's AZT had an uncontested monopoly in the treatment of AIDS during the height of the disease's health crisis.

Due to the expense of AZT and the lack of alternatives, activists had called for Wellcome to lower the price of the treatment. A grassroots organization named ACT UP (AIDS Coalition to Unleash Power) staged a "die-in" protest in March 1987 at the busy, lower-Manhattan intersection of Wall Street and Broadway, near the historic Trinity Church. The early morning protest stopped traffic and caused a major disruption at the peak of rush hour as organizers called for corporate and governmental action to broaden research into new drugs and to make AZT more affordable for patients.

Wellcome stood firm on its pricing, and ACT UP increased its pressure. On September 14, 1989, ACT UP upped the ante by creating a disruption that interfered with the opening of the New York Stock Exchange. A group of seven ACT UP members snuck into the exchange, chained themselves to the VIP balcony, sounded handheld foghorns that completely drowned out the sound of the opening bell, and threw fake $100 bills onto the exchange floor while unfurling a banner reading "SELL WELLCOME."

Trading on the exchange was halted until the protesters could be removed, but photos of the protest action were distributed worldwide through wire services and four days later, Wellcome announced it would lower the price of AZT by 20 percent to $6,400 per year.

ACT UP continued to lobby politicians to encourage the greater use of experimental treatments in cases when treatments were not otherwise available, and the threat of severe human health impacts were large. The grassroots campaign succeeded in increasing scientific, governmental, and corporate attention on AIDS treatment—eventually allowing for modern treatments that essentially render AIDS to be little more than an inconvenience for patients, rather than a death sentence.

Despite the enormous effect the ACT UP protests had on public opinion about AIDS research and treatment and on government policy, the effects on Wellcome's stock price were much more muted, mirroring the effects of antiapartheid protests on the South African market. AZT eventually lost ground in the market for AIDS treatments as its efficacy was questionable. It was the best first treatment for AIDS, but as time passed, not the best treatment for AIDS. In January 1995, English pharmaceutical company Glaxo offered to pay 23 times Wellcome's prior year's earnings, and Wellcome's share price soared over 45 percent on the announcement day. To put it another way, an investor that was invested in Wellcome's shares throughout the ACT UP crisis may have had a few unpleasant days, but in the end would have come out trousering a nice profit.

The examples here relate to social investment considerations—the "S" of the ESG triad. While these movements generate a good deal of press, it is hard to say that they have much of an effect on market capitalizations (think about the muted effects on the market capitalization of Saudi Aramco or ExxonMobil in the face of climate change protests).

While social movements do not, I believe, create investable opportunities, I do think that the most prominent factor related to social investment considerations is the treatment of employees by a company's management. This is one area that at least shows correlation to investment returns and to market capitalization.

Corporate concepts related to employee satisfaction have changed over the years. In an earlier age, the existence of happy employees meant the company was committing the mistake of either underworking or overpaying their workers. Both conditions destroy value for shareholders, so employee satisfaction and well-being were generally considered at best incidental and at worst value destructive. In the new conception, high employee satisfaction leads to more effective employees, which in turn leads to the creation of value for the firm and the shareholders.

The original focus in this area was to ensure that company employees' health, safety, and access to basic benefits were available. Indeed, Jonathan Cohn and Malcolm Wardlaw showed that high levels of employee injury rates lower the value of employer firms (Cohn & Wardlaw, 2016). Cohn and Wardlaw saw a clear relationship between financial stress—negative cash flow shocks and high leverage—and higher injury rates. As such, it is likely that investors are using injury rates as a data point serving as a proxy for financial constraints that are not yet obvious in the publicly available financial statements.

Over the past generation, companies have extrapolated the lessons about workplace safety and general healthcare and incorporated more and more varied perquisites into their corporate culture to help bring about a higher sense of purpose and happiness in their employees. Again, this shift started with a practical, hard-nosed goal of creating more productive workers by offering them opportunities for education and career advancement. However, over time, this trend has expanded to enable employees the famed American "pursuit of happiness" or more recently, "work-life balance" and "doing good." Today, it seems almost cruel and inhuman if a company does not offer free soft drinks and snacks in its cafeterias and break rooms.

Seeing these trends, it is worth asking whether or not the corporate largesse to its workers results in boosts to investors. Alex Edmans's paper "Does the Stock Market Fully Value Intangibles? Employee Satisfaction and Equity Prices" (Edmans, 2011) examines this question by leveraging data from the *100 Best Companies to Work for in America*, first published in 1984. Indeed, Edmans finds that high levels of employee satisfaction generate superior long-horizon returns in the range of 3 to 4 percent, even when controlling for various risk factors. These findings imply that equity investors have thus far failed to incorporate intangible assets into their considerations regarding firm valuation.

With the attention placed on this issue, it is unclear whether this return effect will persist, the hypothesis being that investors were caught off guard because they did not understand the relationship of employee satisfaction to return. Now that this effect is better understood, it is possible that the relationship will break down. Even if the relationship continued to hold, there is the matter of an investor attempting to quantify and measure employee satisfaction correctly. Given my experience with consultants and human resource departments, this will prove to be a difficult task. Intangibles are inherently difficult to measure and thus to incorporate into investment criteria.

On the other hand, employee satisfaction could be a new area of potential innovation for alternative data providers. A 2019 paper published by Clifton Green and colleagues and entitled "Crowdsourced Employer Reviews and Stock Returns" found returns for firms whose employees reported improved satisfaction on crowd source sites like Glassdoor.com were significantly better than returns of firms whose employees reported declining satisfaction (Green et al., 2019). Digging a bit deeper, the academics found that the relationship was particularly strong with regard to self-reported assessments of career opportunities and views of senior management and was completely unrelated to work-life balance issues.

As a manager, I understand that it is easier to attract and retain talented employees when they are drawn to a company's mission, believe they have the opportunity to do interesting work and be recognized by peers and colleagues, and are happy with their working conditions. I think, however, to outsmart other investors with this insight is not very likely.

Changing Perceptions of Corporate Governance in the Nineties

Just as social factors in investing were strongly influenced by American culture, I believe the radical change in attitudes toward corporate governance also has roots in the evolution of the American company.

US companies had a very good run in the postwar period. European and Japanese competitors' production capacity had been badly degraded during the war, national infrastructure was in shambles anywhere bombs fell and bullets flew, and many citizens lost their entire asset base over the course of the conflict.

Coca-Cola, General Motors, and others expanded into the commercial vacuum created by the decimation of local industry, so they ran virtually competitively unopposed in many markets. In this kind of environment, it is easy to mistake luck for skill. And while Europe and Japan rebuilt and tried to figure out how they could compete against American corporate giants, the American corporate giants took for granted that their dominance was ensured.

Imagine the shock then when German luxury cars started to flood the American market in the 1970s, only to be followed by a wave of what many American carmakers perceived as tiny, shoddy cars from Japan. And imagine the increased shock when American consumers traded in their gas-guzzling domestic cars for those "tiny, shoddy cars" during the oil shock of the early 1970s.

The sprawling US blue chip conglomerates took a big hit during the bear market of the early 1970s and performed worse than the market as a whole all the way through the early 1980s. Suddenly, some smart investors started thinking about what might be done to turn around the fortunes of the suddenly moribund American companies.

Low stock valuations and easier access to debt capital sparked a wave of leveraged buyouts (LBOs) starting in the 1980s. The corporate raiders of this period—people such as Carl Icahn and Nelson Peltz—became emblematic of the new face of American capitalism. Their strategy was to take over poorly performing firms—firms, in other words, whose management was doing a poor job of allocating resources and generating value for shareholders—cut costs, sell off noncore divisions, and put a sharp focus on raising the stock price.

This strategy made these titans of the LBO world rich(er) and more famous; fictionalized images of such larger-than-life characters became memorialized in movies such as *Other People's Money*, *Wall Street*, and *Pretty Woman*.

There were likely two different dynamics that played a part in the ability of LBO artists to step in and make so much money at this time.

Michael Jensen believes that the wave of 1980 takeovers were the result of internal governance mechanisms (Jensen, 1993). Starting in the 1930s and accelerating after the war, the original founder/owners of large American corporations retired to be replaced by managers with much smaller ownership stakes. Shares were split between many more owners, each of which had proportionally less stake in the company's success and less ability to make changes through board intervention. Boards—then like today—had close relationships with senior managers and tended to take the side of those managers in issues of strategy. In other words, shareholder rights weakened, both due to increasingly dilute ownership interests and ineffective representation at the board level.

The other contributing factor to the 1980s LBO boom was identified by Gordon Donaldson, who found that while individuals' shareholdings were more dispersed, institutional shareholding became more concentrated. From 1980 to 1996, large institutional investors nearly doubled their share of US corporate ownership from under 30 percent to over 50 percent (Gompers & Metrick, 2001). This shift toward institutional ownership made it easier for investors like Icahn and Peltz to acquire large blocks of shares. Rather than convincing thousands of investors by calling for a special shareholder vote, LBO artists could spend time talking with a few dozen large portfolio managers, trying to sway them toward action.

By the time a few waves of barbarians[3] had pounded down a few dozen gates, corporate titans in the United States took the hint and started effecting the changes themselves that they would have otherwise been forced to take by activist investors.

Poor shareholder focus and increased institutional ownership helped start the LBO fire that burnt through the prairies of the American corporate landscape, but stock-based compensation also played a part. Activist investors wanted CEOs to be aligned with shareholder interests, so they architected compensation packages that skewed toward the fulfillment of stock price–based goals. The average annual CEO option grant increased almost sevenfold between 1980 and 1994 (Hall & Liebman, 1998). As a result, equity-based compensation made up almost 50 percent of total CEO compensation in 1994, compared to less than 20 percent in 1980.

While the current state of affairs may seem normal today, thinking about how much the corporate governance environment changed in a relatively short period of 10 to 15 years; the shift is little short of amazing. US managers have become much more focused on short-term stock price fluctuations—a fact that some longer-term investors find frustrating—and this focus has created a great deal of value for some investors. The initial change was brought about by sticks (corporate raiders) but is nicely maintained now by carrots (incentive-based compensation). I believe that this more market-oriented style of corporate governance is here to stay.

While certain elements of this American-style market focus have taken hold in other parts of the world, some of these changes are difficult for to incorporate into the social and legal traditions of other countries. However, slowly but surely American-style governance systems have begun to converge toward the US norm.

To read the preceding summary, one might be forgiven for thinking that the American style of corporate governance, complete with incentive-based awards and a focus on stock market valuations, was adopted without major incident, but of course, there were plenty of cases where a combination of greed, short-termism, and access to capital markets made for an unpleasant combination.

Scandals at Tyco, Enron, and Worldcom, not to mention years of high-tech companies issuing options with strike prices tailored to allow executives to enjoy spectacular gains the instant the options were authorized—all these incidents pointed to potential weaknesses with market-oriented governance systems when clever managers were allowed to put their thumbs on the scale.

Interestingly, though, the common take-away from these obvious governance failures is that governance can and does significantly affect investor wealth. A fact that was also well documented by academics. Governance measures that lead to weakened shareholder rights correlate with lower returns, or in other words, better governance leads to higher returns (Gompers et al., 2003; Bebchuck et al., 2009). Today, there is a consensus that good governance affects firm value through improved and persistent operational performance.

The problem is that the boost from trading based on this information disappeared in the aughts as more and more asset owners and managers grew savvy to which companies displayed good governance and which took a page out of the Worldcom playbook (Bebchuck et al., 2013), and the governance perspective lost its informational advantage.

FUNDAMENTAL SUSTAINABILITY— THE CHALLENGE FOR ASSET MANAGERS

The asset management industry must focus its attention and capital on issues that are normally termed *ESG* investing but that I like to think about in terms of sustainability.

If you prefer to think about this topic in more tightly focused economic terms, I would say that the reason it is imperative to focus on ESG issues now is because the societal preferences of asset owners is shifting powerfully to focus on sustainability. Whether you as an asset manager prefer to frame this choice as saving the world or simply taking advantage of a long, strong secular trend, it behooves you to pay attention to sustainability issues.

For asset management, shifting focus to sustainable investing strategies can cause difficulties, and that is where I would like to turn to now. Asset management is a global industry, and as we saw in prior chapters, it thrives on scale. For asset managers to succeed in the age of ESG, either they must find universal social values into which investments can be made, or they must somehow propagate the idea that nonpecuniary goals can and should be factored into the industry's objectives.

Do Universal Rights and Wrongs Exist?

ESG investing encompasses ideas of both ethics and morality. Both topics relate to conduct that society perceives as right or wrong, and while they are sometimes used interchangeably, they are different. Ethics refers to rules provided by an external authority or force (e.g., codes of conduct in workplaces or societal mores that frown on people wearing only underwear when they come to the office for a meeting). Morality refers to an individual's own principles regarding proper actions and activities and is often a reflection of one's cultural and/or religious upbringing.[4]

This distinction is important in the realm of ESG because morally motivated investments often reflect religious values (e.g., Sharia-compliant investments). Morally motivated investments are challenging for a global industry simply because the traditions and moral sensibilities of one country or region do not automatically cross borders effectively. Ethical investments, on the other hand, are based on rules that are optimally those that many cultures across the world agree about so it can be successfully exported.

The tradition of considering moral or ethical issues in investing goes back centuries. In 1759, before publishing *The Wealth of Nations*, Adam Smith published his first work: *The Theory of Moral Sentiments*. In this book, Smith described the principles of human nature from which societal preferences could be deduced. One question that interested Smith in particular was the source of the ability to form judgments in the face of the seemingly overriding passion for self-interest and self-preservation. Smith believed that within each person was an "inner man"[5] who plays the role of an impartial spectator that condemns or approves the actions of oneself and others. In Smith's conception, the inner man provided a rational actor that acted to counterbalance the self-serving and passionate part of the person and allow them to work effectively with other rational, self-seeking individuals. Smith's famous observation about the "invisible hand" of the markets was made first in *The Theory of Moral Sentiments*; the invisible hand was, in Smith's conception, the result of all rationally self-interested individuals acting together in a society to react to the production and consumption demands of that society.

This idea ended up being incorporated into Vilfredo Pareto's theory of the optimal allocation of resources, but Smith's original idea of an inner man—or I will say an "impartial spectator" to pull Smith's verbiage into the modern day—implies more than just an actor determining an optimal allocation of resources. In my opinion, the impartial spectator serves an ethical purpose as an arbiter for the rules upon which individuals in a society can all agree. Notice that I say "ethical" rather than "moral." In my definition of these terms, ethics represents agreed-upon rules, so Smith's first book would have been named *The Theory of Ethical Sentiments*.

So what are the universal ethics—the rules to which everyone on the planet can agree—with which asset manager can work?

The term *ESG* was officially coined in 2004 with the publication of the UN Global Compact Initiative's "Who Cares Wins" report. That year, the then secretary-general of the United Nations, Kofi Annan, asked major financial institutions to collaborate with the United Nations and the International Finance Corporation in identifying ways to integrate environmental, social, and governance concerns into capital market decision-making.

Two years later, Annan traveled to the southern tip of Manhattan to hold a kickoff event at the New York Stock Exchange for the Principles for Responsible Investment (PRI) program—the real-world manifestation of the collaborative effort. Annan was joined by a group of top executives from leading institutional investing companies from 16 countries with aggregate assets under management of $2 trillion. Since that time, PRI signatory growth has been spectacular, and the aggregate asset base has swelled more than fiftyfold to almost $120 trillion.

In 2015, less than 10 years after PRI had kicked off, all—I repeat *all*—UN member states adopted the 2030 Agenda for Sustainable Development. This document provides 17 Sustainable Development Goals, 169 targets measured by 231 unique indicators (SDGs; see Table 13.1), which were agreed upon as the necessary building blocks for a peaceful, prosperous community of nations sharing a healthy global ecosystem. In other words, at least on paper, all the nations of the world have agreed on an ethical framework for investing and on specific indicators that allow progress to be measured. This advance demonstrates a clear sign of how much modern access to data can accomplish.[6]

While ESG began as an outgrowth of decisions made by transnational negotiators and government elites, I believe it does reflect a bona fide societal preference that has coalesced as businesses have globalized, communication technologies have improved, and various issues and imbalances have been recognized as negative.

TABLE 13.1 Sustainable Development Goals

GOAL	TARGETS		INDICATORS	
	#	Example	#	Example
No Poverty	7	By 2030, eradicate extreme poverty for all people everywhere (people living on less than $1.25 a day)	13	Proportion of the population living below the international poverty line
Zero Hunger	8	By 2030, end hunger and ensure access by all people to safe, nutritious and sufficient food	14	Prevalence of undernourishment
Good Health and Well-Being	13	By 2030, reduce the global maternal mortality ratio to less than 70 per 100,000 live births	28	Maternal mortality ratio
Quality Education	10	By 2030, ensure that all girls and boys complete free, equitable, and quality primary and secondary education	12	Completion rate (primary education, lower secondary education, upper secondary education)
Gender Equality	9	End all forms of discrimination against all women and girls everywhere	14	Whether or not legal frameworks are in place to promote, enforce, and monitor equality
Clean Water and Sanitation	8	By 2030, achieve universal and equitable access to safe and affordable drinking water for all	11	Proportion of population using safely managed drinking water services
Affordable and Clean Energy	5	By 2030, ensure universal access to affordable, reliable, and modern energy services	6	Proportion of population with access to electricity
Decent Work and Economic Growth	12	By 2030, devise and implement policies to promote sustainable tourism	16	Tourism direct GDP as a proportion of total GDP and in growth rate
Industry, Innovation, and Infrastructure	8	By 2030, upgrade infrastructure and retrofit industries to make them sustainable	12	CO_2 emission per unit of value added

GOAL	TARGETS #	TARGETS Example	INDICATORS #	INDICATORS Example
Reduced Inequalities	10	Adopt policies, especially fiscal, wage, and social protection policies	14	Redistributive impact of fiscal policy
Sustainable Cities and Communities	10	By 2030, ensure access for all to adequate, safe, and affordable housing and basic services	15	Proportion of urban population living in slums, informal settlements, or inadequate housing
Ensure Sustainable Consumption and Production Patterns	11	By 2030, achieve the sustainable management and efficient use of natural resources	13	Material footprint, material footprint per capita, and material footprint per GDP
Climate Action	5	Strengthen resilience and adaptive capacity to climate-related hazards and natural disasters in all countries	8	Deaths, missing persons, and directly affected persons attributed to disasters per 100,000 population
Life Below Water	10	Minimize and address the impacts of ocean acidification	10	Average marine acidity (pH) measured at agreed suite of representative sampling stations
Life on Land	12	By 2020, ensure the conservation, restoration, and sustainable use of freshwater ecosystems	14	Forest area as a proportion of total land area
Peace and Justice and Strong	12	By 2030, provide legal identity for all, including birth registration	24	Proportion of children under 5 years of age whose births have been registered with a civil authority
Partnerships for the Goals	19	Mobilize additional financial resources for developing countries from multiple sources	24	Volume of remittances (in United States dollars) as a proportion of total GDP

Are Nonpecuniary Objectives
Valid for Asset Managers?

The cornerstone of ESG investing is the provision of measurable nonpecuniary rewards to asset owners alongside the pecuniary rewards asset management has attempted to maximize during its entire history. This begs the question as to whether or not setting nonpecuniary objectives is even a valid goal, consistent with an asset manager's fiduciary responsibilities. After all, Erasmus recorded the ancient Roman adage "If you run after two hares, you will catch neither." By pursuing ethical goals simultaneous to pecuniary ones, are modern asset managers chasing two hares?

While this is the question that many in the asset management industry are asking themselves right now, I like to think the very premise of the question is mistaken.

The first reason for my desire to push back on the question is that the distinction between pecuniary and nonpecuniary rewards are, from an economic perspective, irrelevant. Economists focus their work on an unobservable and intangible concept of utility and the desire for people to maximize it. Money is often taken as a marker for utility, but one that does not completely capture it. There is good evidence to show that especially in the field of sustainable investments, asset owners prefer the broader goal of maximizing utility to solely maximizing financial returns. Theoretical models consider the implications of these nonpecuniary preferences in a variety of settings, yet these models start from a relatively untested assumption that nonpecuniary motives affect the allocation of capital in a way that reflects an intentional willingness to pay for impact. The evidence for the intentional willingness to pay for nonpecuniary characteristics of investments is compelling (Barber et al., 2021).

Rob Bauer, Tobias Ruof, and Paul Smeets conducted two field surveys with a pension fund that granted its members a real vote on its sustainable-investment policy (Bauer et al., 2021). In the first study, a majority (two-thirds) of the plan participants expressed willingness to support increased engagement with companies based on the selected SDGs.[7] In the second study, a majority again supported more sustainable investments when participants could see how the pension fund implemented an increased focus on sustainable investments (+44 percent engagement, +33 percent portfolio screening). Most participants responded that they held the belief that a greater focus on sustainability does not come at the expense of financial returns or that they were at least uncertain about the link between sustainability and return. However, even among those who did report the expectation of a reduction in financial returns, the majority still expressed a desire to invest pension money to promote sustainability. This suggests that the pensioners questioned held strong social preferences and derived utility by investing in such a way as to express those preferences through their investment activities.

This preference for ESG investments has been demonstrated time and again through different academic studies and—perhaps a more reliable indicator—through the enormous inflow of assets into ESG funds. Samuel Hartzmark and Abigail Sussman published a study in 2019 that found that funds that had been categorized as "low sustainability" by third-party ratings agencies experienced net outflows of more than $12 billion versus net inflows of more than $24 billion for funds categorized as "high sustainability" (Hartzmark & Sussman, 2019). What's more, the sustainability classification was completely unpredictive of subsequent returns—in other words, some of the $24 billion that flowed into high sustainability funds would have generated higher returns if they had instead been placed in low sustainability ones. Presumably, the investors can see the same data as the authors but keep their assets with the manager that is more accurately expressing their sustainability viewpoint.

Similarly, yet another indication of the power of social preference is that green bonds[8] will sell for a premium over their blander equivalents (in terms of risk) by around five basis points. While five basis points might not strike you as particularly significant, it suggests that green bonds are priced as if they had been assigned a credit rating that was a half-notch higher—in the world of fixed-income investing, this is a pretty big deal (Baker et al., 2022a).

Aside from this distinction between utility and pecuniary return, I question whether or not asset owners may in fact simply be acting in their own self-interest, just on a different time horizon than asset managers are operating. I'll discuss this more later when I touch on the concept of "risk," but I also want to offer an anecdote from the early twentieth century to show that asset owners are often taking real economic effects under consideration when issuers or managers think they are paying attention to something else entirely.

The example is that of the "Liberty Loans" that the US government sold during World War I to finance the bulk of American war expenditures. The secretary of the treasury at that time, William McAdoo, conceived of a brilliant plan that would boost demand for the war bonds while keeping yields (and hence subsequent interest payments) low. The brilliant, and in hindsight deeply cynical, plan was to aggressively "capitalize patriotism." He commissioned America's best-known artists to draw posters advertising the contribution that common people could make by buying war bonds and ran giant "bond rallies" complete with Hollywood stars (who presumably did not speak at the rallies, since this was in the era of silent movies) to convince people to accept low yields for their war bond investments. McAdoo also recruited everyone from Wall Street titans to Boy Scout troops to disperse his Liberty Loans.

Scholars have realized in hindsight that, despite McAdoo's appeal to patriotism, what really created the demand for the Liberty Loans was not the posters or the silent movie stars at the rallies, but instead it was (1) making income from the bonds tax exempt and (2) forcing the Federal Reserve to buy an enormous proportion of the bonds directly or indirectly (Hilt et al., 2021).[9]

This is to say that perhaps investors who are focused on sustainability metrics are actually tuned into "real" economic effects as the buyers of the war bonds were, and even if they are not, they are focused on investing in areas that will boost their utility, perhaps even at the expense of their pension savings.

Who are we as asset managers to say that asset owners are wrong?

CHALLENGES AND BENEFITS
OF ESG INVESTING

Now that we have established that ethical considerations make for valid investment goals and that ESG investing expresses true social preference by asset owners, let us now look more closely at the most important of the practical issues related to ESG.

From what we have seen, each element of ESG is very different in terms of investment considerations. While each of the letters—E, S, and G—show similarities in motivations, history, and original inspiration, each are very different in terms of investing policy.

Specifically, if we are to look at the three letters from a high-level perspective, I believe that the juice has already been squeezed out of the G-Governance orange in terms of investor ability to find excess returns. It is nice (and essential) to have "G" in the mix of an investing policy, but it seems that governance differences are already mostly priced into securities valuations.

The S-Social focus on investing is important—in some cases extremely important—to asset owners, and because it is, I believe that asset managers have a duty to offer products that will allow asset owners to express their convictions through their investment choices. The problem is that quantifying, measuring, then making asset allocation decisions on the basis of a company's "S" score is, in my opinion, years away if it can ever be done at all. I think there are ways for asset managers to help asset owners to invest according to the social convictions they hold, but the model for doing this goes against the way the asset management industry has long worked and may even cause frictions with our long-held concept of fiduciary responsibility.

E-Environmental issues are, I believe, the most critical ones for asset managers to proactively address, but they will also be some of the hardest to do so. Human impact on the earth's climate and biological systems has become so large and pervasive that we hold in our power the ability to destroy the productive capacity of the planet on which we all depend.

Our planet is maybe best described in the form of a complex adaptive system (CAS). These systems—also known as those exhibiting mathematical chaos—can change states very quickly and very permanently if and when they hit certain "tipping points." Unfortunately, modern finance is not well equipped to consider the effects of tipping points and—like all other sciences and semisciences—has a very difficult time of conceiving of CAS. The most basic concept of finance—time value of money—operates on an implicit assumption of continuity and gradual change. I have real questions whether discontinuous change to our environment can even be conceptually captured by the concept of "discount rate."

The topic of the "E" part of the ESG triad is so important, it will be a sole focus in Chapter 14.

Suffice it to say that if the asset management business does not take ecological and environmental investing seriously, our clients' returns may be fine, but our clients' children's returns will be irretrievably negative.

To sum up, of the three letters, E is the most practically important, S is tricky to implement but vital for asset owners to be able to express their investing opinion accurately, and G is largely already built into intelligent investing policies.

Measuring ESG Preferences

We can clearly see that asset owners seem to prefer investments in companies that score high on ESG measures even if they have to give up a little return to do so. The problem is that while asset managers have a good understanding of asset owners' risk preferences, this understanding is not as good for ESG preference.

Indeed, measuring ESG preference is still in its infancy, demonstrated by the fact that different ESG rating agencies sometimes rate the same company very differently.[10]

In addition to measurement problems, there appears to be a reluctance on the part of pension funds to survey beneficiaries for information about their ESG preferences. This reluctance might in part have to do with the suggestion that asking about ESG attitudes implicitly brings up a topic long thought to be out-of-bounds for polite conversation: politics.

Harrison Hong and Leonard Kostovetsky show that mutual fund managers who make campaign donations to the Democratic Party in the United States hold less of their portfolios in companies that are deemed socially irresponsible versus managers that make no donations or donate to the Republican Party (Hong & Kostovetsky, 2012). By "socially irresponsible," the academics meant companies whose primary business was the sale of tobacco, guns, or military items or those that had bad reputations regarding employee relations or hiring diversity.

It is hard to develop an investment policy if no one can agree on what metrics are meaningful!

ESG Investing to Control Risk

The most prominent argument regarding why ESG investing has merit is related to risk, namely that companies that score high on ESG-related measures will suffer less idiosyncratic risk in the future.

A vivid example of how idiosyncratic risk can be avoided through screening on ESG factors is that of Tokyo Electric Power Company (TEPCO), the operator of the Fukushima nuclear plant that was critically damaged in March 2011 by a large offshore earthquake and tsunami. Investors that screened out companies involved in nuclear power generation because of an ESG overlay would have been protected from financial loss after the Daiichi plant went offline and started to overheat.

The difficulty with this example and with ESG factors in general is knowing what factors will be the important ones to screen for and having the conviction to accept potentially lower returns for months, years, or decades due to the inherent uncertainties related to black swan events.

As someone trained in hard sciences with an understanding of the physics of climate change, I have long realized that the burning of fossil fuels is creating an imbalance in the global carbon cycle. As an investor with insight and foresight, I may have then sensibly decided back in January 2011 to invest solely in global nuclear and renewable generation sources. If I would have done this, I would have been "right" in my reasoning but would have suffered a loss on some part of my holdings due to my presumed ownership of TEPCO and its exposure to an unforeseeable, historically rare natural disaster in the form of a massive, megathrust earthquake.[11]

The example underscores well the difference between systematic and idiosyncratic risk. The TEPCO disaster is idiosyncratic and can be diversified away. The former—climate change—cannot be diversified away, so we must start to factor in the possibility of all companies being affected to one extent or another by a global ecological crisis brought about by climate change.

As the effects of climate change become more severe, some businesses will do better than others. A construction firm that bids for contracts to harden infrastructure against rising sea levels will likely experience a boost in business, while a company manufacturing ski boots may suffer, for instance.

However, if and when the planet reaches some critical climactic tipping points that negatively affect agricultural production or the ability for resource-rich countries to maintain the infrastructure needed to bring their raw materials to market, all companies who have workers who eat or use assets made from raw materials will begin to be negatively impacted. This is the systematic risk that cannot be avoided, even using the best ESG metric.

This realization forces asset managers to start thinking more about investing in assets that might be expected to be negatively correlated in an environment of extensive climactic disruption—climate hedges, in other words. For instance, Richard Roll's famous weather hedge—orange juice futures—might be a good instrument to do that (Roll, 1984). But such hedging transactions open an asset manager to idiosyncratic risk, and that risk may fail to pay off in a time frame that is helpful to the manager's clients (or the manager's career).

In fact, common asset pricing logic suggests that the exposure to idiosyncratic hedging risk is avoided by paying with lower expected returns in the future.

ESG Investing to Generate Returns

We have seen that investors value the perceived utility of ESG investments to the extent that they will forgo some monetary returns. Given this observation, a reasonable question to ask is: "How much are investors willing to pay for the impact of their ESG investments?" There are two ways of answering this question: one is by comparing the fees of ESG and non-ESG mutual funds, and another is to compare the performance of ESG investing with traditional approaches.

From a fee comparison perspective, Malcolm Baker and his colleagues published an NBER working paper in December of 2022 that found investors willing to pay 20 basis points per year more to be invested in a fund with an ESG mandate compared to a comparable fund without the ESG mandate (Baker et al., 2022b). There are two ways to read this fee difference based on the premises we suggested earlier: either investors believe that the ESG investments are worth 20 basis points of unobservable utility to themselves, or they expect that future returns are going to be commensurately higher.

Performance comparison of ESG funds is more challenging, simply due to the difficulties inherent in analyzing investment performance. Analyzing performance, a researcher needs to take into account a wide variety of factors from investment approach, research frameworks, definition of metrics and benchmarks, data quality, sample period, fees, and so on. It is a truly daunting task to do well.

ESG investing adds yet another complication to the analysis. Namely, because there is no single agreed-upon definition of the characteristics of ESG investing; funds that are counted in the same ESG peer group may have very different investment objectives.

ESG funds have been around for a long time—they existed as far back as the 1990s, when I was just joining the investing business as an "ESG analyst"—so it is not as if there is a paucity of data. Even still, there has been no clear sign to date that ESG investing has provided superior returns with respect to conventional, actively managed funds.

My personal thought is that ESG investing during the early years of the field probably did lead to superior investment performance. However, the effects of the clean-tech boom-bust cycle in the early 2000s, as well as an increasing recognition of the importance of ESG factors, are making it more difficult to generate alpha in this area now.

Meeting Societal Preferences: The Climate Challenge

I started my professional life as an environmental chemist but could not find a job to save my life. When I eventually switched career paths, took a PhD in finance, and began working in the asset management business, the term *ESG* did not even exist. Today, the trickiest hires are invariably environmental scientists with good numeracy and data analysis skills. Environmental issues touch so many aspects of a potential investment on both the risk and reward side, so people who understand the technical details represent valuable fonts of talent. It is amazing to see how much has changed in such a short time!

A fundamental switch this fast is exactly what one would expect when living through the beginning of a wave of globally converging societal preferences. And environmental concerns are and will be on the top of the agenda for humanity's future—whether you like it or not. Asset managers will inevitably have to get a good grip on how to integrate these issues in their investment process. This chapter explains why.

EARLY ENVIRONMENTAL DISASTERS

In the twenty-first century, the biggest environmental concerns are global: climate change and ecosystem diversity loss. However, historically, environmental problems had been local rather than global.

Because of the high population density of Japan, which is exacerbated by the fact that arable floodplains suitable for population centers are relatively scarce on the mountainous archipelago, some of the first recognized cases of environmental pollution causing human illness were recorded there. These are known in Japan as "four major pollution diseases."

Of these four, the first to be recognized was "itai-itai" disease.[1] In 1912, farmers in rural areas bordering the Jinzu River in Toyama Prefecture, Japan, began complaining of debilitating pain, bone fractures, skeletal deformities, anemia, and kidney disorders. The source of the Jinzu River lies in the mountains of Gifu Prefecture to the south, which had been recognized for centuries for its rich mines. Mining activity picked up at the turn of the twentieth century to support a domestic military buildup prior to the Russo-Japanese War and to supply the Allies during World War I. In 1910, cadmium, a mining byproduct that is toxic to animal life, began being released upstream. The toxic water was used to flood rice fields and for drinking, bathing, and washing and also affected riverine fish eaten by the farmers.

For years, locals believed the painful condition was caused by a bacterial infection, but as military demands for metals increased before and during World War II, greater quantities of cadmium were released, sickening more people. In 1946, doctors recognized itai-itai disease as a condition separate from bacterial infection, but it was a decade before a Japanese doctor pinpointed the cause of the condition to cadmium poisoning originating from the Mitsui Mining and Smelting Company's mines in Gifu. The Japanese government—renowned for its close and supportive relationship to large industrial concerns—recognized a causal connection between the mining pollution upstream and itai-itai disease only in 1968 and only finally settled with victims of the condition in 2013—101 years after the initial complaints were recorded.

Itai-itai disease and other pollution-related conditions (Minamata disease and Niigata Minamata disease—both cases of methylmercury poisoning—and Yokkaichi asthma—caused by heavy oil-fired power generation plants without Sarbanes-Oxely Act controls) during the period of Japan's rapid industrialization in the 1960s underscore the myriad problems of environmental pollution, in addition to the toll on human lives and well-being. Symptoms may be reported but are misattributed to other causes, true causal links with pollutants and facilities may take a long time to be scientifically established and longer to be legally recognized, and cleanup and remediation efforts are costly, complex, and large-scale.

While Japan was the first country to recognize the deleterious effects of industrial pollution on human health and was thus the first to have to deal with the legal and public safety repercussions, it was certainly not the last. The list of disasters is frustratingly inexhaustible.

Shock over the Japanese accidents and others around the world resulted in the drafting of the Rio Declaration on Environment and Development, adopted at the 1992 UN Earth Summit. The Rio Declaration is a summation of lessons learned from the impact of environmental damage worldwide. The fifteenth principle in the Declaration applies particularly to itai-itai disease in that it states that "where there are threats of serious or irreversible damage, lack of full scientific certainty shall not be used as a reason for postponing cost-effective measures to prevent environmental degradation."

This principle is remarkable in that it shifts the burden of proof to the polluter rather than to the party claiming damage and filing suit. This shift of the burden of proof should tend to focus corporate interests on prevention in cases where the science is not yet definitive. The notion that protective measures may be adopted in the face of significant uncertainties surrounding the likelihood or magnitude of potential risks is wonderful in principle, but as we have seen from everything from smoking to climate change, corporate pressure groups often point to "scientific uncertainty" to maintain a franchise in businesses that are well understood to be causing damage to human health or the ecosystem.

THE TRAGEDY OF THE COMMONS

In all industrial pollution cases to date, there have been a small number of people who are directly and severely affected. The legal answer to this situation is clear—the affected people can file a lawsuit and force the polluting entity to bear the cost of remediating the damage caused and paying compensation to the victims.[2]

These cases, while tragic, are limited to distinct regions and to a relatively small number of people. However, more and more, we are coming to understand that some environmental issues are inherently global in scale. The "tragedy of the commons" is a term used to describe a situation in which individual entities undertake legal, self-interested actions that are rational from the perspective of the entity, but which end up damaging the interests of the community (or humanity) and which are thus irrational from a collective standpoint. These situations arise when a resource—such as a bay or an ocean basin or our atmosphere—is not owned by any single entity but instead is used communally by a group. Each member of the group receives the benefit of access to that resource whether or not they contribute to the value of the resource. An actor who receives the benefits of a resource without paying for it is known in economics as a free rider.

An illustration of the tragedy of the commons issue that has ended up affecting political and commercial policy and prompting widespread social interest in ecological issues is that of the insecticide dichloro-diphenyl-trichloroethane (DDT). DDT was first formulated by an Austrian scientist in the mid-1870s, but its use as an insecticide was only discovered in the late 1930s by Dr. Paul Müller, a Swiss scientist. During World War II, DDT was hailed as a miracle chemical that could be used to quickly wipe out populations of malarial mosquitoes in the South Pacific and delouse military troops in Europe. Its most useful feature was that while it appeared safe to humans, it was instantly toxic to insects—making it a perfect solution for insect infestations.

DDT was approved for civilian use after the war, and it came under widespread use in the United States, both in agricultural settings and in mosquito-prone urban and suburban areas. Within several years, cases of malaria in the United States had disappeared and Dr. Müller had been awarded the Nobel Prize in Physiology and Medicine for his discovery.

While moderate DDT exposure did not seem to have deleterious effects on humans, DDT had a hidden quality that became apparent only after years of repeated exposure. Namely, once ingested, DDT is stored in fat cells within an animal. When another animal eats an animal with DDT in its fat, the predator also ends up storing the DDT in its fat. This process is termed *bioaccumulation* or *biomagnification*, and its effects can be very great from the standpoint of an ecological community.

In 1962, a former marine biologist for the US Fish and Wildlife service, Rachel Carson, published the book *Silent Spring*, which investigated the ecological repercussions of synthetic pesticides in general and the effects of DDT spraying in particular. In the book—meant to evoke the image of a world without birdsong due to ecosystem degradation—Carson writes about the mysterious death of birds and livestock after aerial DDT spraying and suggests that chemical companies had misrepresented the safety of various synthetic pesticides. The book was serialized in the influential magazine the *New Yorker*, and excerpts of it were also published by the Audubon Society—one of the oldest nonprofit environmental organizations.

While the book garnered a great deal of public interest on its own, its effect on the political environment in the United States was made more profound by the fact that DDT ended up threatening the US national bird, the bald eagle, with extinction. Due to its bioaccumulation, the effects of DDT are magnified for predator species and especially for the top predator species that feed on other predators. Accumulated DDT ended up changing the chemical composition of bald eagle eggs, making them brittle and easily broken, leading to a precipitous fall in the majestic bird's population. In the 1950s, there was a point at which the bald eagle population in the continental United States had fallen to a few thousand.

To bring this anecdote about DDT back to the discussion of the tragedy of the commons, let us consider a farmer spraying DDT on his crops to cut down on loss due to insect infestations. To the farmer, buying the relatively cheap chemical that's easy to apply to his fields makes perfect sense. If his yield increases by a few percentage points, he will have generated enough revenues to pay for several applications of DDT, so his economic self-interest is clearly to apply DDT. On the other hand, if we think about the population of bald eagles as a shared resource, every additional application of DDT increases the stress upon this resource. The eagles have little or no economic value from the farmer's perspective, but as the symbol of the United States have an enormous cultural value to the wider society.

The publication of *Silent Spring* brought ecological issues into the world of politics. And while Carson had not called for the banning of DDT, within 10 years, DDT was not only banned from use in the United States, but a new executive agency, the Environmental Protection Agency (EPA), was established to help research and regulate similar environmentally impactful industrial products or byproducts. *Silent Spring* provided the spark that ignited the fuel of public opinion to turn the gears of government.

FROM ENVIRONMENTAL DISASTERS TO A GLOBAL TRAGEDY

As broad of an effect that DDT had on ecosystems, its global effect was limited due to its chemical nature. DDT is preserved in fat molecules, which means that after it is sprayed, it is effectively locked into the physiology of the species living in the area over which it was applied. This "locking" feature is not the case for volatile organic compounds (VOCs) such as carbon dioxide or methane. "Volatile" means that a substance has a very low boiling point, so it is found as a gas unless specially processed. When VOCs are released, they act as any gas does—spreading evenly throughout whatever container into which they are released, whether that container is a lab beaker or the atmosphere. This quality of room temperature and pressure volatility means that any effect of releasing a VOC into the atmosphere is going to be global, since the atmosphere covers the entire globe.

The first political consideration related to an industrial pollution incident with global repercussions was that of chlorofluorocarbons (CFCs) and their effect on the ozone layer. CFCs are one class of VOC that was used commercially in chemical refrigerants, aerosol propellants, and solvents. Once released, CFCs drift into the atmosphere and chemically react with ozone molecules in an area of the lower stratosphere where ozone concentrations are at their highest.

The ozone layer absorbs all but 1 to 3 percent of the sun's medium-frequency ultraviolet light. Because life on earth evolved with low exposure to these frequencies of solar radiation, a lowered concentration of atmospheric ozone threatens the lives of plants and animals living close to the earth's surface. A reduction in stratospheric ozone concentrations was discovered in the mid-1970s, and this discovery led to bans of CFCs for certain applications, but not all. In 1985, a group of scientists discovered that, in contrast to relatively modest declines of ozone in mid-latitudes, millions of square miles of area around the poles had experienced extreme reductions of nearly 50 percent. The realization that ozone-depleting chemicals were causing such severe damage to the ozone layer and had the potential for disrupting life worldwide led to both the United States and Britain supporting a phase-down and phase-out of these chemicals. The phase-out schedule was agreed as part of the 1987

Montreal Protocol and has since been agreed upon by all the countries in the world.

The good news is that since the bans were put into place, the depletion of the ozone layer has slowed significantly. In January 2023, the United Nations reported the successful phase-out of 99 percent of ozone-depleting chemicals and projected that concentrations of ozone in the ozone layer would return to their 1980 values by midcentury, though recovery for the Antarctic region would take relatively longer due to the very severe depletion occurring there (United Nations, 2023).

There are a few important takeaways from our close call with the ozone layer.

First, we can clearly see the difference between global ecological damage caused by volatile substances compared to the local damage inflicted by chemicals like DDT. But the ecological differences are not the only ones. Because the problems associated with VOCs are inherently global, legal negotiations and agreements had to take place at the international level, rather than at a state or national one. The Montreal Protocol treated the responsibility of developing nations differently than that of developed ones—with the latter responsible for a much more rapid phase-out than the former (under the theory that developed nations had greater resources to bring to bear on the problem and had been the chief sources of the problem in the first place).

Second, it's interesting to see how large a difference in effect can be caused by a relatively dilute atmospheric concentration of a given molecule. Climate change deniers often talk about how paltry of a share carbon dioxide makes up in the atmosphere (historically around 280 ppm versus around 420 ppm now) without admitting that the depletion of the even more diffuse molecule ozone (around 10 ppm on average) has necessitated a worldwide all-hands-on-deck emergency siren.

Last, it's nice to see that, at least on this one topic, it seems like international coordination, agreement, and action is possible.

THE CHALLENGE OF A CHANGING CLIMATE

Today, without a doubt the most severe, pressing, and publicly debated environmental topic is climate change. The chemistry and physics of climate change is well-understood after over 100 years of peer-reviewed academic studies and studies from industry scientists that were pointedly *not* exposed to the peer-review process, but come to the same (dire) conclusions.[3]

There is so much high-quality information about the science of climate change that I will not address the physical effects here. Suffice it to say that for an analyst who is used to gleaning information about trends by looking at graphical representations of data, seeing a chart with this clear of an anomalous pattern is enough to stop one in one's tracks (Figure 14.1).

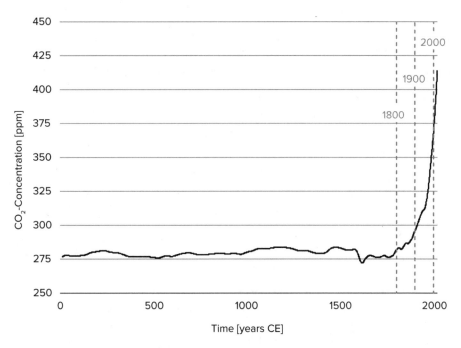

FIGURE 14.1 Long-term Keeling Curve

Source: Data from UCSD and Scripps Institution of Oceanography.

Atmospheric carbon dioxide is one of the important drivers of the earth's climactic temperature regulation process, acting as a comfy blanket that keeps surface temperatures in the "just right" temperature range that has allowed such a wonderful diversity of plant and animal species to evolve on this planet.

Agriculture, the basis for our advanced civilization, developed around 10,000 years ago as the last Ice Age's glaciers retreated back to the poles. Glacial retreat allowed more liquid water to be freed up for plant growth and opened up much more land for cultivation; milder temperatures created conditions much more supportive of larger populations of plants and animals.

The level of atmospheric carbon dioxide stayed at a level between 250 ppm and 280 ppm from the start of agriculture until the Second Industrial Revolution. From that time forward, the combustion of coal and subsequently of oil pushed many trillions of tons' worth of additional carbon dioxide into the atmosphere. The proportion of carbon dioxide now in the atmosphere is around 420 ppm. I don't think one needs arcane knowledge to know that if you pull nearly twice the number of blankets over you when you are in bed, you will warm up.

The geophysical theory predicting my simple blanket insight was first discovered 200 years ago in 1824, and the first experimental verification of the theory—now termed the "greenhouse effect"—occurred about a quarter century after that. For many years, the volume of the atmosphere seemed so vast and our inputs into it so small, no one paid much attention to the possible repercussions of unrestrained and unmitigated burning of fossil fuels. But as the first wave of societal preference (industrialization) met with the second wave of societal preference (consumerization), the amounts of carbon dioxide entering into the atmosphere started to become material and geophysicists started to get worried.

The first scientific papers on the topic of greenhouse gas emissions and atmospheric warming appeared in the 1970s, and economists started talking about the potential economic effects around the same time.

THE ECONOMICS OF CLIMATE CHANGE

Limits to Growth—the gloomy study written by Donna Meadows and colleagues mentioned in the last chapter—was published in 1972. The conclusions reached by the *Limits to Growth* team were difficult for policymakers to swallow: the business-as-usual approach to natural resource exploitation would soon reach hard, physical limits. Even today, the *Limits to Growth* message is a difficult one to hear: finite systems cannot grow indefinitely and tend to crash when growth outpaces resource availability.

Despite the fact that the computers used in the *Limits to Growth* study were primitive and the study was forced to simplify modeled interdependencies as a result, I believe the multidisciplinary approach used by the Meadows' team was correct, and the subsequent reanalysis using the *Limits to Growth* conceptual framework demonstrates the original team was indeed on the right track. Environmental issues are exceedingly complex—requiring an understanding of physics, biology, chemistry, and social sciences—so do not lend themselves well to single-discipline analyses. Suffice it to say, though, that the conviction to tackle environmental issues in an interdisciplinary way did not prevail in the 1970s.

Thanks to the "inconvenient" conclusions, the complexity in solving global environmental issues and the continuation of societal preferences for consumerism, the policy sphere did not pick up the topic; the *Limits to Growth* was largely dismissed in the 1970s and 1980s and was totally forgotten by the time the 1990s rolled around. And I am afraid to say that essentially humanity lost a generation's worth of potential policy discussions and response regarding natural resource use and pollution as a result.

The 1990s saw another important advance in theory of the economics of climate change with the publication of a model describing the economic effects of climate change. The model was called the Dynamic Integrated Climate-Economy (DICE) model and was published by the 2018 Nobel laureate William Nordhaus.

In contrast to the gloomy *Limits to Growth* model, Nordhaus's DICE model showed something that policymakers and captains of industry could really get behind. Its conclusions were that the economic effects of climate change will be minimal and will only have an impact many years in the future.

As for the first part of that summary—that the economic effects will be minimal—Nordhaus's model's base assumptions raise plenty of eyebrows in the climate science community. His ideas of an "optimal" temperature rise are so high that climate scientists doubt that widespread agriculture will be able to be practiced, for instance. His model's climate change conclusions—were they to represent a purely theoretical finding—might make for the centerpiece of an interesting and lively academic debate at a conference room at Yale. However, due to the reputation of the institution from which Nordhaus hails and the strength of his own reputation among economists, his ideas are considered authoritative and have had a powerful effect on policymakers' thinking (see Box 14.1).

BOX 14.1 The Predictions of the DICE Model

William Nordhaus's DICE model (Nordhaus, 1992) became the go-to economic modeling tool used by government agencies in the United States (the EPA uses the model to calculate its social cost of carbon—SCC) and by international organizations.

The DICE model is structured along a circular flow. It basically models the circular connection of CO_2 emissions to climate, from climate to impacts, from impacts to policies, and closing the circle from policies to CO_2 emissions.

This circular flow needs to be parametrized and quantified. For example, economic activity is linked to emissions of CO_2, the concentration of CO_2 in the atmosphere is linked to the global temperature, and the global temperature is linked to an impact on the global ecosystem as well as the global economy. And if that circularity is not enough, the societal responses to climate change also need to be factored in.

The DICE model has the mathematical form of a constrained non-linear dynamic optimization model with an infinite horizon. This means it maximizes the discounted utility of consumption for the world population subject to complex constraints specified using exogenous variables such as the world population and given parameters such as climate sensitivity. In total, around 20 equations represent the circular flow model and optimization calculus previously described.

As you can tell by this overview description, all in all, it is a tricky model that is hard to digest in its entirety. Rather than working through the details, I think it's better to focus on the big picture and the message.

In a simplified economic language, the DICE model estimates the future economic output taking into account abatement costs—costs associated with removing negative environmental impacts on production—and climate change damages.

The most relevant variable in the model is the price of CO_2—think of the price as a tax or a cap on CO_2 emissions. The lower/higher the price, the higher/lower the emission, the more/less global warming, the higher/lower the abatement costs and climate change damages. The DICE model is designed to allow users to find the optimal price of CO_2—the CO_2 price that produces the highest discounted utility of consumption, in other words.

According to Nordhaus the optimal SCC is very close to the SCC of the base scenario (i.e., the business-as-usual case). Consequently, GDP projections in the optimal case do not differ greatly between the optimal and the base scenario. Obviously, this is surprisingly unrealistic.[4]

Let me explain my thinking by starting with a quote out of William Nordhaus's Nobel lecture in 2018 describing the results of the DICE model (Nordhaus, 2019): "The base path (which is essentially the path the globe is following) continues to have rising temperature, passing 4°C by 2100."

But what does Nordhaus's base path of 4°C by 2100 mean in reality? The World Bank describes the direct and indirect effects of 4°C as the following (The World Bank, 2012).

Direct consequences will be that extreme heat waves become normal (from now once in several hundred years to every year) and the sea level will rise up to one meter leaving many cities located in Mozambique, Madagascar, Mexico, Venezuela, India, Bangladesh, Indonesia, the Philippines, and Vietnam, as well as many small islands, very vulnerable to flooding.

Indirect consequences are even more severe. Impacts that will come together in the areas of agriculture, water resources, human health, biodiversity, and ecosystem will consequently lead to large-scale displacement of populations and jeopardize the stability of established political and economic systems. This all paints a dark picture.

In sum, the effects of 4°C are extremely disruptive no matter how you look at it.

A future conforming to the base scenario of the DICE model will irretrievably change the world we live in. How this world will look is simply unknown, but I (and a lot of scientists and economists) believe it will have catastrophic economic effects.

One other way to try to understand the amplitude of change of a 4°C increase is a look way back in the past of the earth. According to climate scientists, the average global temperature during the last ice age, the Last Glacial Maximum, was about 6°C cooler than today (Tierney et al., 2020). Back then, around 20,000 years ago, massive layers of icy glaciers stretched across the globe, covering around a quarter of the earth's land while woolly mammoths and giant ground sloths roamed the remaining land.

It looks like assuming a 4°C rise will allow for an almost unchanged economy from the one we enjoy now is dangerously risky.

With respect to this model risk, the conclusion of "The Stern Review: The Economics of Climate Change" (Stern, 2006) is probably the safer bet for the generations to come: "Using the results from formal economic models, the Review estimates that if we don't act, the overall costs and risks of climate change will be equivalent to losing at least 5% of global GDP each year, now and forever."

The second part of the summary—that any effects will occur far in the future—provides the ammunition for policymakers to hold off on taking mitigation steps for many years and forms the basis of an argument around discount rates to which I hinted in the last chapter.

The fundamental rule of finance is that future cash flows are worth less than present ones—known as the time value of money. Working from this fundamental principle, if climate change effects will be small and the cash flow impacts will occur far in the future, the discounted value of those effects on taxpayers and consumers brought back to the current day are negligible. In contrast, the cash outflows in the present day related to capital improvements designed to mitigate climate change (e.g., altering current industrial infrastructure to either avoid the use of fossil fuels or capture any carbon dioxide emissions that result from their combustion) are enormous. Comparing the large present cash outflows to the tiny future benefits, no one in their right mind would allocate public or private money to climate-change mitigation efforts.

Thanks to the fact that Nordhaus's "Don't Worry, Be Happy" message was seized upon by conservative businesspeople, combined with what can only be described as a massive disinformation campaign by companies whose profits flowed from the mining, refining, and sales of fossil fuel–based products, essentially another decade and a half of mitigation potential was lost in the 1990s and the early 2000s.[5]

In 2006, former US Vice President Al Gore starred in a documentary entitled *An Inconvenient Truth*—a multimedia version of a presentation Gore had been making regarding the science of climate change. Gore's lecture series and the film based on it captured the attention of audiences in the United States and Europe, and Gore's role as a former top-level politician added gravitas to the message.

That same year, Sir Nicholas Stern published a massive, 700-page report entitled "The Stern Review: The Economics of Climate Change" at the request of UK Chancellor of the Exchequer, Gordon Brown. While the report was commissioned by Her Majesty's Government, the report covered the economic impacts of climate change worldwide.

The Review's broad-brush perspective is that climate change is the greatest and widest-ranging market failure ever seen and one that presents a unique challenge for economics. Its conclusion is 180 degrees from that of Nordhaus's—namely, Stern found that the benefits of strong, coordinated, and early action to mitigate the effects of climate change far outweigh the costs of delaying action.

Whereas Nordhaus's DICE model analysis projected a truly trivial discounted cost to climate change effects, Stern found that without action, the overall costs of climate change would be material (best case) to catastrophic (worst case). Specifically, Stern's calculations estimated that continuing a business-as-usual emission posture would, best case, cost the world the equivalent of at least 5 percent and, worst case, 20 percent of global GDP *per year* from 2006 through perpetuity.

I won't opine on which model is more correct but will point out that after the IPCC's (Intergovernmental Panel on Climate Change) fourth Assessment Report was published in 2007, the United Nations decided to abandon Nordhaus's DICE model to forecast economic effects for future reports.

The problem with the Gore-Stern/politics-economics one-two punch was that—even though both men were basing their conclusions on sound science—the individuals presenting the conclusions were both supporters of left-of-center political parties (Democratic Party for Gore, Labour Party for Stern). In the United States and the United Kingdom, the right-of-center parties turned the issue of climate change from a scientifically proven threat to all humanity to a partisan ploy to increase the overweening interference in free markets by effete intellectuals at the expense of common people's jobs and the semisacred dictum of national self-determination.

Only within the last few years has mass public support started to (slowly) incentivize politicians to take more active measures restricting emissions. In 2015, the Paris Agreement was adopted by 196 countries worldwide, all of which agreed on a goal of maintaining global average temperatures well below 2°C (3.6°F) above preindustrial levels and preferably below 1.5°C (2.7°F). The agreement formalizes the understanding that emissions should be reduced as soon as possible and reach net-zero by the middle of this century. It also aims at developing mechanisms to mobilize the financial resources necessary to reduce emissions so rapidly; in order, for example, to be on track for only a 1.5°C increase, the world would have to cut emissions by 50 percent by 2030.

Even though the political will appears to be in place, making such drastic, rapid changes to our industrial and commercial infrastructure creates a host of logistical issues.

For instance, in a 2019 paper by Söhnke Bartram, Kewei Hou, and Sehoon Kim entitled "Real Effects of Climate Policy: Financial Constraints and Spillovers," the researchers found that even when one jurisdiction implemented greenhouse gas emission restrictions, corporations would engage in "regulatory arbitrage" (i.e., moving to a jurisdiction with less restrictive regulations), creating what is known as the "spillover" effect (Bartram et al., 2019). The dreary conclusion of the group's detailed study of California's cap-and-trade program was that "overall, [wealthier] firms do not reduce their total emissions, whereas [less wealthy ones] increase their total emissions [N.B. by moving to another state], undermining the effectiveness of the policy."

Between dueling economic projections from left- and right-of-center economists, intense political lobbying by fossil fuel interests, and the politicization of scientific findings that have been vetted for 200 years, we have ended up wasting the opportunity to put mitigation policies in place for nearly another generation.[6]

HOW CAN ASSET MANAGERS HELP?

Pulling up the forward price-to-earnings ratio of US retailer Walmart today, I get a value of around 20 times. This means that Walmart's stock price is 20 times what analysts expect it to earn over the next 12 months. Put another way, next year's earnings only make up 5 percent (1/20) of the value of the stock. The remaining 95 percent of the value of the stock price is associated with the idea that Walmart will continue to generate earnings growth in perpetuity.

Considering that the Stern Review is projecting an annual GDP *decline* of anywhere from 5 to 20 percent from now through the end of time, one cannot help but feel a sense of cognitive dissonance when seeing the implicit market assumption that Walmart is going to *expand* its earnings a few percentage points per year in perpetuity. How is that going to work, I wonder? Even if you do not accept Stern's economic projections into infinity, one look at what the science says we can expect over the next 50 years (close enough to "perpetuity" from a financial economics standpoint), one still starts to think that *ceteris paribus* either Walmart's revenues will fall, its costs will increase, or both—any of which situations would lead to shrinking profits.

What are scientists forecasting? Increased flooding, unlivable wet-bulb temperatures in the tropics, increasing sea levels, increasing numbers of tropical cyclones, crop failures due to drought and/or destructively severe rainfall patterns, increasing ocean acidification, and perhaps even increased levels of crime are all on the menu of the climate change café.

Hard to forecast eternally rising profits in an environment like that.

What are asset managers saying? According to a survey by Philipp Krueger, Zacharias Sautner, and Laura Starks about climate risk perceptions published in February 2020,[7] institutional investors believe climate risks have financial implications for companies in their portfolios and that these risks, particularly those related to regulatory matters, have already started to materialize (Krueger et al.,

2020). Many investors, especially the long-term, larger, and specifically ESG-oriented ones consider risk management and corporate engagement (i.e., more activism à la Blackrock's Larry Fink's letters) to be more effective strategies than divestment.

Another survey by Johannes Stroebel and Jeffrey Wurgler of 861 finance academics, professionals, public sector regulators, and policy economists published in 2021 shows similar results (Stroebel & Wurgler, 2021). These respondees mentioned regulatory risk as the most important over the next 5 years, but view physical risk as the top concern over the next 30 years. This group also believes that "asset prices underestimate climate risks rather than overestimate them."

Whether regulatory risk or the financial impact of climate change on companies will force asset managers to include climate change in their investment decisions, climate change as a topic is here to stay and will undoubtfully become one, if not the most, of the relevant drivers of societal preferences in the decades to come. For asset managers ready for future success, climate change must be a reality today.

So how can asset managers contribute?

Asset managers must first accept the idea that the third wave of societal preference—a preference for sustainability—is rising. With the present mania for ESG, this should not be a hard pill for my fellow asset managers to swallow. Even though I have mixed views about the impact of "S" and "G" factors, as mentioned in the last chapter, my unalloyed conviction of the critical importance of the environmental factor plus pure considerations of valuation such as those mentioned in my preceding Walmart example make me think that "E" will soon be recognized among the investing community as widely as it has been among the larger society.

Many asset owners are deeply concerned about climate change and are seeking investments in companies that offer mitigation and adaptation technologies and services. The problem is that publicly traded securities of companies in this sector are still hard to find. The SPAC phenomenon in the 2020–2022 period did result in the listing of a few climate tech companies such as New Zealand–US company LanzaTech. LanzaTech has developed a commercial solution to solve the carbon footprint issue related to steel, nonferrous metals, oil refining, and even municipal solid waste using bioreactors containing genetically engineered anaerobic bacteria that consume carbon molecules and excrete carbon-negative commodity chemicals used in a myriad of common consumer products and that can even be converted to carbon negative jet fuel.

But the number of listed sustainability companies like LanzaTech is small, their market capitalizations are tiny, and the floats of their stocks are limited. There is a larger pool of private climate tech companies, but investments in these firms are mainly restricted to institutions and HNW investors.

I believe that the asset management industry, working as financial intermediaries, has the capacity to solve this problem by transforming liquidity and risk and bringing investments in hybrid public-private portfolios to the wider investing world. To do this, though, regulations also need to be altered because most countries' securities laws prevent nonaccredited investments in privately held firms.

During the dot.com boom, I saw firsthand the extent to which capital flowing into an industry could radically transform it, creating a powerful and self-sustaining virtuous cycle of capital flowing to the best ideas, the best ideas flourishing and changing the world, only to attract more capital.

Today, in the first quarter of what I believe will be the most important century for the entirety of human history, we desperately need to create such a virtuous cycle around sustainable infrastructure, transportation, communications, and consumer goods.

PART IV

A Moral Imperative for Asset Managers

A Vision for the Future of the Asset Management Industry

We have covered a good bit of ground in this book—charting out a map of the asset management industry, describing the driving forces that have created the structure we see today, and looking at what I believe are the four important areas that asset managers must concentrate on during the later three-fourths of the twenty-first century.

Having read this far, you must have a good idea of my vision of the future, but allow me a few pages to spell things out explicitly.

Asset management must change to address the most pressing matters of human civilization and to alter humanity's fate for the better. Asset managers must find a way to draw the best and brightest talent to the industry if the human civilization that has been painstakingly constructed over the past 100 centuries is to survive and progress into the next one.

We must, above all, shift our focus away from outmoded models to one that truly serves asset owners and society at large.

WE MUST STOP CLINGING TO THE ACTIVE-PASSIVE DICHOTOMY

The passive approach, pioneered by John Bogle at Vanguard nearly 50 years ago, has served two important purposes. Namely, it has shown over and over how terribly difficult it is for an active manager to add value to an asset owner, and it has vividly demonstrated the importance of lowering fees.

Passive investing has done a great service to the industry and continues to serve an important role in helping determine which purportedly active managers truly possess investing skill and which ones are phoning it in from the yacht club.

The enormous problem with passive investing has not yet become apparent, however, and this weakness represents the mother of all blind spots. Passive investing works well as one wave of societal preferences are building and heading toward a peak. As explained in Chapter 13, the societal preference for consumerism began building in the 1950s and 1960s and displaced the preference for industrialism sometime in the early 1970s. The most prominent positions of the most famous investor in the world—Warren Buffett—perfectly reflect the societal preference for consumerism. Buffett, who began to be recognized as an important investor in the 1960s, built his reputation largely on the strength of positions in the products and services under great demand in a consumerist society: See's Candies, Coca-Cola, American Express, Disney, and the property and casualty insurer Geico.

I would argue that Buffet's portfolio of consumer-focused investments outperformed the passive index not only because of his added leverage from the insurance company "float," as described in a prior chapter, but also because the index always looks backward. The index, therefore, contained industrial names that capped returns as societal preferences shifted to consumerism.

The fact is that during times of a paradigm shift, making decisions based on what one sees in the rearview mirror is a great way to hit a wall. I believe we should take the lessons that passive investing has taught us about fees and about the rarity of true investment talent and incorporate those into a model that really works.

The one thing that I will say is that it is not only asset managers who must make this conceptual shift. The role of regulators will also become very important. Regulations are not the types of theoretical constructs usually associated with the adjectives "creative" or "nimble" (and with good reason), but I believe that to the extent possible regulators must acknowledge the necessity of change and adapt to a world that understands that paradigms are shifting. Regulating the excesses of the last crisis will not help prevent the disasters of the next one.

WE MUST SHIFT TO A WORKABLE FRAMEWORK

Throughout Part III, I have laid out a framework for the asset management business that relies upon the first principle of acting as an effective financial intermediary. I believe that the asset managers who are relentless in their execution of this model and who build organizations based upon this model will win and those who cling to the frameworks of the path will inevitably lose.

To win the century and help—without hyperbole or lack of seriousness—save civilization as we know it, asset managers must achieve laserlike focus on the following four elements:

1. Lowering the cost of investing
2. Better enabling and enhancing investment risk sharing
3. Lowering information asymmetry between owners and managers
4. Serving societal preferences

Managers who accomplish the above best and most quickly will win. Those who do not, will lose.

An important nuance is that due to regional differences in regulation, savings vehicles, and societal preferences, I believe that progress along these lines will be lumpy from jurisdiction to jurisdiction.

For example, in the United States the onus of responsibility for building retirement savings is placed much more on the individual than in Europe or Asia. In the United States, most people save using 401(k) or individual retirement accounts (IRAs), whereas in Europe and Asia, savings mechanisms are much more geared toward institutional investors like pensions. The difference in the importance of the asset manager and of the relative financial literacy of each set of owners will invariably mean that development along the lines I have specified will proceed at different rates in Asia, Europe, and the United States.

Regulators in different countries also move at different speeds and operate according to different social norms and preferences. An excellent example of this phenomenon is the difference in sustainable investing in Europe and the United States. In Europe, there is much greater political acceptance of the reality of climate change, so investment restrictions designed to encourage sustainable investing are already in place. Contrast that environment to the one in the United States, where state attorneys general are suing investment companies for breach of fiduciary responsibility if the company uses ESG criteria in its asset selection process.

Despite these regional variances, however, if there is one positive that stemmed from the GFC it was to demonstrate the degree of interconnectedness of economies and capital markets globally. I am convinced that as the economic consequences of climate change become more profound, everyone will see the wisdom of asset managers using sustainability overlays in asset selection decisions.

Lowering Investment Costs

While investment cost is just one of the three driving forces of the industry, it is the one most often discussed. And because the most visible cost associated with investments is the management fee, most people focus on this to the exclusion of other costs.

As fees for index-tracking portfolios fall to zero, there is not much more room for discussion about reductions in explicit fees.

Instead, I believe the measurement and control of the other costs of investing—opportunity costs, search costs, and behavioral costs—are those to which asset managers must turn their attention now.

This is not to say that there is no room for a rethinking of active management fees—fees which, as we have seen, are remarkably and persistently high and often poorly structured. For active managers, I do like the idea of fulcrum fees, as I believe this structure is the quickest to weed out pseudo-active from truly skillful active investors. Even if fulcrum fees are implemented, however, it may be overly optimistic to think that managers with true investing skill—especially in the hedge fund world—will not continue to benefit as much or more from a rich fee structure as the asset owners themselves. This dynamic obviously has something to do with behavioral costs that asset owners inflict upon themselves, a topic about which I will turn my attention to shortly.

To lower opportunity and search costs, I see two developments as potentially very helpful. The first is an increase in financial literacy. Before you say that financial literacy has stayed low for years and will not be moved by anything, I beg you to think back to the early 1980s, a time within living memory of many asset management industry leaders today. Even in the 1980s, if you surveyed 10 people on the street to see if they knew what a P/E ratio was or asked them about their favorite investor, you would have likely come back with at least nine blank stares.

However, after regulations in the United States changed and the burden of asset management shifted away from institutional investors to the future retirees themselves, one could easily walk into an office anywhere in the world and see people day-trading stocks on their employers' dime and talking knowledgeably about P/E ratios, operating leverage, and more. This vast improvement in basic financial literacy was aided by technology, of course. As cable TV and the internet became more ubiquitous, the number of programs and sites offering free financial information to the common person exploded.

The second development is the use of technology. Just as cable TV and the internet helped the new DIY investors of the 1990s, in our age, I see the potential for AI tools to offer a significant boost to investors looking for financial information.

If a single person tries to go online and sort through the many thousands of actively managed funds, it will take years before she could come to a reasoned conclusion as to which of the funds was best given her constraints and proclivities. However, the ever-growing sophistication of AI algorithms holds enormous potential to offer retail investors a much more comprehensive, quick, and accurate sense of which portfolio will be most suited to them. As the task of selecting assets becomes easier and perhaps even more enjoyable, the likelihood that people will increase their own level of financial literacy increases concomitantly.

Of course, some costs can also be lowered through lowering behavioral costs to investors through nudging processes. These have been effective in the past, and I continue to see a role for them going forward, but we must all admit that they serve as dull policy instruments, not scalpels. To decrease opportunity and behavioral costs for retail asset owners, technology-driven improvements in literacy are still the most effective tool I see.

Creating AI-powered financial "shopping agents" that allow for an easy winnowing and comparison of products is my preferred theoretical solution. However, even I admit that the creation of such tools will be difficult, given the abstract and heterogenous nature of financial products (i.e., every product sells a unique vision of the future, so trying to get a machine to extrapolate the analysis of these visions is nontrivial).

Until search and behavioral costs can come down, it is hard for me to see the overall cost of investing coming down substantially. There might even be the chance that search costs especially will go up as the number of financial products increases faster than AI-enabled search engines can come up to speed.

One trend that I do see in institutional management that has the potential to lower behavioral costs is that of quantitative investing.

As a quantitative investor myself, I am painfully aware that I am "talking my own book" here, but I think there is a case to be made for this view. Even the best human decision makers are human. All humans share behavioral and cognitive biases that have been baked into the hardware of our brains over the last few hundred thousand years of evolution. We can always find reasons to hold onto a beloved security as the price falls. We can always find reasons to sell after we have generated what we consider a "reasonable" or "adequate" profit on a position.

Algorithms are programmed by humans, so it is impossible to say that human biases do not creep into the programs to become ghosts in the machine. However, programming requires humans to use reason during moments of dispassionate consideration. Many of the behavioral biases that hurt investors so badly are those that are related to having to make reactionary decisions under conditions of extraordinary stress. Machines, for all their weaknesses, do not suffer from stress. They can calculate the square root of a very large number just as quickly whether it is sunny or cloudy outside and whether the market is down by 5 percent or up by as much.

The one enormous weakness that I acknowledge machines have that are difficult to overcome, especially as investing paradigms shift is that algorithms are typically built by looking at what happened in the past and extrapolating what might happen in the future based upon the history. Just as passive investing suffers from a rearview mirror bias, those of us who command the services of machines must acknowledge the awesome power of regime shifts.

Despite all the difficulties, the example of the growth of passive investing demonstrates clearly that costs are important to investors. Managers who can figure out how best to control search and behavioral costs, as well as to lower explicit fees, will be richly rewarded.

Lowering Investing Information Asymmetry

There are two main forces that will affect information asymmetry between asset owners and managers going forward. The first is regulation, which may include what I will term *voluntary self-disclosure*. The second is sustainable investing.

We have seen the dangers of poorly conceived regulation in the example of European rules on sustainable investing. Those kinds of problems can only be corrected at the political and administrative levels.

However, we have also seen the ridiculous and meaningless regulation Kabuki that offers little information to asset owners but ends up giving them plenty of additional costs. To the extent that the Kabuki show needs to continue for as long as the regulator wants to watch, this frustrating and value destructive practice will continue. However, I cannot help thinking that an asset manager who puts some time and energy into considering more meaningful and value creative ways to lower information asymmetry will be justly rewarded in the marketplace.

At the root of this voluntary self-disclosure is confidence that one is indeed an asset manager with genuine skill rather than just a faux-active manager attracted to the business with the lure of fat fees and easy living. In my opinion, the form this enlightened self-disclosure would take is that of an accounting of investing costs versus marketing costs and the history of both overlain with the return history. In my experience, the amount an asset manager is spending to nurture and maintain a competitive advantage compared to the amount the manager is spending to create flashy brochures is a good measure of the processes that are most important to that manager.

Regarding sustainable investing, while I believe this is the most important theme for asset managers, owners, and everyone else during the coming century, I realize that as the inclusion of ESG factors into the investment process becomes standard, the information asymmetry between investors and managers will invariably become larger.

The sources of potential information asymmetry are myriad: the ESG measures themselves are still in the process of being refined, there is little understanding of how ESG scores of the past relate to those of the present (let alone the future), and real questions as to how effective the process of extrapolation of historical measures will be as the economic impacts of climate change and environmental degradation become more intense and impactful.

In the early days there were many specialized asset managers who focused on ESG—they were the pioneers and they had unique and genuine insight into investing in this realm. Today however, every asset manager takes ESG into account and many of them claim they have always been focused on these measures—they are the followers who are simply trying to keep up with regulatory mandate and/or client interest. Because they view the work on ESG factors as compulsory, they try to economize on the raw materials (i.e., research talent and time and high-quality data) while maintaining a premium pricing model.

In my opinion, it is this dynamic that is and will drive information asymmetry to become more pronounced and is something about which regulators should be aware.

There are regulatory efforts to increase ESG-related transparency, but I cannot help thinking that the thrust of this effort can be classified in the Kabuki category. For example, the ESMA's disclosure template runs to 21 pages in all! It is not clear to me what the purpose of such a lengthy disclosure requirement is, but it will force asset managers to focus additional resources into completing and updating it, and it is hard to imagine that those costs will not get passed through to owners.

Enabling Investment Risk Sharing

With the advent of fractional shares and customized SMAs, risk sharing through diversification has reached a plateau. Technically, the blueprint for the global asset management industry exists, and it is hard to see that much more can be done in the area of diversification.

In fact, the potential for diversification effects to regress due to automatically customized SMAs is one we should acknowledge and consider. In Hal Varian's textbook *The Economics of Information Technology*, he discusses the possibility of the construction of a "market of one," and this dynamic represents a theoretically possible end point for asset management (Varian et al., 2010). Varian's argument is that information technology allows for extreme customization of products for an extremely low cost, and it is certainly easy to see how the computer-aided construction of customized portfolios could follow this route. While this "mass customization" trend is attractive for an asset owner in some respects, customization implies the ability of the provider to increase prices. It is hard to imagine that society at large and the regulators that represent it would allow price discrimination for retirement pensions and social security products.

Another challenge related to diversification involves societal preference in general and, I believe, sustainable investing in particular.

Diversification means selecting from a wide group of assets whose value and prices are related to different fundamental drivers. However, the idea of sustainable investing is—as is true for all thematic investment styles—to concentrate assets into a collection that have precisely the same driver. This type of concentration, especially when it becomes widespread across the industry, has an obvious effect on prices that will also become difficult for asset managers to handle. Since asset management is as much of an art as a science, I believe balancing the conflicting goals of true diversification and concentration in a specific theme is a topic that requires the artistic talent of a manager.

It is the sharing of the other good risk—the risk inherent in innovation—that will be most important when addressing sustainable investing, and the best model is that of Israel's Yozma.

Regulation might be tempting—certainly government subsidies, as with Yozma, are a sort of quasi-regulatory intervention—but too much regulation is risky as it tends to stifle rather than encourage innovation in the long run.

In the end, I believe the managers who will be most successful are those who can balance the benefits of diversification with the benefits of customization, overlain with the benefits that come from conscientious concentration in sustainable investments.

Serving Societal Preferences

As described in Chapters 13 and 14, I believe that the most relevant societal preference for the rest of my life and career and certainly for the lives and careers of those who will follow me is how society faces the issue of climate change. What risk can be more systematic than the risk that a large swath of humanity will not be able to feed itself or that widespread commercial activity will be disrupted or halted due to environmental disasters and supply chain disruptions?

Think about the disruption from the COVID-19 pandemic. Now try to imagine a COVID-19 pandemic that (1) worsens over time and (2) cannot be resolved in one or even two lifetimes! This thought experiment should offer you a glimpse at the grave nature of the threat that confronts us.

How can asset managers support the goals of mitigating (to the extent still possible) and adapting to a post-climate change world?

Taking one extreme case as a hypothetical, if humanity—or rather the policymakers who direct the productive capacity of humanity—decides to do nothing in the face of climate change, our civilization will end up altering the course of life on earth to an extent never seen before. Nihilists and those who are mentally imbalanced might accept this future, but I would like to think that most normal, healthy people would not.

Taking the other extreme case as the contrasting hypothetical, if asset owners and managers simultaneously decided to divest from any industry whose production and distribution include the combustion or use of fossil fuels, our civilization would be thrown back into, if not the Stone Age, at least the Bronze Age. Obviously, such a move would also have a "nontrivial effect" on equity and bond market valuations. Such a drastic course of action would not only destroy the wealth and standard of living of everyone on this planet, but it would also cost millions, perhaps even billions, of human lives.

My optimistic perspective is that while policymakers have been slow to act and have gotten sidetracked at times, the corporate and the investment worlds are both beginning to agree and to move forward. Policymakers have gotten the message and are following along. Subsidies laid out in the US Inflation Reduction Act of 2022 (IRA) and the recently promulgated Carbon Border Adjustment Tax in the European Union are two very visible and effective policy tools encouraging a global shift to a "Climate Revolution" paradigm to replace the Industrial Revolution one.

From the previous examples of the antiapartheid divestment campaign and the campaign to shame Wellcome into lowering the prices of AIDS drugs, I strongly believe that the answer to the climate crisis is not going to come about through the organization of divestment campaigns. In my mind, societal preference for sustainability will only and can only be promoted by engaging with the governments who set the rules and the corporations who (mostly) play by them.

The most powerful incentive the world has found to date is the incentive of people to receive the monetary and social benefits of innovating a product or service that ends up becoming widely admired and used. To a very real extent, asset managers exist at the fulcrum of the lever that allows that incentive to move people. In my mind, it is imperative that we asset managers move that fulcrum as near to the burden as possible to allow creative people all over the world a chance at shifting the burden with the least amount of energy possible. Put simply, this means allocating resources to companies with credible—though perhaps unproven or even outlandish—plans to mitigate or adapt to climate change.

A MANIFESTO FOR THE INDUSTRY

While what I have written here makes it sound like it will be a straightforward process for the asset management industry to lower the cost of investing, encourage risk sharing, lower information asymmetry between owners and managers, and respond to the overwhelmingly important societal preference of sustainability, just looking at the task list should convince you that this process will not be an "easy lift."

In my mind, the most difficult part in making the changes I am recommending stems from conflicting and interdependent trends.

Namely, in thinking about these driving forces, I realize that meeting the societal preference of sustainability—the one thing that I have harped on for the better part of two chapters—conflicts to a certain extent with all the other intermediary goals.

The introduction of sustainable investing's additional, nonpecuniary focus naturally increases information asymmetry. Managers thrive on information asymmetry, but this can cause the problems already discussed to asset owners. Meeting societal preferences also introduces an extra layer of work for managers, and managers will want to be paid for the additional work—thus put the break on lowering investing cost. The added complexity of the focus on sustainability will increase search costs—again causing overall investing cost to rise. As I discussed previously, concentrating assets in such a way as to favor sustainable investing also lowers the degree to which diversification of risk is possible.

The challenges are myriad, but the rewards could not be greater. Nothing less than the future of our civilization rests on the asset management industry's ability to move the great and heavy ship of the global economy.

The challenges are myriad, but we must overcome them. It is a moral imperative.

REFERENCES

PREFACE

Polman, Paul. "Conscious Quitting Has Arrived." February 16, 2023, https://www.paulpolman.com/conscious-quitting-has-arrived/.

CHAPTER 2

Barth, Daniel, Juha Joenväärä, Mikko Kauppila, and Russ Wermers. 2020. "The Hedge Fund Industry Is Bigger (and Has Performed Better) Than You Think." *OFR Working Paper* 20–01. http://dx.doi.org/10.2139/ssrn .3544181.

Getmansky, Mila, Peter Lee, and Andrew Lo. 2015. "Hedge Funds: A Dynamic Industry in Transition." *Annual Review of Financial Economics* 7, no. 1: 483–577. https://doi.org/10.1146/annurev-financial-110311-10 1741.

Global SWF. n.d. "Sovereign Wealth Funds & Public Pension Funds." Global SWF (website). Accessed April 1, 2023. https://globalswf.com/.

IOSCO. 2022. "Investment Funds Statistics." IOSCO Investment Funds Statistics Report (January 2022). https://www.iosco.org/library/pubdo cs/pdf/IOSCOPD693.pdf.

Kaplan, Steven, and Berk Sensoy. 2015. "Private Equity Performance: A Survey." *Annual Review of Financial Economics* 7, no. 1: 597–614. https://doi.org/10.1146/annurev-financial-111914-041858.

Korteweg, Arthur. 2019. "Risk Adjustment in Private Equity Returns." *Annual Review of Financial Economics* 11, no. 1: 131–152. https://doi.org /10.1146/annurev-financial-110118-123057.

McKinsey. 2022. "Private Markets Rally to New Heights." *Global Private Markets Review* (March 2022).

Mukerjee, Meghna. 2021. "Top 25 Global Wealth Management Firms Market Monitor, 2021." Aite-Novarica Group, November 3, 2021 (website). https://aite-novarica.com/report/top-25-global-wealth-management-firms-market-monitor-2021.

OECD. 2022. "OECD Insurance Statistics 2021." OECD Publishing, Paris. https://doi.org/10.1787/2307843x.

OECD. 2023. "OECD Pension Market in Focus 2022." OECD Publishing, Paris. www.oecd.org/finance/pensionmarketsinfocus.htm.

Thinking Ahead Institute. "The World's Largest 500 Asset Managers." Thinking Ahead Institute and Pensions & Investments (October 2022). https://www.thinkingaheadinstitute.org/content/uploads/2022/10/PI-500-2022_final_1013.pdf.

CHAPTER 3

SIFMA. "2022 Capital Markets Fact Book." SIFMA (July 2022). https://www.sifma.org/wp-content/uploads/2022/07/CM-Fact-Book-2022-SIFMA.pdf.

CHAPTER 4

Arrow, Kenneth. 1962. "Economic Welfare and the Allocation of Resources for Invention," in *The Rate and Direction of Inventive Activity: Economic and Social Factors*, National Bureau of Economic Research: 609–626. https://www.nber.org/system/files/chapters/c2144/c2144.pdf.

Del Guercio, Diane, and Paula Tkac. 2008. "Star Power: The Effect of Morningstar Ratings on Mutual Fund Flow." *Journal of Financial and Quantitative Analysis* 43, no. 4: 907–936. http://www.jstor.org/stable/27647379.

Greenspan, Alan. 1987. "Testimony Before the Committee on Banking, Housing & Urban Affairs, United States Senate." FRASER (website). Accessed April 1, 2023. https://fraser.stlouisfed.org/title/452/item/8368.

Moss, David, and Eugene Kintgen. "The Dojima Rice Market and the Origins of Futures Trading." Harvard Business School Case 709–044, January 2009. (Revised November 2010.) https://www.hbs.edu/faculty/Pages/item.aspx?num=36846.

CHAPTER 5

Boustanifar, Hamid, Everett Grant, and Ariell Reshef. 2018. "Wages and Human Capital in Finance: International Evidence, 1970–2011." *Review of Finance* 22, no. 2: 699–745. https://doi.org/10.1093/rof/rfx011.

Carhart, Mark. 1997. "On Persistence in Mutual Fund Performance." *Journal of Finance* 52, no. 1: 57–82. https://doi.org/10.1111/j.1540-62 61.1997.tb03808.x.

Frazzini, Andrea, David Kabiller, and Lasse Heje Pedersen. 2018. "Buffett's Alpha." *Financial Analysts Journal* 74, no. 4: 35–55. https://doi.org/10 .2469/faj.v74.n4.3.

Ippolito, Richard. 1995. "Toward Explaining the Growth of Defined Contribution Plans." *Industrial Relations: A Journal of Economy and Society* 34, no. 1: 1–20. https://doi.org/10.1111/j.1468-232X.1995.tb00 357.x.

Jensen, Michael. 1968. "The Performance of Mutual Funds in the Period 1945–1964." *Journal of Finance* 23, no. 2: 389–416. https://doi.org/10 .2307/2325404.

Mallaby, Sebastian. "Learning to Love Hedge Funds." *Wall Street Journal*, June 11, 2010. https://www.wsj.com/articles/SB1000142405274870330 2604575294983666012928.

Philippon, Thomas, and Ariell Reshef. 2012. "Wages and Human Capital in the U.S. Finance Industry: 1909–2006." *Quarterly Journal of Economics* 127, no. 4: 1551–1609. https://doi.org/10.1093/qje/qjs030.

Sharpe, William. 1964. "Capital Asset Prices: A Theory of Market Equilibrium Under Conditions of Risk." *Journal of Finance* 19, no. 3: 425–442. https://doi.org/10.1111/j.1540-6261.1964.tb02865.x.

CHAPTER 6

Ben-David, Itzhak, Jiacui Li, Andrea Rossi, and Yang Song. 2022. "What Do Mutual Fund Investors Really Care About?" *Review of Financial Studies* 35, no. 4: 1723–1774. https://doi.org/10.1093/rfs/hhab081.

Berk, Jonathan, Jules van Binsbergen, and Binying Liu. 2017. "Matching Capital and Labor." *Journal of Finance* 72, no. 6: 2467–2504. https://doi .org/10.1111/jofi.12542.

Berk, Jonathan, and Richard Green. 2004. "Mutual Fund Flows and Performance in Rational Markets." *Journal of Political Economy* 112, no. 6: 1269–1295. https://doi.org/10.1086/424739.

Chen, Joseph, Harrison Hong, Ming Huang, and Jeffrey Kubik. 2004. "Does Fund Size Erode Mutual Fund Performance? The Role of Liquidity and Organization." *American Economic Review* 94, no. 5: 1276–1302. https://doi.org/10.1257/0002828043052277.

Edelen, Roger. 1999. "Investor Flows and the Assessed Performance of Open-End Mutual Funds." *Journal of Financial Economics* 53, no. 3: 439–466. https://doi.org/10.1016/S0304-405X(99)00028-8.

Evans, Richard. 2010. "Mutual Fund Incubation." *Journal of Finance* 65, no. 4: 1581–1611. https://doi.org/10.1111/j.1540-6261.2010.01579.x.

Gara, Antoine. 2022. "Tiger Global Blames Inflation After 50% Drop in Flagship Hedge Fund." *Financial Times*, August 4, 2022. https://www.ft.com/content/87347d49-390d-408b-9059-2e5a42b5787c.

Getmansky, Mila. 2012. "The Life Cycle of Hedge Funds: Fund Flows, Size, Competition, and Performance." Available at SSRN: http://dx.doi.org/10.2139/ssrn.2084410.

Goyal, Amit, and Sunil Wahal. 2008. "The Selection and Termination of Investment Management Firms by Plan Sponsors." *Journal of Finance* 63, no. 4: 1805–1847. http://www.jstor.org/stable/25094490.

Jain, Prem, and Joanna Shuang Wu. 2000. "Truth in Mutual Fund Advertising: Evidence on Future Performance and Fund Flows." *Journal of Finance* 55, no. 2: 937–958. https://doi.org/10.1111/0022-1082.00232.

Joenväärä, Juha, Mikko Kauppila, Robert Kosowski, and Pekka Tolonen. 2021. "Hedge Fund Performance: Are Stylized Facts Sensitive to Which Database One Uses?" *Critical Finance Review* 10, no. 2: 271–327. http://dx.doi.org/10.1561/104.00000104.

Kokkonen, Joni, and Matti Suominen. 2015. "Hedge Funds and Stock Market Efficiency." *Management Science* 61, no. 12: 2890–2904. http://www.jstor.org/stable/24551566.

Loomis, Carol. 1966. "The Jones Nobody Keeps Up With." *Fortune* 74 (April): 237–247. https://fortune.com/2015/12/29/hedge-funds-fortune-1966/.

Lopez-de-Silanes, Florencio, Ludovic Phalippou, and Oliver Gottschalg. 2015. "Giants at the Gate: Investment Returns and Diseconomies of Scale in Private Equity." *Journal of Financial and Quantitative Analysis* 50, no. 3: 377–411. https://doi.org/10.1017/S0022109015000113.

Pástor, Ľuboš, Robert Stambaugh. 2012. "On the Size of the Active Management Industry." *Journal of Political Economy* 120, no. 4: 740–781. https://doi.org/10.1086/667987.

Pástor, Ľuboš, Robert Stambaugh, and Lucian Taylor. 2015. "Scale and Skill in Active Management." *Journal of Financial Economics* 116, no. 1: 23–45. https://doi.org/10.1016/j.jfineco.2014.11.008.

Perold, André, and Robert Salomon. 1991. "The Right Amount of Assets Under Management." *Financial Analysts Journal* 47, no. 3: 31–39. https://www.tandfonline.com/doi/abs/10.2469/faj.v47.n3.31.

Pollet, Joshua, and Mungo Wilson. 2008. "How Does Size Affect Mutual Fund Behavior?" *Journal of Finance* 63, no. 6: 2941–2969. http://www.jstor.org/stable/20487954.

Rohleder, Martin, Hendrik Scholz, and Marco Wilkens. 2011. "Survivorship Bias and Mutual Fund Performance: Relevance, Significance, and Methodical Differences." *Review of Finance* 15, no. 2: 441–474. https://doi.org/10.1093/rof/rfq023.

Sirri, Erik, and Peter Tufano. 1998. "Costly Search and Mutual Fund Flows." *Journal of Finance* 53, no. 5: 1589–1622. https://doi.org/10.1111/0022-1082.00066.

Vangelisti, Marco. 2006. "The Capacity of an Equity Strategy." *Journal of Portfolio Management* 32, no. 2: 44–50. https://doi.org/10.3905/jpm.2006.611802.

Yin, Chengdong. 2016. "The Optimal Size of Hedge Funds: Conflict Between Investors and Fund Managers." *Journal of Finance* 71, no. 4: 1857–1894. https://www.jstor.org/stable/43868371.

Zhu, Min. 2018. "Informative Fund Size, Managerial Skill, and Investor Rationality." *Journal of Financial Economics* 130, no. 1: 114–134. https://doi.org/10.1016/j.jfineco.2018.06.002.

CHAPTER 7

Aggarwal, Rajesh, and Nicole Boyson. 2016. "The Performance of Female Hedge Fund Managers." *Review of Financial Economics* 29, no. 1: 23–36. https://doi.org/10.1016/j.rfe.2016.02.001.

Atkinson, Stanley, Samantha Baird, and Melissa Frye. 2003. "Do Female Mutual Fund Managers Manage Differently?" *Journal of Financial Research* 26, no. 1: 1–18. https://doi.org/10.1111/1475-6803.00041.

Berzins, Janis, Crocker Liu, and Charles Trzcinka. 2013. "Asset Management and Investment Banking." *Journal of Financial Economics* 110, no. 1: 215–231. https://doi.org/10.1016/j.jfineco.2013.05.001.

Bucher-Koenen, Tabea, Rob Alessie, Annamaria Lusardi, and Maarten van Rooij. 2017. "How Financially Literate Are Women? An Overview and New Insights." *Journal of Consumer Affairs* 51, no. 2: 255–283. https://doi.org/10.1111/joca.12121.

Bucher-Koenen, Tabea, Rob Alessie, Annamaria Lusardi, and Maarten van Rooij. 2021. "Fearless Woman: Financial Literacy and Stock Market Participation." NBER Working Paper no. 28723. http://www.nber.org/papers/w28723.

Buffett, Warren. 1984. "The Superinvestors of Graham-and-Doddsville." Columbia Business School (website). Accessed April 1, 2023. https://www8.gsb.columbia.edu/sites/valueinvesting/files/files/Buffett1984.pdf.

Burry, Michael. 2010. "I Saw the Crisis Coming. Why Didn't the Fed?" *New York Times*, April 3, 2010. https://www.nytimes.com/2010/04/04 /opinion/04burry.html.

Carhart, Mark. 1997. "On Persistence in Mutual Fund Performance." *Journal of Finance* 52, no. 1: 57–82. https://doi.org/10.1111/j.1540-62 61.1997.tb03808.x.

Chevalier, Judith, and Glenn Ellison. 1999. "Are Some Mutual Fund Managers Better Than Others? Cross-Sectional Patterns in Behavior and Performance." *Journal of Finance* 54, no. 3: 875–899. https://doi .org/10.1111/0022-1082.00130.

Dunleavey, M.P. "A Trillion-Dollar Question: Why Don't More Women Run Mutual Funds?" *New York Times*, January 13, 2017. https://www .nytimes.com/2017/01/13/business/mutfund/a-trillion-dollar-question -why-dont-more-women-run-mutual-funds.html.

Ferreira, Miguel, Pedro Matos, and Pedro Pires. 2018. "Asset Management Within Commercial Banking Groups: International Evidence." *Journal of Finance* 73, no. 5: 2181–2227. https://doi.org/10.1111/jofi.12702.

Gil-Bazo, Javier, and Pablo Ruiz-Verdú. 2009. "The Relation Between Price and Performance in the Mutual Fund Industry." *Journal of Finance* 64, no. 5: 2153–2183. https://doi.org/10.1111/j.1540-6261.2009.01497.x.

Gruber, Martin. 1996. "Another Puzzle: The Growth in Actively Managed Mutual Funds." *Journal of Finance* 51, no. 3: 783–810. https://doi.org /10.1111/j.1540-6261.1996.tb02707.x.

Gu, Pu. 2020. "The Effects of Social Bias Against Female Analysts on Markets." *Journal of Corporate Finance* 64, no. 101681: 1–28. https://doi .org/10.1016/j.jcorpfin.2020.101681.

Niessen-Ruenzi, Alexandra, and Stefan Ruenzi. 2019. "Sex Matters: Gender Bias in the Mutual Fund Industry." *Management Science* 65, no. 7: 3001–3025. https://doi.org/10.1287/mnsc.2017.2939.

Pedersen, Lasse Heje. 2018. "Sharpening the Arithmetic of Active Management." *Financial Analysts Journal* 74, no. 1: 21–36. http://dx.doi .org/10.2139/ssrn.2849071.

Sharpe, William. 1991. "The Arithmetic of Active Management." *Financial Analysts Journal* 47, no. 1: 7–9. http://www.jstor.org/stable/4479386.

Swolfs, John. "Arnott: It's Relatively Easy to Beat the Market." ETF.com, May 4, 2017. https://www.etf.com/sections/features-and-news/arnott -its-relatively-easy-beat-market.

van Rooij, Maarten, Annamaria Lusardi, and Rob Alessie. 2011. "Financial Literacy and Stock Market Participation." *Journal of Financial Economics* 101, no. 2: 449–472. https://doi.org/10.1016/j.jfineco.2011.03.006.

Wermers, Russ. 2000. "Mutual Fund Performance: An Empirical Decomposition into Stock-Picking Talent, Style, Transactions Costs, and Expenses." *Journal of Finance* 55, no. 4: 1655–1695. http://www.jst or.org/stable/222375.

CHAPTER 8

Appel, Ian, Todd Gormley, and Donald Keim. 2016. "Passive Investors, Not Passive Owners." *Journal of Financial Economics* 121, no. 1: 111- 141. https://doi.org/10.1016/j.jfineco.2016.03.003.

Arnott, Robert, Jason Hsu, and Philip Moore. 2005. "Fundamental Indexation." *Financial Analysts Journal* 61, no. 2: 83–99. https://doi.org /10.2469/faj.v61.n2.2718.

Azar, José, Miguel Duro, Igor Kadach, and Gaizka Ormazabal. 2021. "The Big Three and Corporate Carbon Emissions Around the World." *Journal of Financial Economics* 142, no. 2: 674–696. https://doi.org/10 .1016/j.jfineco.2021.05.007.

Coles, Jeffrey, Davidson Heath, and Matthew Ringgenberg. 2022. "On Index Investing." *Journal of Financial Economics* 145, no. 3: 665–683. https://doi.org/10.1016/j.jfineco.2022.05.007.

Cremers, Martijn, Miguel Ferreira, Pedro Matos, and Laura Starks. 2011. "The Mutual Fund Industry Worldwide: Explicit and Closet Indexing, Fees, and Performance." AFA 2012 Chicago Meetings Paper. http://dx .doi.org/10.2139/ssrn.1785552.

Grossman, Sanford, and Joseph Stiglitz. 1980. "On the Impossibility of Informationally Efficient Markets." *American Economic Review* 70, no. 3: 393–408. http://www.jstor.org/stable/1805228.

Hill, Simon. 2013. "A Complete History of the Camera Phone." Digital Trends, August 11, 2013. https://www.digitaltrends.com/mobile/came ra-phone-history/.

Langton, James. 2019. "FCA Sanctions Firm for Closet Indexing." Investment Executive, November 20, 2019. https://www.investmentex ecutive.com/news/from-the-regulators/fca-sanctions-firm-for-closet -indexing/.

Libson, Adi, and Gideon Parchomovsky. 2021. "Reversing the Fortunes of Active Funds." *Texas Law Review* 99, no. 3: 581–620. http://dx.doi.org /10.2139/ssrn.3517849.

McCahery, Joseph, Zacharias Sautner, and Laura Starks. 2016. "Behind the Scenes: The Corporate Governance Preferences of Institutional Investors." *Journal of Finance* 71, no. 6: 2905–32. http://www.jstor.org /stable/44155408.

McNabb, William. "Getting to Know You: The Case for Significant Shareholder Engagement." *Harvard Law School Forum* (blog), June 24, 2015. https://corpgov.law.harvard.edu/2015/06/24/getting-to-know -you-the-case-for-significant-shareholder-engagement.

Norman, David. "Outing 'Closet' Indexing." FT Advisor, February 17, 2016. https://www.ftadviser.com/2016/02/17/investments/equities/outing -closet-indexing-5J8YAhOPLtKW6tLE62rU5J/article.html.

Roll, Richard. 1977. "A Critique of the Asset Pricing theory's Tests Part I: On Past and Potential Testability of the Theory." *Journal of Financial Economics* 4, no. 2: 129–176. https://doi.org/10.1016/0304-405X(77)9 0009-5.

Shiller, Robert. 1987. "Investor Behavior in the October 1987 Stock Market Crash: Survey Evidence." NBER Working Paper no. 2446. https://www .nber.org/papers/w2446.

Treynor, Jack. 2005. "Why Market-Valuation-Indifferent Indexing Works." *Financial Analysts Journal* 61, no. 5: 65–69. https://doi.org/10.2469/faj .v61.n5.2757.

Tobin, James. 1958. "Liquidity Preference as Behavior Towards Risk." *Review of Economic Studies* 25, no. 2: 65–86. https://doi.org/10.2307 /2296205.

Wigglesworth, Robin. "How Passive Are Markets, Actually?" *Financial Times*, September 5, 2022. https://www.ft.com/content/73a6527d-cd59 -498e-9923-af5143cbb952.

CHAPTER 9

Mishkin, Frederic, and Stanley Eakins. 2018. Financial Markets and Institutions. The Pearson Education series in finance. Pearson. https:// www.pearson.com/store/p/financial-markets-and-institutions-global -edition/P200000005053/9781292215006.

CHAPTER 10

Abel, Andrew. 1990. "Asset Prices Under Habit Formation and Catching up with the Joneses." *American Economic Review* 80, no. 2: 38–42. http://www.jstor.org/stable/2006539.

Benartzi, Shlomo, and Richard Thaler. 2007. "Heuristics and Biases in Retirement Savings Behavior." *Journal of Economic Perspectives* 21, no. 3: 81–104. https://www.aeaweb.org/articles?id=10.1257/jep.21.3.81.

Ben-David, Itzhak, and Justin Birru and Andrea Rossi. 2022. "The Performance of Hedge Fund Performance Fees." NBER Working Paper no. 27454. http://dx.doi.org/10.2139/ssrn.3630723.

Cai, Cynthia. 2020. "Nudging the Financial Market? A Review of the Nudge Theory." *Account & Finance* 60, no. 4: 3341–3365. https://doi.org/10.1111/acfi.12471.

Cremers, Martijn, Miguel Ferreira, Pedro Matos, and Laura Starks. 2016. "Indexing and Active Fund Management: International Evidence." *Journal of Financial Economics* 120, no. 3: 539-560. https://doi.org/10.1016/j.jfineco.2016.02.008.

French, Kenneth. 2008. "Presidential Address: The Cost of Active Investing." *Journal of Finance* 63, no. 4: 1537–1573. https://doi.org/10.1111/j.1540-6261.2008.01368.x.

Gennaioli, Nicola, Andrei Shleifer, and Robert Vishny. 2015. "Money Doctors." *Journal of Finance* 70, no. 1: 91–114. https://doi.org/10.1111/jofi.12188.

Hirshleifer, David. 2015. "Behavioral Finance." *Annual Review of Financial Economics* 7, no. 1: 133–159. https://doi.org/10.1146/annurev-financial-092214-043752.

Hortaçsu, Ali, and Chad Syverson. 2004. "Product Differentiation, Search Costs, and Competition in the Mutual Fund Industry: A Case Study of S&P 500 Index Funds." *Quarterly Journal of Economics* 119, no. 2: 403–456. http://www.jstor.org/stable/25098690.

Ibert, Markus, Ron Kaniel, Stijn Van Nieuwerburgh, and Roine Vestman. 2018. "Are Mutual Fund Managers Paid for Investment Skill?" *Review of Financial Studies* 31, no. 2: 715–772. https://doi.org/10.1093/rfs/hhx105.

Kim, Christine, and Sebastian Sinclair. "The Art of the Prank: How a Hacker Tried to Fake the World's Most Expensive NFT." CoinDesk, September 14, 2021 (website). https://www.coindesk.com/markets/2021/04/27/the-art-of-the-prank-how-a-hacker-tried-to-fake-the-worlds-most-expensive-nft/.

Khorana, Ajay, and Henri Servaes. 2012. "What Drives Market Share in the Mutual Fund Industry?" *Review of Finance* 16, no. 1: 81–113. https://doi.org/10.1093/rof/rfr027.

Kostovetsky, Leonard, and Jerold Warner. 2020. "Measuring Innovation and Product Differentiation: Evidence from Mutual Funds." *Journal of Finance* 75, no. 2: 779–823. https://doi.org/10.1111/jofi.12853.

Malkiel, Burton. 2013. "Asset Management Fees and the Growth of Finance." *Journal of Economic Perspectives* 27, no. 2: 97–108. https://doi.org/10.1257/jep.27.2.97.

Newall, Philip, and Love, Bradley. 2015. "Nudging Investors Big and Small Toward Better Decisions." *Decision* 2, no. 4: 319–326. https://doi.org/10.1037/dec0000036.

Roussanov, Nikolai, Hongxun Ruan, and Yanhao Wei. 2021. "Marketing Mutual Funds." *Review of Financial Studies* 34, no. 6: 3045–3094. https://doi.org/10.1093/rfs/hhaa095.

Shiller, Robert. 2003. "From Efficient Markets Theory to Behavioral Finance." *Journal of Economic Perspectives* 17, no.1: 83–104. https://www.aeaweb.org/articles?id=10.1257/089533003321164967.

Slovic, Paul. 1973. "Behavioral Problems of Adhering to a Decision Policy." N.p., Print. http://hdl.handle.net/1794/23607.

Smith, Simon, and Allan Timmermann. 2022. "Have Risk Premia Vanished?" *Journal of Financial Economics* 145, no. 2: 553–576. https://doi.org/10.1016/j.jfineco.2021.08.019.

Thaler, Richard, and Cass Sunstein. 2008. *Nudge: Improving Decisions About Health, Wealth, and Happiness.* Penguin, New York, 2008. https://www.penguin.co.uk/books/56784/nudge-by-richard-h-thaler-cass-r-sunstein/9780141999937.

CHAPTER 11

Aghion, Philippe, John Van Reenen, and Luigi Zingales. 2013. "Innovation and Institutional Ownership." *American Economic Review* 103, no. 1: 277–304. http://dx.doi.org/10.1257/aer.103.1.277.

Barber, Brad, and Terrance Odean. 2000. "Trading Is Hazardous to Your Wealth: The Common Stock Investment Performance of Individual Investors." *Journal of Finance* 55, no. 2: 773–806. https://doi.org/10.1111/0022-1082.00226.

Bartlett, Robert, Justin McCrary, and Maureen O'Hara. 2022. "A Fractional Solution to a Stock Market Mystery." Available at SSRN. http://dx.doi.org/10.2139/ssrn.4167890.

Bertrand, Marianne, and Sendhil Mullainathan. 2003. "Enjoying the Quiet Life? Corporate Governance and Managerial Preferences." *Journal of Political Economy* 111, no. 5: 1043–1075. https://doi.org/10.1086/376950.

Brandon, Emily. 2015. "How Your Retirement Account Balance Compares to Your Peers." U.S. News, July 6, 2015 (website). Accessed April 1, 2023. https://money.usnews.com/money/retirement/articles/2015/07/06/how-your-retirement-account-balance-compares-to-your-peers.

Brav, Alon, Wei Jiang, Song Ma, and Xuan Tian. 2018. "How Does Hedge Fund Activism Reshape Corporate Innovation?" *Journal of Financial Economics* 130, no. 2: 237–264. https://doi.org/10.1016/j.jfineco.2018.06.012.

Brown, James, Steven Fazzari, and Bruce Petersen. 2009. "Financing Innovation and Growth: Cash Flow, External Equity, and the 1990s

R&D Boom." *Journal of Finance* 64, no. 1: 151–185. https://doi.org/10.1111/j.1540-6261.2008.01431.x.

Brown, James, Gustav Martinsson, and Bruce Petersen. 2012. "Do Financing Constraints Matter for R&D?" *European Economic Review* 56, no. 8: 1512–1529. https://doi.org/10.1016/j.euroecorev.2012.07.007.

Charles Schwab. n.d. "Schwab Stock Slices." Schwab (website). Accessed April 1, 2023. https://www.schwab.com/fractional-shares-stock-slices.

Gârleanu, Nicolae, Leonid Kogan, and Stavros Panageas. 2012. "Displacement Risk and Asset Returns." *Journal of Financial Economics* 105, no. 3: 491–510. https://doi.org/10.1016/j.jfineco.2012.04.002.

Hall, Bronwyn. 2002. "The Financing of Research and Development." *Oxford Review of Economic Policy* 18, no. 1: 35–51. https://doi.org/10.1093/oxrep/18.1.35.

Hull, John, Andrew Lo, and Roger Stein. 2019. "Funding Long Shots." Rotman School of Management Working Paper no. 3058472. http://dx.doi.org/10.2139/ssrn.3058472.

Kerr, William, and Ramana Nanda. 2015. "Financing Innovation." *Annual Review of Financial Economics* 7, no. 1: 445–462. https://doi.org/10.1146/annurev-financial-111914-041825.

Keynes, Maynard. 1937. "The General Theory of Employment." *Quarterly Journal of Economics* 51, no. 2: 209–223. https://doi.org/10.2307/1882087.

Kortum, Samuel and Joseph Lerner. 2000. "Assessing the Contribution of Venture Capital to Innovation." *Rand Journal of Economics* 31, no. 4: 674–692. https://doi.org/10.2307/2696354.

Lhabitant, François-Serge, and Michelle Learned. 2002. "Hedge Fund Diversification." *Journal of Alternative Investments* 5, no. 3: 23–49. https://doi.org/10.3905/jai.2002.319062.

Lucas, Robert. 1978. "Asset Prices in an Exchange Economy." *Econometrica* 46, no. 6: 1429–1445. https://doi.org/10.2307/1913837.

Malkiel, Burton. 2003. *A Random Walk Down Wall Street: The Time-Tested Strategy for Successful Investing.* New York: W.W. Norton. https://wwnorton.com/books/9781324002185.

Moshirian, Fariborz, Xuan Tian, Bohui Zhang, and Wenrui Zhang. 2021. "Stock Market Liberalization and Innovation." *Journal of Financial Economics* 139, no. 3: 985–1014. https://doi.org/10.1016/j.jfineco.2020.08.018.

Sahlman, William. 1990. "The Structure and Governance of Venture-Capital Organizations," *Journal of Financial Economics* 27, no. 2: 473–521. https://doi.org/10.1016/0304-405X(90)90065-8.

Schumpeter, Joseph A. 1942. *Capitalism Socialism and Democracy*. First ed. New York: Harper & Brothers. https://www.harpercollins.com/products /capitalism-socialism-and-democracy-joseph-a-schumpeter?variant=3 2122832879650.

CHAPTER 12

Akerlof, George. 1970. "The Market for 'Lemons': Quality Uncertainty and the Market Mechanism." *Quarterly Journal of Economics* 84, no. 3: 488–500. https://doi.org/10.2307/1879431.

Ben-David, Itzhak, and Jiacui Li, Andrea Rossi, Yang Song. 2022. "What Do Mutual Fund Investors Really Care About?" *Review of Financial Studies* 35, no. 4: 1723–1774. https://doi.org/10.1093/rfs/hhab081.

Brown, David, and Shaun Davies. 2017. "Moral Hazard in Active Asset Management." *Journal of Financial Economics* 125, no. 2: 311–325. https://doi.org/10.1016/j.jfineco.2017.05.010.

Candelon, Bertrand, Jean-Baptiste Hasse, and Quentin Lajaunie. 2021. "ESG-Washing in the Mutual Funds Industry? From Information Asymmetry to Regulation." *Risks* 9, no. 11: 199. https://doi.org/10.33 90/risks9110199.

deHaan, Ed, Yang Song, Chloe Xie, and Christina Zhu. 2021. "Obfuscation in Mutual Funds." *Journal of Accounting and Economics* 72, no. 2–3. https://doi.org/10.1016/j.jacceco.2021.101429.

Del Guercio, Diane, and Jonathan Reuter. 2014. "Mutual Fund Performance and the Incentive to Generate Alpha." *Journal of Finance* 69, no. 4: 1673–1704. https://doi.org/10.1111/jofi.12048.

Deuskar, Prachi, Joshua Pollet, Jay Wang, and Lu Zheng. 2011. "The Good or the Bad? Which Mutual Fund Managers Join Hedge Funds?" *Review of Financial Studies* 24, no. 9: 3008–3024. https://doi.org/10.1093/rfs /hhr057.

Flammer, Caroline. 2021. "Corporate Green Bonds." *Journal of Financial Economics* 142, no. 2: 499–516. https://doi.org/10.1016/j.jfineco.2021 .01.010.

Guan, Yuyan, Congcong Li, Hai Lu, and Franco Wong. 2019. "Regulations and Brain Drain: Evidence from Wall Street Star Analysts' Career Choices." *Management Science* 65, no. 12: 5766-5784. https://doi.org/10 .1287/mnsc.2018.3182.

He, Zhiguo, and Wei Xiong. 2013. "Delegated Asset Management, Investment Mandates, and Capital Immobility." *Journal of Financial Economics* 107, no. 2: 239–258. https://doi.org/10.1016/j.jfineco.2012 .08.010.

Holmström, Bengt. 1979. "Moral Hazard and Observability." *Bell Journal of Economics* 10, no. 1: 74–91. https://doi.org/10.2307/3003320.

Kacperczyk, Marcin, Clemens Sialm, and Lu Zheng. 2008. "Unobserved Actions of Mutual Funds." *Review of Financial Studies* 21, no. 6: 2379–2416. https://doi.org/10.1093/rfs/hhl041.

Prat, Andrea. 2005. "The Wrong Kind of Transparency." *American Economic Review* 95, no. 3: 862–77. http://www.jstor.org/stable/4132745.

Tetlock, Philip, and Dan Gardner. 2015. *Superforecasting: The Art and Science of Prediction.* First ed. New York: Crown.

Zetzsche, Dirk, and Linn Anker-Sørensen. 2022. "Regulating Sustainable Finance in the Dark." *European Business & Organization Law Review* 23: 47–85. https://doi.org/10.1007/s40804-021-00237-9.

CHAPTER 13

Baker, Malcolm, Daniel Bergstresser, George Serafeim, and Jeffrey Wurgler. 2022a. "The Pricing and Ownership of US Green Bonds." *Annual Review of Financial Economics* 14, no. 1: 415–437. https://doi.org/10.1146/annurev-financial-111620-014802.

Baker, Malcolm, Mark Egan, and Suproteem Sarkar. 2022b. "How Do Investors Value ESG?" NBER Working Paper no. 30708. https://www.nber.org/papers/w30708.

Barber, Brad, Adair Morse, and Ayako Yasuda. 2021. "Impact Investing." *Journal of Financial Economics* 139, no. 1: 162–185. https://doi.org/10.1016/j.jfineco.2020.07.008.

Bauer, Rob, Tobias Ruof, and Paul Smeets. 2021. "Get Real! Individuals Prefer More Sustainable Investments." *Review of Financial Studies* 34, no. 8: 3976–4043. https://doi.org/10.1093/rfs/hhab037.

Bebchuk, Lucian, Alma Cohen, and Allen Ferrell. 2009. "What Matters in Corporate Governance?" *Review of Financial Studies* 22, no. 2: 783–827. https://doi.org/10.1093/rfs/hhn099.

Bebchuk, Lucian, Alma Cohen, and Charles Wang. 2013. "Learning and the Disappearing Association Between Governance and Returns." *Journal of Financial Economics* 108, no. 2: 323–348. https://doi.org/10.1016/j.jfineco.2012.10.004.

Burrough, Bryan, and John Helyar. 1989. *Barbarians at the Gate.* New York: Harper & Row. https://www.harpercollins.com/products/barbarians-at-the-gate-bryan-burroughjohn-helyar?variant=32206878539810.

Castillo, Greg. 2005. "Domesticating the Cold War: Household Consumption as Propaganda in Marshall Plan Germany." *Journal of Contemporary History* 40, no. 2: 261–88. http://www.jstor.org/stable/30036324.

Chambers, Matthew, Carlos Garriga, and Don Schlagenhauf. 2009. "Accounting for Changes in the Homeownership Rate." *International Economic Review* 50, no. 3: 677–726. http://www.jstor.org/stable/2562 1484.

Cohn, John, and Malcom Wardlaw. 2016. "Financing Constraints and Workplace Safety." *Journal of Finance* 71, no. 5: 2017–2058. https://doi .org/10.1111/jofi.12430.

Edmans, Alex. 2011. "Does the Stock Market Fully Value Intangibles? Employee Satisfaction and Equity Prices." *Journal of Financial Economics* 101, no. 3: 621–640. https://doi.org/10.1016/j.jfineco.2011.03.021.

Gompers, Paul, Joy Ishii, and Andrew Metrick. 2003. "Corporate Governance and Equity Prices." *Quarterly Journal of Economics* 118, no. 1: 107–155. http://dx.doi.org/10.2139/ssrn.278920.

Gompers, Paul, and Andrew Metrick. 2001. "Institutional Investors and Equity Prices." *Quarterly Journal of Economics* 116, no. 1: 229–259. https://doi.org/10.1162/003355301556392.

Green, Clifton, Ruoyan Huang, Quan Wen, and Dexin Zhou. 2019. "Crowdsourced Employer Reviews and Stock Returns." *Journal of Financial Economics* 134, no. 1: 236–251, https://doi.org/10.1016/j.jfin eco.2019.03.012.

Hall, Brian, and Jeffrey Liebman. "Are CEOs Really Paid Like Bureaucrats?" *Quarterly Journal of Economics* 113, no. 3: 653–91. http://www.jstor.org /stable/2586870.

Hartzmark, Samuel, and Abigail Sussman. 2019. "Do Investors Value Sustainability? A Natural Experiment Examining Ranking and Fund Flows." *Journal of Finance* 74, no. 6: 2789–2837. https://doi.org/10.11 11/jofi.12841.

Hilt, Eric, Matthew Jaremski, and Wendy Rahn, 2022. "When Uncle Sam Introduced Main Street to Wall Street: Liberty Bonds and the Transformation of American Finance." *Journal of Financial Economics* 145, no. 1: 194–216. https://doi.org/10.1016/j.jfineco.2021.06.043.

Hong, Harrison, and Marcin Kacperczyk. 2009. "The Price of Sin: The Effects of Social Norms on Markets." *Journal of Financial Economics* 93, no. 1: 15–36, https://doi.org/10.1016/j.jfineco.2008.09.001.

Hong, Harrison, and Leonard Kostovetsky. 2012. "Red and Blue Investing: Values and Finance." *Journal of Financial Economics* 103, no. 1: 1–19. https://doi.org/10.1016/j.jfineco.2011.01.006.

Jensen, Michael. 1993. "The Modern Industrial Revolution, Exit, and the Failure of Internal Control Systems." *Journal of Finance* 48, no. 3: 831–880. https://doi.org/10.1111/j.1540-6261.1993.tb04022.x.

Kotsantonis, Sakis, and Georg Serafeim. 2019. "Four Things No One Will Tell You About ESG Data." *Journal of Applied Corporate Finance* 31, no. 2: 50–58. https://doi.org/10.1111/jacf.12346.

Meadows, Donella, et al. 1972. *The Limits to Growth*. New York: Universe Books. https://www.clubofrome.org/publication/the-limits-to-growth/.

Roll, Richard. 1984. "Orange Juice and Weather." *American Economic Review* 74, no. 5: 861–80. http://www.jstor.org/stable/549.

Teoh, Siew Hong, Ivo Welch, and Paul Wazzan. 1999. "The Effect of Socially Activist Investment Policies on the Financial Markets: Evidence from the South African Boycott." *Journal of Business* 72, no. 1: 35–89. https://doi.org/10.1086/209602.

United Nations, 2023. "SDG Indicators." Sustainable Development Goal (website). https://unstats.un.org/sdgs/indicators/indicators-list/.

University of California. 2018. "How Students Helped End Apartheid." University of California, May 2, 2018 (website). https://www.university ofcalifornia.edu/news/how-students-helped-end-apartheid.

CHAPTER 14

Bartram, Söhnke, Kewei Hou, and Sehoon Kim. 2022. "Real Effects of Climate Policy: Financial Constraints and Spillovers." *Journal of Financial Economics* 143, no. 2: 668–696. https://doi.org/10.1016/j.jfin eco.2021.06.015.

Krueger, Philipp, Zacharias Sautner, and Laura Starks. 2020. "The Importance of Climate Risks for Institutional Investors." *Review of Financial Studies* 33, no. 3: 1067–1111. https://doi.org/10.1093/rfs/hh z137.

Nordhaus, William. 1992. "An Optimal Transition Path for Controlling Greenhouse Gases." *Science* 258, no. 5086: 1315–1319. http://www.jst or.org/stable/2880417.

Nordhaus, William. 2019. "Climate Change: The Ultimate Challenge for Economics." *American Economic Review* 109, no. 6: 1991–2014. https://www.aeaweb.org/articles?id=10.1257/aer.109.6.1991.

Stern, Nicholas. 2006. "Stern Review: The Economics of Climate Change." HM Treasury, London. https://webarchive.nationalarchives.gov.uk /ukgwa/20100407172811/https:/www.hm-treasury.gov.uk/stern_review _report.htm.

Stroebel, Johannes, and Jeffrey Wurgler. 2021. "What Do You Think About Climate Finance?" *Journal of Financial Economics*, 142, no. 2: 487–498. https://doi.org/10.1016/j.jfineco.2021.08.004.

Supran, Geoffrey, Naomi Oreskes, and Stefan Rahmstorf. 2023. "Assessing Exxon Mobil's Global Warming Projections." *Science* 379, no. 6628: 1–9. https://www.science.org/doi/10.1126/science.abk0063.

The World Bank. "New Report Examines Risks of 4 Degree Hotter World by End of Century" November 18, 2012 (website). https://www.world bank.org/en/news/press-release/2012/11/18/new-report-examines-risks -of-degree-hotter-world-by-end-of-century.

Tierney, Jessica, et al. 2020. "Glacial Cooling and Climate Sensitivity Revisited." *Nature* 584: 569–573. https://doi.org/10.1038/s41586-020 -2617-x.

United Nations. "Ozone Layer Recovery Is on Track, Due to Success of Montreal Protocol." United Nations, January 9, 2023 (website). https:// news.un.org/en/story/2023/01/1132277.

CHAPTER 15

Varian, Hal, Joseph Farrell, and Carl Shapiro. 2010. *The Economics of Information Technology: An Introduction* (Raffaele Mattioli Lectures). Cambridge: Cambridge University Press. https://doi.org/10.1017/CBO 9780511754166.

NOTES

CHAPTER 1

1. The largest "investment projects" were always those involving wars. The first large issuers were monarchs and aristocrats who raised money from syndicates of entities with excess cash.
2. A process by which financial *intermediaries* are *dis*carded.
3. In the field of financial economics, an efficient market is one in which asset prices reflect all available information about the value of the asset.
4. The primary market is where securities are first issued. The secondary market is where already issued securities are traded. Typically, people think of the stock market when talking about the secondary market.

CHAPTER 2

1. Estimates from Barth et al., 2020, of the AUM are substantially higher in the range of 5 trillion for 2016. Additionally, the authors estimate the total gross AUM, which represent assets purchased with equity capital and borrowing, above $8 trillion for 2016.
2. The distribution of the AUM by region is similar.
3. In the words of one VC, "How are you going to use a spreadsheet to value two guys, a golden retriever, and a PowerPoint deck?"
4. FoHF fees tend to be lower than that of hedge funds—1-and-10 rather than 2-and-20—but are modeled on the management fee and performance fee structure typical for all alternative managers.

CHAPTER 3

1. For those of you already in the business, "sales and research" does not sound like the natural pairing, since the term "sales and trading" is the one always used to discuss the "front office" of a sell-side institution. I

will explain the reason to group sell-side jobs this way throughout this chapter.

2. Issuers also speak with sell-side research analysts, but these discussions differ from conversations with investment bankers in an important way that I will discuss later in this chapter.

3. To make the nomenclature more confusing, a sell-side salesperson is talking to a buy-side trader. Buy-side traders do not deal with the exchange but with sell-side salespeople, and their job is simply to make sure that the decisions of the asset managers are communicated correctly to the sell side for execution on the market.

4. In Europe, MiFID II restricts asset managers from receiving any material third-party nonmonetary benefits. However, managers are allowed to receive research if they pay for it.

CHAPTER 4

1. In a testimony on the first of December 1987, Alan Greenspan (Greenspan 1987) said that "it would be appropriate at this time to concentrate on the specific proposal contained in the Financial Modernization Act to repeal the Glass-Steagall Act."

CHAPTER 5

1. A basis point is 1/100 of a percentage point. So if one invests $100 in a fund that has a 1-basis point management fee, one pays $100 × 0.0001 = $0.01 to the money manager as a fee.

2. "Float" in this context is the amount of money paid into an insurance company in premia and that the insurance company can invest before a claim is made or the policy expires worthless.

3. Sometimes these contracts with expert networks cross over from "gray zone" discussions to illegal ones when background information related to industry developments becomes insider information about a certain company's internal developments. Rajakumaran "Raj" Rajaratnam's, the founder of Galleon, conviction in 2009 for insider trading and subsequent 11-year prison sentence and $60 million disgorgement of ill-gotten gains stems from just this sort of case. In order not to cross over from that gray zone into the black and white striped zone of prison, a Rolls-Royce manager must also pay a hefty fee to fancy lawyers wearing well-cut suits to advise her on how far she can lean forward with questions to an expert network's expert. Networks often include top management of prestigious companies. As a consequence of the Galleon scandal, the worldwide CEO of McKinsey & Company, Rajat Gupta, was convicted and went to prison in 2014.

CHAPTER 6

1. A fund's investment mandate is like a country's constitution. It lays out all the things that fund cannot do, and for most mutual funds anyway, being invested in a private company (i.e., one not traded on any exchange) would violate their mandates and so would be prohibited.
2. A 5 percent position means that the manager is dedicating 5 percent of the fund's assets to a single stock.
3. I should point out that this contention is controversial. Zhu (2018), for one, disagrees.

CHAPTER 7

1. This measure of turnover assumes that the investor buys new shares with cash and invests the proceeds from corporate repurchases in cash as well.
2. Apparently, the United States is not the only country in the world to have such a low proportion of female fund managers. The statistics are also around one-in-ten for funds in Germany, Brazil, India, and Poland.
3. The title of this paper comes from the statue of the young girl staring down the statue of the Wall Street bull in lower Manhattan. The authors are searching for clues how fearless girls can become fearless, stock market participating women.

CHAPTER 8

1. There are various ways how to deduct the superior risk return profile of the market as a whole. One example would be James Tobin's (painful to read) "separation theorem" (Tobin, 1958). The problem, however, lies in testing this claim. Typically, the hypothesis is "the market portfolio is mean-variance efficient." This means that the market portfolio provides the best ratio between return and risk. The problem with testing this hypothesis is known as Roll's critique (Roll, 1977). Roll's critique suggests it is impossible to define the true market portfolio, since it would include every marketable asset under the sun.
2. A few good academic resources look at the issue of how institutional asset managers influence corporations. One example is "Behind the Scenes: The Corporate Governance Preferences of Institutional Investors" (McCahery et al., 2016), which recounts a survey the academics conducted with institutional investors that found active managers used their influence with company managers and boards to influence strategic decision-making. They also found that 40 percent of the managers surveyed believed that they wielded influence due to the implicit threat

they would sell off the position if management did not listen to their concerns.

3. Obviously, this is a provocative statement in the eyes of a financial economist. If the market is a collection of the best ideas, it obviously reflects the forward-looking perspective of the average investor, that is, the collective view of the future.

CHAPTER 9

1. Of course, there are notable exceptions, but in general, portfolios constructed using passive management strategies outperform active ones on average. One of the main reasons for the outperformance is the higher fees charged by active managers, but even pre-fee returns tend to be better with passive over time. I believe the reason for this passive outperformance is simply that investing in a passive fund offers a saver consistent access to systematic risk without taking on idiosyncratic (i.e., stock-specific) risk. And in a highly efficient market, stock-specific risk means that bad news is essentially just a coin flip away.

2. For illustration purposes it is assumed performance fees are calculated before deducting the management fee.

CHAPTER 10

1. Differences in perspective are not the only difficulty in talking about costs. There are all sorts of jargon regarding costs that vary depending on jurisdiction, sales channel, and investor type. *Management fees* in one setting are termed *advisory fees* in another and might be confused with a *load* in the United States.

2. Mutual fund fees can also either be front-loaded, back-loaded, or both. If front-loaded, the fees must be paid at the initiation of the investment. A back-loaded fee is charged when one redeems the investment.

3. Dollar cost averaging just means investing a certain dollar amount automatically at regular intervals, independent of the asset's value at that time.

4. Relative utility is often referred to as "catching up with the Joneses" in asset pricing (Abel, 1990).

5. The equity risk premia on the US market varies between 3.3 percent after and 6.7 percent between 1950 and 2018 (Smith and Timmermann, 2022).

6. Resolving temporal risk-return trade-offs is a hallmark of human thinking processes, and it takes until our mid-twenties before we show much ability to do it at all. This is one of the main reasons that nations enlist 18-year-olds in the military rather than 30-year-olds.

7. Passive managers have built up sophisticated technological infrastructure to be able to accurately track an underlying index and to react

quickly to any changes in that index. With nominal fees for market indices headed toward zero, the only way passive managers can increase profits is by finding newly "flavored" indices such as those that focus on ESG ratings, to which their infrastructure investments can be applied. As long as a data supplier is defining a given ESG index, a passive fund manager can incorporate the new basket into its infrastructure and charge clients something more than zero for the resultant product.

8. Moore's Law, named for one of the cofounders of Intel, Gordon Moore, roughly says that semiconductors double processing power at the same price once every 18 months or so. This was originally a description of historical semiconductor development at the time Moore was writing, but it has become accepted as a predictive rule of thumb rather than just as a historical artifact.

9. The UCITS framework, which is often used for retail clients, allows for performance fees. However, ESMA issued a clear guidance for setting up these kinds of fees.

10. While this thought experiment provides good theoretical justification for not implementing incentive fees, research on incentive fees in the context of mutual funds has repeatedly failed to find evidence that incentive fees are associated with better risk-adjusted performance. Instead, the research finds that mutual fund managers receiving incentive fees tend to invest in riskier investments to attempt to pump up their own compensation.

11. "From Efficient Markets Theory to Behavioral Finance" by Robert Shiller is an easy reading introduction (Shiller, 2003).

CHAPTER 11

1. It is termed *phantom volume* because the company offering the fractional shares creates them out of their own inventory of the base shares. In other words, a brokerage such as Schwab will buy Berkshire Hathaway shares into its own inventory, then sell fractional shares to its own clients. As such, the volume of shares trading on the exchange does not represent the demand for the shares at that price.

2. Which people pronounce as "cap-em."

3. Gârleanu et al., 2012, model displacement risk due to innovation within an asset pricing model. While innovation increases productivity, it also increases competitive pressure on existing firms and their employees, eroding profits and human capital. This systematic risk created by innovation is not included in today's financial markets, since the benefits of the innovation are captured by "unborn" new companies and employees.

4. Consider, for example, a thematic fund investing with a view that renewable energy will increase its share of generation capacity. This fund might invest in obvious beneficiaries of this trend—solar panel and wind turbine manufacturers—but also might invest in engineering companies with significant exposure to renewable construction projects, specialized software firms that manage charging and discharging timing for grid storage installations, and networking firms with novel solutions to allow power producers to report bids to supply power to the grid on a near real-time basis. These companies clearly cross industrial and sector boundaries, though, interestingly, the portfolio constructed with holdings in them would have limited diversification benefits. The idea of a thematic investment is to be diversified away from individual company risk, but to accept nonsystematic risk related to a particular theme.

5. *Yozma* means "initiative" in Hebrew.

CHAPTER 12

1. Asset managers address agency conflicts with defined, well-documented policies and procedures. These policies and procedures articulate to all relevant parties, above all to the regulators, the processes and the check and balances installed. Setting up these policies and procedures is a mammoth task, and typically a whole team of lawyers, compliance experts and consultants are on the task writing hundreds of pages. In particular, good policies and procedures make it easier to audit compliance with them. However, often these policies are so difficult and long that everyone falls asleep when reading them. So the enforcement of policies can be difficult. At the end the most important element in solving agency problems is the underlying culture of an investment team. If investor take their fiduciary responsibility seriously, many conflict of interest do not exist.

2. A "lemon," in addition to being a sour, yellow citrus fruit, is the nickname for a defective product. If one buys a new car, for instance, that needs repairs immediately after it is driven off the lot and is out of commission for a certain amount of time, the buyer may appeal to that state's lemon law and force the seller to replace their car with a new one.

3. To a modern reader, this may seem like a nonissue because the build quality for new cars is so high. However, in the mid-1960s when Akerlof had started thinking about these issues, the build quality for American cars could be quite poor and the existence of lemons was well-documented. Competition from Japanese automakers in the 1980s

forced American manufacturers to improve their build quality, and today, buyers simply expect cars to work properly right off the lot.

4. One approach to disclosure is to require funds to submit reports about the assets they hold—this allows asset owners to assess the investments a manager is making directly and draw their own conclusions about risk and potential return. For example, in the United States, the SEC requires different types of managers to file different reports listing current holdings. An institutional investor managing over $100 million, such as Warren Buffet's Berkshire Hathaway, must submit form 13F to the SEC within 45 days of the end of each calendar quarter. There are some exceptions to this rule—an asset manager can petition the SEC to delay the publication of certain securities in which they are building a position. Also, short positions need not be disclosed, so any funds running a long-short strategy essentially need to disclose only one side of their book. Another blind spot with the 13F reporting process is that the disclosures can sometimes be of little use for quantitative funds that may swap out different assets on a weekly or even more frequent basis. Essentially, looking at the 13F of a quant investor like D. E. Shaw, for instance, one gets a snapshot of the holdings as of the end of the quarter, but no clue into the fund's present portfolio (Many hedge fund managers spend time looking through other of their colleagues' 13F filings to get investment ideas or a general sense of positioning). Mutual funds and ETFs are not subject to 13F requirements. Instead, they must submit an N-PORT filing on a monthly basis, though only quarterly N-PORT reports are made available to the public. This type of disclosure might certainly be automated, and funds are required to post positions to the internet on a more regular basis. However, there is enormous pushback from the industry—understandable in my opinion—to doing this. Especially large funds, which must take weeks or months to build a position in a given security, would be directly harmed by this level of disclosure. Every investor would be able to front run a large asset manager and benefit from the manager's subsequent purchases. In the end, disclosure is meant to decrease issues related to information asymmetry to help asset owners. However, it is hard to see how helping small hedge funds to build positions in advance of a large fund making a purchase gets society closer to that goal.

CHAPTER 13

1. Look at a history of General Electric, Siemens, or Mitsubishi to get a sense of this observation.

2. A few months after his release from prison, Mandela visited Berkeley and made a speech at the Oakland Coliseum to a crowd of 58,000 people.

3. *Barbarians at the Gate,* written in 1989 by Bryan Burrough and John Helyar, is for many the best business book ever written (Burrough & Helyar, 1989). The book is about the leveraged buyout of RJR Nabisco.

4. The following example nicely illustrates the difference between ethics and morals. Imagine a lawyer whose moral belief is that killing is wrong and should be punished. She works for a client who confesses that he murdered his wife. The lawyer would be acting according to her moral convictions if she were to stand up in court and confess on behalf of her client but would be undertaking an action that is extremely unethical from a professional standpoint.

5. Incredibly, the female gender did not exist in the eighteenth century.

6. Interested readers may be directed to https://ourworldindata.org/ for further insights.

7. The UN SDGs have created societal and political pressure for companies and investors to promote sustainability.

8. A special class of fixed-income instruments that satisfy ESG criterions are "green bonds." According to the *Green Bond Principles* formulated by the International Capital Market Association, green bonds are associated with "several broad categories of eligibility for Green Projects to address key areas of environmental concern such as climate change, natural resources depletion, loss of biodiversity, and air, water or soil pollution." This would typically include projects targeted at renewable energy, efficiency, sustainable waste management and land use, biodiversity conservation, clean transportation, and clean water. Green bonds are issued by corporations, national and local governments, as well as international organizations.

9. As fate would have it, the Federal Reserve came into existence at the end of 1913, just in time to help manage the country's finances when the guns of August 1914 began to fire.

10. Indeed, measuring ESG preference is still in its infancy, demonstrated by the fact that different ESG rating agencies sometimes rate the same company very differently. Kotsantonis and Serafeim, 2019, provide an in-depth analysis.

11. The 2011 Tōhoku earthquake was the single most powerful earthquake ever recorded in Japan and the fourth most powerful earthquake around the world since the beginning of scientific recordkeeping in 1900. Note that normal approaches to adjusting cost of capital to account for risk are completely inappropriate for cases such as this. A review of TEPCO's 2010 financial statements show that for its bonds

issued during the twenty-first century, the maximum coupon rate was 2.4 percent and the minimum was 0.7 percent. Clearly receiving a coupon of 2.4 percent of one's principal investment yearly did not reflect the risk inherent in TEPCO's operations.

CHAPTER 14

1. 痛い! (itai) in Japanese doubles as the word for "pain" and as an exclamation used when one hurts oneself, similar to the English "ouch!" The pain of cadmium poisoning is said to be excruciating.

2. A case similar to the Japanese four major pollution diseases, Pacific Gas & Electric (PG&E) dumped a carcinogenetic compound into unlined waste pools at a remote location in the Mojave Desert during the 1950s and 1960s. The chemical soaked into the groundwater of the small rural town of Hinkley, California. Even though Erin Brockovich became famous for helping affected Hinkley residents win a $330 million arbitration in 1996, PG&E paid out a total of $315 million more over the next 12 years, as well as spending approximately $750 million in remediation efforts. The underground plume of the carcinogenic chemical continues to grow, and PG&E representatives estimate that cleanup will not be complete until around 2050—roughly 100 years after initial dumping.

3. The Supran et al., 2023, study entitled "Assessing ExxonMobil's Global Warming Projections" published in the journal *Science* found that from the late-1970s on, atmospheric scientists and Exxon (later, ExxonMobil) had used proprietary data sources and projected average atmospheric warming that was extremely accurate compared to actual subsequent warming and agreed with work being published by academic colleagues. The problem was that while its scientists were saying they were confident in their modeling and that their models agreed with others, the company was spending millions of dollars every year on marketing and lobbying campaigns that explicitly called such mathematical models inaccurate and claimed there was considerable scientific uncertainty regarding the science of climate change. This calls into question what legal liability this oil major and others may have.

4. Due to commonly known flaws of the GDP concept regarding economic performance, it is probably not the best measure to begin with.

5. Perhaps I am being too pessimistic. In 1997, the Kyoto Protocol was signed and ratified by 192 parties. This was the first international treaty to set legally binding greenhouse gas emission reduction targets. The positive effect of the protocol was attenuated because the US Senate failed to ratify the treaty after the Clinton administration had already

signed. The United States is one of the largest emitters in the world, so nonratification encouraged other countries not to take their own emission targets quite as seriously. The proof is in the pudding, they say. As you can see by the Keeling Curve in Figure 14.1, atmospheric carbon dioxide concentrations rose by 7 percent from 1993 through 2006, an annualized rate roughly 20 percent higher than the 9 percent increase seen between 1972 and 1992.

6. Even with a slowdown triggered by the GFC and another deep slowdown as a result of the COVID crisis, atmospheric carbon dioxide concentrations increased 9 percent during the 2007–2022 period, an annual rate 11 percent faster than the 1993–2006 period. We can remain hopeful about the Paris Agreement—signed in 2015 and going into force the year after—and nations' commitments to keeping the average rise in global temperatures below 2 degrees Celsius. However, it would have been a lot easier and much less disruptive to make adjustments in the 1980s rather than in the 2020s.

7. Note that the survey data was collected before COVID was known. I wonder what institutional investors would think about a global natural disaster risk now.

INDEX

ABOUT THE AUTHOR

Daniel is a seasoned asset manager with over 25 years of experience in various prominent roles within the industry. He has successfully led and executed diverse investment processes across multiple countries, asset classes, and investments strategies, catering to some of the largest institutional investors worldwide.

Known for his expertise in quantitative investing, Daniel's passion lies in the broad field of asset management. He takes immense pride in never losing sight of the higher purpose of his work: helping individuals save for retirement, facilitating intergenerational wealth transfer, and contributing to the betterment of society through investments in transformative ideas and companies.

Guided by a strong belief in the power of markets and asset management, Daniel excels in translating the principles of financial market science into investment strategies for his institutional clientele. His journey in the financial world began in 1997 as an ESG analyst at a forward-thinking "green" venture capital boutique. Over time, he transitioned to partner and chief investment officer roles at a hedge fund-of-fund and later at a quantitative asset management firm investing in public markets. At the latter, he managed several tens of billions in assets under management with a sizable multinational team of investment experts located in various countries.

Recently, Daniel embarked on a new venture in the field of asset management, trying to tackle the challenges described in this book with his characteristic drive and determination.

Daniel's career is built upon extensive expertise as a practitioner fortified by his academic background. He holds a PhD and a master's degree in financial and capital markets theory from the University of St. Gallen. In addition, he possesses a master's degree in environmental sciences from ETH Zurich, further augmenting his well-rounded knowledge.

Daniel resides in Switzerland with his partner, Monika, where they raise their daughter, Annick. During his leisure time, Daniel enjoys immersing himself in the realms of finance, investing, and asset management. Drawing upon his passion, professional expertise, and academic background, he actively engages in teaching finance and asset management courses at the University of St. Gallen.